KV-455-991

Credit and Debt:
the PSI report

The Policy Studies Institute (PSI) is Britain's leading independent research organisation undertaking studies of economic, industrial and social policy, and the workings of political institutions.

PSI is a registered charity, run on a non-profit basis, and is not associated with any political party, pressure group or commercial interest.

PSI attaches great importance to covering a wide range of subject areas with its multi-disciplinary approach. The Institute's 40+ researchers are organised in teams which currently cover the following programmes:

Family Finances
Health Studies and Social Care
Innovation and New Technology
Quality of Life and the Environment
Social Justice and Social Order
Employment Studies
Arts and the Cultural Industries
Information Policy
Education

This publication arises from the Family Finances programme and is one of over 30 publications made available by the Institute each year.

Information about the work of PSI, and a catalogue of available books can be obtained from:

Marketing Department, PSI
100 Park Village East, London NW1 3SR

This report is one of a series of PSI studies of the use of credit and the problems of debt supported by the Joseph Rowntree Foundation.

Credit and Debt: the PSI report

Richard Berthoud and Elaine Kempson

Policy Studies Institute,
London

The publishing imprint of the independent
POLICY STUDIES INSTITUTE
100 Park Village East, London NW1 3SR
Telephone: 071-387 2171 Fax: 071-388 0914

PSI Report No. 728

ISBN 0 85374 497 1

A CIP catalogue record of this book is available from the British Library.

1 2 3 4 5 6 7 8 9

How to obtain PSI publications
All bookshop and individual orders should be sent to PSI's distributors BEBC Ltd, 9 Albion Close, Parkstone, Poole, Dorset, BH12 3LL.
Books will normally be despatched in 24 hours. Cheques should be made payable to BEBC Ltd.

Credit card and telephone/fax orders may be placed on the following freephone numbers
FREEPHONE: 0800 262260
FREEFAX: 0800 262266

Booktrade Representation (UK & Eire)
Book Representation Ltd
P O Box 17, Canvey Island, Essex SS8 8HZ

PSI Subscriptions
PSI publications are available on subscription.
Further information from PSI's subscription agent
Carfax Publishing Company Ltd
Abingdon Science Park, P O Box 25, Abingdon OX10 3UE

Typesetting and Origination by PNA Associates, London SW10
and Studio Set, Fleet, Hants.

Printed in Great Britain by BPCC Wheatons Ltd, Exeter

Acknowledgements

The research on which this report is based was supported by a consortium of 54 commercial companies, public agencies and voluntary organisations, listed overleaf. Two of those sponsors played a crucial role. The Joseph Rowntree Foundation paid a quarter of the total costs of the study, and provided a platform on which the rest of the consortium could be built. The National Westminster Bank was the first subscriber in the private sector, and started the snowball rolling.

The research team has been advised by a consultative group drawn from the consortium, chaired by Peter Barclay. We very much appreciated the interest and support of its members.

The survey of households in Great Britain was undertaken by PAS Survey Research Ltd. Nick Smith and his colleagues at PAS made a substantial contribution to the success of the survey through their commitment throughout the fieldwork and data preparation stages. Fieldwork in Northern Ireland was carried out by Ulster Marketing Surveys Ltd, led by Olwen Davies. We thank the interviewers who worked hard on a highly complex survey; and the thousands of men and women in the sample who gave up time to answer detailed questions about their money matters.

At PSI, the research was the joint responsibility of Richard Berthoud and Elaine Kempson. Mike Joyce joined the project on secondment from the Bank of England, to carry out multivariate analysis of factors associated with the use of credit and the risk of debt. Other colleagues who contributed directly to the study included Rosemary Lewin, Stephen McKay and Karen Mackinnon.

Sponsors

In Great Britain

Joseph Rowntree Foundation
National Westminster Bank
Midland Bank
Department of Social Security
Department of the Environment
Bank of England
Retail Credit Group
Abbey National Building Society
National & Provincial Building Society
Nationwide Anglia Building Society
Infolink
Britannia Building Society
Royal Bank of Scotland
British Credit Trust
Credit & Data Marketing Services
HFC Bank
United Dominions Trust
Credit Services Association
AIB Group
American Express
Forward Trust
Beneficial Bank
Security Pacific
Economic and Social Research Council
Barclays Bank
National Consumer Council
Office of Fair Trading
British Gas
Trustee Savings Bank
Bradford & Bingley Building Society
Woolwich Equitable Building Society
Halifax Building Society
Lloyds Bank
Finance Houses Association
Thorn EMI Financial Services
Co-operative Bank
Chelsea Building Society
First National Bank
Yorkshire Bank Retail Services
Sears Financial Services
Diners Club UK
House of Fraser
London Scottish Bank
Gas Consumers' Council
Northern Rock Building Society

In Northern Ireland

Department of Economic Development
Department of Health and Social Services
Northern Ireland Electricity Service
Bank of Ireland
Northern Bank
Department of Finance and Personnel
General Consumer Council
Northern Ireland Housing Executive
Halifax Building Society
Ulster Bank

Contents

Detailed tables of contents appear at the beginning of each Part

1 Introduction

Three concerns dominate the debate about household finances in the 1990s: the increasing gap between rich and poor; the rising use of consumer credit; and the growing number of households in debt.

The 1980s was a period of growing prosperity for many people. After allowing for inflation the average household was 25 per cent better off in 1989 than it had been a decade earlier. But not everyone shared equally in this increased prosperity. The incomes of the poorest tenth of households have at best stood still, so that the gap between rich and poor widened over the decade.

High levels of unemployment, the continued increase in the number of lone parents, and decisions to increase social security benefits in line with inflation rather than wages have all played a part. At the same time poor people have faced increasing demands on their budgets: both rents and mortgage payments have increased faster than inflation; the community charge and separate payments for water rates have added to their commitments. A number of research studies have examined the household budgets and money problems of poor and unemployed people.[1] The budgets of middle- and high-income households have not received the same attention.

Over the same decade the volume of outstanding consumer credit more than doubled in real terms. Twenty years ago a royal commission, set up to consider the potential problems of consumer credit, concluded that

> *on balance consumer credit is beneficial, since it makes a useful contribution to the living standards and the economic and social well-being of the majority of the British people.*[2]

This conclusion was still valid at the end of the 1980s when average incomes were rising. Yet consumer credit seems to worry the public conscience. Credit is condemned as a 'bad thing' which encourages people to live beyond their means, and to buy luxury goods they have not earned. Credit is said to be advertised and promoted too energetically, and too easy to obtain. Journalists have several times demonstrated how easy it is to obtain goods in the high street in return for a signature – with few questions asked, and no apparent check on the accuracy of the answers. There are, therefore, frequent calls for creditors to adopt 'more responsible lending policies'. This means crying their wares less vigorously, directing their promotions at people who can afford to repay, and enquiring into the circumstances of candidates for loans, both directly, and through credit referencing services.

There is also unease about the terms and conditions on which loans are made. Do people understand the agreements they are signing? Are they putting their homes at risk in return for quite small advances? What rate of interest are they being charged? Do they know how much they will eventually have to repay?

Much of the discussion is directed at the potential problems for households with low incomes. They may need credit facilities to manage a budget with a very small cash flow. On the other hand, they can least afford to repay what they have borrowed, let alone the extra cost of interest. They may be excluded from the services offered in the mainstream credit market to 'good risks', but, perhaps, be especially susceptible to the blandishments of unscrupulous operators on the margins of the law.

Given the size of the credit market and the degree of public interest in its potential problems, there has been remarkably little detailed study of its operation. Official statistics record the total amount of money advanced by the financial services industry to private households.[3] Lenders will have conducted surveys into the markets at which their particular products are aimed, but naturally have not made the results available for wider discussion.

There have, however, been three surveys of public attitudes to consumer credit that collected some details of borrowings. These were commissioned by the Crowther Commission,[4] the National Consumer Council[5] and the Office of Fair Trading.[6] The first two were conducted 10 and 20 years before our own study, and allow some comparisons to be made of changes over the years.

In spite of these official surveys, there has been almost no systematic description of credit use by households in the United Kingdom, setting it within the wider context of household budgets. Neither do we have an analysis of the social and economic influences on the pattern of borrowing.[7]

Concerns about poverty and consumer credit almost inevitably lead to discussion about the problem of debt. The words credit and debt are often used interchangeably, but throughout this report we will distinguish between *credit,* which is the money that people borrow, and *debt* which is commitments that are causing them financial problems. We can assume that people want 'credit', but that they do not want 'debt'. Debt includes arrears on all types of household commitment, such as rents, mortgages and fuel bills, as well as on consumer credit.

It is often assumed that the huge increase in the volume of consumer credit over the past ten years or so must have been accompanied by an increase in indebtedness. In fact there is so little information about the extent of debt that it is difficult either to substantiate or contradict this conclusion. The great majority of credit transactions do not fall into arrears. And, as our survey shows, the majority of arrears are not owed to consumer creditors, but to landlords and fuel boards. It is known that the number of people falling behind with mortgage repayments has soared, but there are no equivalent figures for arrears on most other types of commitment.

It is clear, though, that debt is a widespread problem. Citizens Advice Bureaux, alone, report half a million requests for help with debt every year,[8] and specialist money advice services have sprung up all over the country.

Compared with credit use, there has been rather more research into various aspects of debt. Arrears to different types of creditor have been subject to separate studies: fuel debts,[9] rent arrears,[10] mortgage arrears;[11] but there has been no overall study of consumer debts. General consideration of the experiences of debtors has been based on the clients of specialist debt-counselling services.[12] Other studies have looked at the roles played by organisations, and examined enforcement procedures adopted by creditors[13] or the courts.[14] The work of money advice services to help people get out of debt has also been described.[15]

A number of research overviews and policy statements have been based on this work over the past 10 years.[16] Many of the detailed studies have investigated particular issues far more thoroughly than is possible in the wider-ranging survey which forms the backbone of this report, and they will be referred to as appropriate to provide background to our own findings. But, just as there has been no systematic analysis of the pattern of use of credit, there has been no attempt even to count the total number of debtors in the country, still less to assess the risk of different categories of household falling into particular types of debt.

While household budgets, the use of credit and the problems of debt are each areas of study in their own right, it is the inter-relationships between them that are poorly understood.

This research

The PSI study was therefore undertaken with three linked aims:

- to identify spending commitments and methods of budgeting among households at different levels of income, focusing especially on the problems faced by families with resources unequal to their needs;
- to measure and analyse the detailed pattern of credit use by private households, covering the complete range of credit from bank loans to mail order instalments and borrowing from family and friends. The use of different sources for different purposes was set in the wider context of household budgets, linking it to the needs and resources of the family, so that credit use could be assessed as one element in the micro-economy of the household;

- to obtain detailed information about the nature and extent of indebtedness. Almost nothing was known about the extent to which individuals experienced difficulties in meeting their obligations, and how many fell seriously into debt. The problem needed to be examined in the light of households' financial and other circumstances, their budgeting habits and their household commitments as well as the pattern of credit use identified by the same study.

The study was supported by more than 50 organisations, listed on page vi. Although there are some notable absentees from the list, the consortium, which is led by two organisations specialising in the support of independent research, includes the majority of the public agencies responsible for policy in this area, most of the biggest banks and building societies, the representative organisations of retailers and finance houses, and a range of individual companies in the financial services industry.

The original motive for organising the research in this way was the difficulty of persuading one organisation to support the whole project, but multiple sponsorship has had unexpected advantages. Each sector of the consortium – the commercial, the public sector, the academic – has contributed ideas about the objectives of the research from its own perspective, which have forced us to consider the design and the analysis from every point of view. Each sector has provided information about its own activities. We hope that the inputs from so many sources have helped to produce a rounded and well-balanced research design. By the same token, no organisation or sector has been in a position to exert the direct or indirect pressure on our interpretation of the brief which a single funder might have assumed, and this has guaranteed an independent approach to a controversial subject. Finally, every organisation with a stake in the research had a direct interest in the results.

This report is based on a detailed survey of the household budgets, the uses of personal credit and the problems of debt, of a sample of 2,212 households in the United Kingdom. The sample is described briefly in Box A, and in more detail in Appendix 1.

Previous surveys of credit have interviewed adults as independent potential credit users. But, as we discovered, one third of all active consumer credit facilities operated by married people are in the joint names of husband and wife. A very large proportion of household commitments such as rent, mortgage and fuel bills are paid out of a general household budget. Where the owner or tenant of an address was married, a single interview covered the income, spending and credit use of *both husband and wife*. Almost all of the findings of the survey refer to households, taking husbands and wives as a joint unit. Where partners had individual commitments, however, it possible to analyse them separately – as, for example, in Chapter 2.

Some adults live in accommodation where someone else (not their husband

Box A Sample

1,732 interviews were conducted in a sample of 94 postal districts spread across Great Britain; 480 were in Northern Ireland. Almost all of the results in this report are drawn from both these surveys to describe the situation in the United Kingdom as a whole. Separate summaries of the findings on *Credit and Debt in Britain,* and in *Northern Ireland* have already been published.[17]

Because only a small proportion of the population faces debt problems, a straightforward sample would not have provided enough debtors for analysis. The sample was therefore designed in three sections:

- a straightforward random sample of households;
- a random sample of non-pensioner households who either received a low income or had children; we knew from previous research that these groups were most at risk of debt;
- samples of known debtors drawn from the arrears lists of a number of creditors.

This design was successful in covering a total of 1,072 debts, where a simple sample of 2,212 members of the population would have yielded only 497 debts.

The samples were combined at the analysis stage in such a way that the results are truly representative of the overall population – the extra debtors in the sample do **not** mean that the survey has over-estimated the amount of debt in the country.

If a survey is to provide reliable results, it is important that as large a proportion as possible of the people originally selected should agree to take part. We had hoped that the response rate would exceed 70 per cent; in the event, it was about 60 per cent. Checks on the results, however, do not suggest that the resulting sample is seriously biassed; the indications are that refusals to participate were just as common among middle and upper income households reluctant to discuss their family finances as among low income households in debt.

or wife) is the owner or tenant. These 'non-householders' are often the adult sons and daughters of the householder. Where a non-householder aged 18 or more was identified in a survey household, a *separate* interview was conducted. Most of the results in this report refer only to households (that is, householders and their partners); there are, however, some direct comparisons between householders and non-householders. It is important to remember that in any analysis of households by age, the younger age-groups do not include 'young people' in the sense of those who have not yet left home.

The survey was based on detailed face-to-face interviews, which generally took between 45 and 90 minutes depending on the extent of the household's credit commitments or debts. Fieldwork was conducted by the professional interviewers employed by PAS Survey Research Ltd in Great Britain, and Ulster Marketing Surveys Ltd in Northern Ireland.

The results of the survey have been presented in tables, charts and text throughout this report. To avoid confusion between tables and charts, both are numbered in a single sequence within each chapter – thus Table 2.6

Box B Bases for percentages

Each table in the report indicates the total number of cases on which the percentages are based. Because of the complicated sample design, the weighted figures reported in the tables are not an exact count of the number of interviews in each category, though the weighted and unweighted totals are broadly similar.

It is important to understand that the unit of analysis varies from table to table. Throughout the report we analyse the characteristics of *householders*. In Chapters 4 to 7, much of the analysis describes the characteristics of *consumer credit commitments*. In Chapters 8 to 10 the counts are often of *debts*.

follows Chart 2.5. There are references to multivariate analyses of credit use and of levels of debt at appropriate points in the narrative, but these are written up separately in Appendix 2.

The formal survey is not the sole source of information. Some members of the main sample were visited a second time and asked to describe their personal views and experiences in a more informal way than had been possible in a structured interview. Some of their comments are quoted directly from the transcripts of the depth interviews.

Other research, public comment and official statistics are referred to when they are relevant. We have taken 1979 as the start year for comparisons over time. One reason for this is the political watershed of that year which led to so many changes in the legislative and economic environment affecting credit and debt. Another reason for choosing 1979 is that a National Consumer Council survey of attitudes to credit provides a convenient ten year benchmark for our own survey, conducted in the summer and autumn of 1989.

Some statistical series can be quoted to indicate changes which have taken place in the period since the survey. But we have not attempted to address up-to-the-minute issues which might affect short-term policies of lenders or borrowers. This is the first ever comprehensive survey of credit and debt in the United Kingdom, and the analysis is aimed at identifying and clarifying the underlying relationships rather than updating the latest figures.

We begin, in Part I, by looking at *household spending*. It is clear that people's borrowing and repayments will depend partly on how much money they have, and partly on their personal budgeting habits and priorities. We therefore examine the household incomes, budgeting behaviour and general household commitments – rents, mortgages, fuel bills and local taxes – of people in varying circumstances. This provides a background to the rest of the report.

Part II covers *consumer credit*. It analyses the growing market for short- and medium-term credit in terms of the economic, demographic and personal characteristics of borrowers. We then look in more detail at revolving credit facilities – bank overdrafts, plastic cards and mail-order catalogues. The chapter on one-off credit transactions includes not only hire purchase commitments and commercial loans, but also money borrowed informally from family or friends. Before turning from 'credit' to 'debt', we examine the impact of credit on family budgets.

Part III turns to *arrears and debts*. It describes the households who have had difficulty in meeting their commitments, not only their consumer credit, but also their general household expenses. The pattern of debts to particular types of creditor is analysed in detail. This part of the report concludes with a review of what happened to people who had fallen behind, including their contacts with creditors, the courts and money advisers.

Part IV draws some *conclusions*. No one organisation is responsible for policy relating to household incomes, credit or debt, and the problems identified in this report will have to be addressed by many different people: in government, in the financial services industry, in voluntary organisations and in the public at large.

References

1. E. Evason, *Ends that Won't Meet*, Child Poverty Action Group, 1980; L. Burghes, *Living from Hand to Mouth*, Child Poverty Action Group, 1980; P. Ashley, *The Money Problems of the Poor*, Heinemann, 1983; J. Bradshaw and H. Holmes, *Living on the Edge*, Tyneside Child Poverty Action Group, 1989

2. Crowther Committee, *Report of the Committee on Consumer Credit*, HMSO, 1971

3. Department of Trade and Industry, *Business Monitor SDM6 Credit Business*, HMSO

4. National Opinion Polls, *Consumer Credit: surveys carried out by NOP Market Research Ltd for the Committee on Consumer Credit*, Department of Trade and Industry, 1971

5. National Consumer Council, *Consumers and Credit*, NCC, 1980

6. Public Attitude Surveys, *Consumer Credit Survey*, PAS 1988; Office of Fair Trading, *Overindebtedness*, HMSO, 1989

7. G.T. Ison, *Credit Marketing and Consumer Protection*, Croom Helm, 1979

8. T. Hinton and R. Berthoud, *Money Advice Services*, Policy Studies Institute, 1988

9. R. Berthoud, *Fuel Debts and Hardship*, Policy Studies Institute, 1981; J. Field, *Survey of the Code of Practice Payment Arrangements: a report to the Electricity Council and Electricity Consumers Council*, Social and Community Planning Research, 1989

10. S. Duncan and K. Kirby, *Preventing Rent Arrears*, Department of the Environment, 1983, Audit Commission, *Bringing Rent Arrears under Control*, HMSO, 1984

11. M. Boleat, *Mortgage Repayment Difficulties*, Building Societies Association, 1985; J. Doling, V. Karn and B. Stafford, *Behind with the Mortgage*, National Consumer Council, 1985; J. Doling, J. Ford and B. Stafford (eds) *The Property Owing Democracy*, Avebury, 1988; J. Ford, *The Indebted Society: credit and default in the 1980s*, Routledge, 1988

12. A. Hartropp and others, *Families in Debt*, Jubilee Centre, 1988; G.Parker, *Getting and Spending*, Avebury, 1990

13. P. Rock, *Making People Pay,* Routledge and Kegan Paul, 1973; J. Hesketh, *Inside the System,* Family Welfare Association, 1978; B. Doig and A. Millar, *Debt Recovery – a review of creditors' practices,* Scottish Office, 1981

14. M. Adler and E. Wozniac, *The Origins and Consequences of Default: an examination of the impact of diligence,* University of Edinburgh, 1981; J. Gregory and J. Monk, *Survey of Defendants in Debt Actions,* HMSO, 1981; I. Ramsay, *Debtors and Creditors,* Professional Books, 1986; Touche Ross and Co, *Study of Debt Enforcement Procedures,* 1987; Lord Chancellor's Department, *Civil Justice Review,* LCD, 1988

15. J. Blamire and A. Izzard, *Debt Counselling,* Birmingham Settlement, 1978; National Consumer Council, *Money Advice,* NCC, 1982; T. Hinton and R. Berthoud, *Money Advice Services,* Policy Studies Institute, 1988; E. Kempson, *Debt Recovery and Money Advice,* National Consumer Council, 1988; National Consumer Council *A Report on Debt Advice Provision in the UK,* NCC, 1989; R. Manion, *Dealing with Debt: an evaluation of money advice services,* HMSO, 1991

16. National Consumer Council, *Consumers and Debt,* NCC, 1983; Finance Houses Association, *Consumers and Debt,* FHA, 1985; G. Parker, *Consumers in Debt,* NCC, 1985; M. Adler and R. Sainsbury, *Personal Debt in Scotland,* Scottish Consumer Council, 1988; R. Berthoud, *Credit Debt and Poverty,* HMSO, 1989; J. Ford, *Consuming Credit,* Child Poverty Action Group, 1991

17. R. Berthoud and E. Kempson, *Credit and Debt in Britain;* and *Credit and Debt in Northern Ireland;* Policy Studies Institute, 1990

Part I
HOUSEHOLD SPENDING

2 Family Budgets

Any study of how and why people use credit or get into debt must begin by considering households' income, their savings, styles of budgeting and patterns of consumer spending.

Incomes and the life cycle

The average net income of households in 1989 was £205 per week (see Box C). Economic growth during the 1980s increased the incomes available to private households by about a quarter, after allowing for inflation. But not all households have shared equally in this rise in prosperity. The increased number of two-earner families has to be contrasted with the large number of no-earner families during a period of high unemployment. Among those with jobs, earnings have risen rapidly for those above the national average, but hardly at all for the low paid.[1] Reduced income taxes have created incentives for the well-paid; but social security benefits for the poor have barely kept pace with inflation.

So the distribution of income has been stretched. Chart 2.1 shows that the poorest tenth of households shared between them a mere half of one per cent of the increase in the national disposable income between 1979 and 1988. Meanwhile the richest tenth of households shared nearly half the extra money. As a result the richest tenth enjoyed a 50 per cent increase in their

Box C Money

All income and expenditure figures throughout this report are expressed at 1989 prices.

Although many sources of income are received by the month, and many items of expenditure are paid monthly, all money amounts derived from the survey have been converted to weekly equivalents, because more than half all households think of the week as their normal budgeting period.

In tables and charts grouping money amounts into bands, the dividing line is always a member of the lower band. So households with an income of exactly £150 are in the £100-£150 category; strictly speaking, the £150-£200 category should be labelled £150.01-£200.00.

Our definition of income includes earnings, pensions, investment income and social security benefits; income tax and national insurance contributions have been deducted from the total. 'Household income' refers to the incomes of the householder and partner, but excludes non-householders.

24 per cent of households' income includes an estimate of either the husband's or the wife's earnings, based on his or her occupation. No income estimate could be calculated for 5 per cent of households, and these are excluded from the analysis.

real incomes; the income of the poorest tenth barely changed over the period. Any differences between rich and poor in either the use of credit or the risk of debt will have been exaggerated over the past decade. Better-off households, seeing their income rise steadily, would have been encouraged to borrow against future earnings; but low-income households would not have been influenced by the same expectations.

Chart 2.1 Real increases in weekly income, 1979-1988 - the bottom tenth through to the top tenth of households

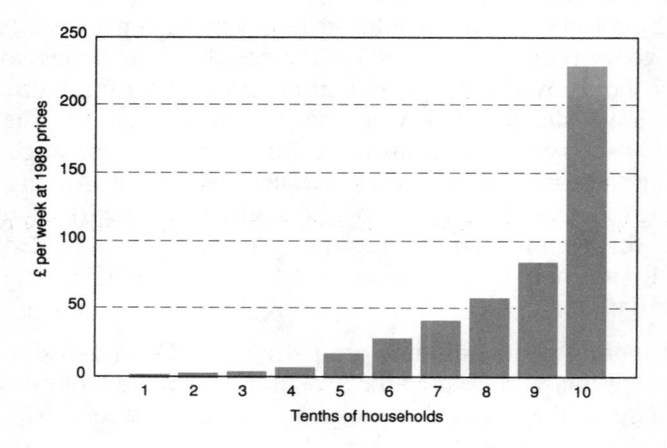

Source: Central Statistical Office [2]

Incomes change over the life-cycle. On average, they rise fairly rapidly early in adult life, and stabilise during the middle working years. They decline slightly in the years before retirement, and again after retirement, with a sharp drop in the early to mid-60s. The pattern of variation in incomes between age groups among members of the survey sample is shown in Chart 2.2. The low incomes of older people are partly the result of life-cycle changes affecting every generation, and partly the result of differences between the lifetime incomes of successive generations.

The economic theory of the life cycle assumes that people are forward-looking, attempting to maximise their lifetime consumption, within the limits set by the total income they expect to receive.[3] They will normally want to acquire goods early, while spreading the expenditure over their lifetime. We would expect borrowing to be concentrated among younger people wanting to 'smooth' their lifetime consumption profile by borrowing against future earnings. In contrast, we would expect elderly people to be drawing on their savings rather than incurring credit to pay off later. We can, therefore,

Chart 2.2 Average household incomes, by age

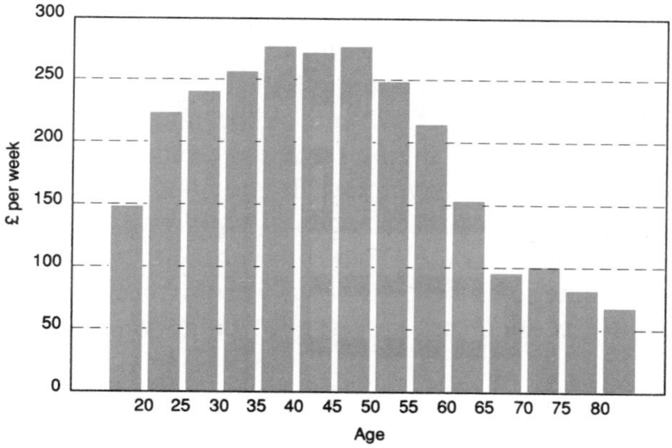

Source: PSI survey; analysis based on all householders

identify four successive phases of borrowing or savings activity over the life cycle:

Period	Income	Change in income	Activity
Young adult	Below lifetime average	Rising fast	Borrowing
Young middle age	Above lifetime average	Rising slowly	Repaying borrowings
Older middle age	Above lifetime average	Falling slowly; big fall expected	Saving
Elderly	Below lifetime average	Falling slowly	Spending savings

Our findings on the use of credit are broadly consistent with this hypothesis, although the detail has to be amended when we consider the difference between long-term mortgages and short-term consumer credit facilities. But whenever differences in behaviour are identified between different age groups, it is necessary to consider whether age is an indication of the stage people have reached in their lifetime income profile, or whether it is an indication of the generation they were brought up in.

It is also important to distinguish between two types of household with low incomes. Those past retirement age are at a low-income stage in their life cycle. They are similar to other members of their age group, and do not expect things to get better. People below pension age who have low incomes because of unemployment, ill-health, lone-parenthood or low pay are worse off than the other members of their age group, and may hope for an improvement in their situation. In order to maintain the distinction, *we keep the term 'low-income households' to refer to people with low incomes who are below pensionable age. Pensioners' attitudes and behaviour are presented in terms of their age.*

The period of child-rearing is important to many analyses of the life cycle, not only because income can be depressed, but also because the available money has to be stretched to feed and clothe more people. It is not clear what effect having children might have on credit usage, compared with people of the same age who have none. It is common to adjust total income to take account of the number and ages of children for analysis of what is known as 'equivalent income', but this combination of two items of information can sometimes be confusing. *Throughout this report income is calculated simply as total net receipts, without regard to the number of children.*

Savings

Saving and borrowing are opposites in two senses. One would expect any particular household to have savings or borrowings, but in the long run it would not make sense to have both at the same time. And looking at the market as a whole, the money saved by one group of households is available to be borrowed by others. The processes at work are more complex than either of those two simple statements implies, but there remain clear links between savings and borrowing.

> **Box D Savings**
>
> Respondents were asked whether they had any savings with a building society, a bank deposit account, a post office savings account or in other investments.
>
> If they did, they were asked to indicate the total amount on a scale which effectively asked how many digits there were in the answer.
>
> 12 per cent of the sample did not answer one half of the question or the other; they have been omitted from the base for the estimate.

Chart 2.3 Total liquid assets, 1979-1989

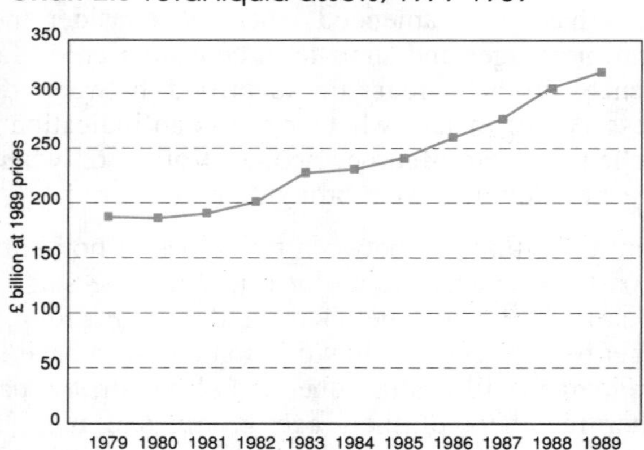

Source: Council of Mortgage Lenders [4]

Much macro-economic analysis of saving is based on simple calculations which subtract total spending from total income. It is appropriate to include capital assets such as housing and future pension rights. For our own purposes, however, we are more concerned with savings in the sense of liquid assets – money held in banks, building societies, national savings and so on. Chart 2.3 shows that the total stock of savings increased by more than 70 per cent in the 1980s, after taking account of inflation.

Our survey was about borrowing, not saving. A crude question was designed to distinguish those with substantial savings from those who had none:

No savings at all	29%
Savings less than £100	9%
Savings £101 to £1,000	20%
Savings £1,001 to £10,000	27%
Savings over £10,000	15%

Chart 2.4 (left) shows that older people were far more likely than younger ones to have significant savings, exactly in line with the life-cycle theory. Among non-pensioners, the higher the household income the greater the probability of having substantial savings (Chart 2.4 right).

Chart 2.4 Proportion of households with more than £1,000 in savings, by age and by household income

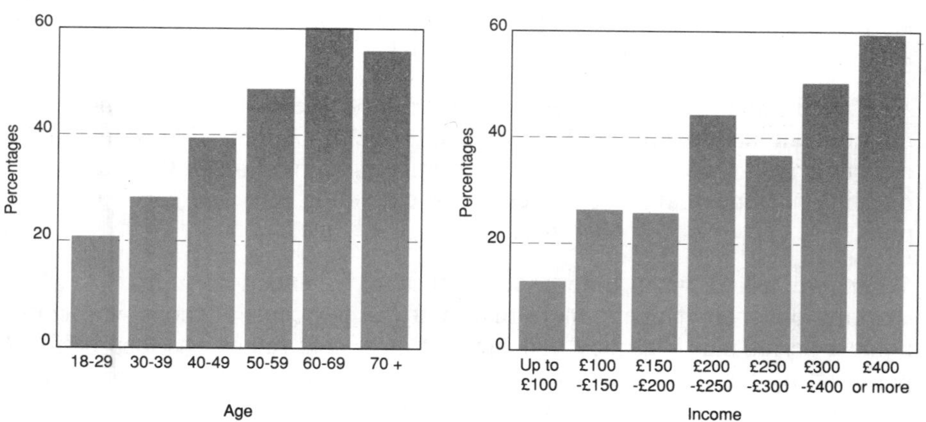

Source: PSI survey; analysis by age based on all householders; analysis by income based on non-pensioner householders.

Banking and budgeting

A current bank or building society account can influence household budget management in three different ways. First, the availability of statements, a cheque book and other non-cash methods of payment probably make a difference to the way in which money is organised. Second, the account can often be used as a source of short-term credit in its own right, in the form of an overdraft. Third, possession of a current account is one of the important factors in credit-scoring systems used to assess applications for other forms of credit.

The long-term increase in the use of cheque accounts was particularly rapid during the 1970s. As recently as 1969 only a third of adults had a bank account.[5] By 1979 the proportion had increased to three-quarters.[6] Our own survey showed that the number of people with a current account was very similar in 1989 – eight adults out of ten had current accounts with either a bank or a building society. Building societies were not allowed to offer banking facilities until 1986, but have taken up a substantial share of the market since then. One fifth of the accounts identified by our own survey were with building societies; the remaining four-fifths with banks.

Almost all householders currently in employment had a current account (92 per cent). Employees without an account were mostly weekly-paid workers, with low earnings and/or recent experience of unemployment. A quarter of pensioners (28 per cent) handled their money without a current account; the older they were, the fewer of them had an account. This is almost certainly a generation effect, reflecting the lower penetration of banking services in the days when they were at work. But nearly a half (48 per cent) of householders who were out of work for other reasons – unemployed, lone parents or disabled people – appeared to operate a purely cash budget. Looked at another way, it seems that benefit claimants were much less likely to have an account than workers were.

As a result, non-account holders were mostly people with low incomes. This might mean that the households with small weekly budgets did not feel that a current account would be helpful; alternatively, it could mean that banks and building societies have not succeeded in extending effective services to the poor.

When we asked what time-period households tended to think of when working out their budgets, more than half (53 per cent) of those who could name a period said that they budgeted by the week; rather less than half (39 per cent) by the month; a few mentioned other cycles such as a fortnight, a quarter or a year. The great majority of the people without a current account were weekly budgeters; conversely almost all the monthly budgeters had a current account. The intermediate group, therefore, consisted of people using a current account in combination with a weekly budget.

Most householders who were not in work used a weekly or fortnightly cycle: 70 per cent of pensioners, and 72 per cent of non-workers below pensionable age. Among those in employment, the choice of a budgeting period was strongly influenced by the frequency with which earnings were paid. There was, therefore, a strong link with occupational status. Most families of non-manual workers budgeted by the month, while manual workers, especially at lower skill levels, were more likely to adopt a weekly cycle. As would be expected, therefore, monthly budgeting was associated with high levels of income. Even so, a significant minority of high-earning households budgeted by the week: getting on for a quarter of those with incomes above £400 per week.

There were some signs that the frequencies of payment of the main household commitments were adapted to the budgeting cycles of the majority of each organisation's customers, but were not sensitive to the preferences of individuals. For example, the majority of tenants budgeted by the week; rents were usually paid weekly; but those tenants who operated a monthly cycle still had to pay by the week. Similarly, almost all mortgages were paid monthly, even though some borrowers would probably have preferred a weekly schedule. About the only sign of customers being able to suit their payment methods to their own budgets was in the payment of electricity and gas bills. Nearly two-thirds of both utilities' customers were still invoiced quarterly, but among the third who paid more frequently, the choice of monthly, weekly or daily (through a meter) was closely linked to the household's preferred budgeting cycle.

People were asked which of two statements best described their own attitude towards money:

If the money is there, I find it just goes	26%
I always try to keep some money in hand for emergencies	74%

A quarter of householders thought of themselves as spenders. This approach was three times as common among people in their twenties and thirties (38 per cent) as it was for pensioners over the age of 70 (13 per cent). It is possible to interpret this in terms of the harsher economic environment in which the older generation grew up – 'when I were a lad we had to worry about where the next meal was coming from'. But we suspect that this comparison between old and young remains true for each succeeding generation and that an increasingly cautious approach is a natural feature of ageing.

The important thing to note is that there was no systematic link between attitudes to money and level of income, confirming that we were, in fact, looking at attitudes, not at strain on the household budget.

Husbands and wives

Most surveys of consumer credit have examined the activities of adults, without taking account of the fact that many married couples share their budgets.[7] Meanwhile, most research into family income and expenditure has looked at the household or the couple as an economic unit. Only recently have researchers turned their attention to the way that money is controlled and managed within households. Almost all this work has been qualitative in nature, looking in detail at the financial arrangements of a small number of couples.[8]

A number of different systems of household budget management have been identified, with most research studies drawing a distinction between control and management of household resources.

Control is concerned with who holds the bank account, who decides how much is to be allocated to the general household budget, who has control over personal spending money and who has the final say over major financial decisions.[9] Just over half (55 per cent) of the current accounts held by couples in our survey were in joint names. The remainder were split evenly between those in the husband's name and those in the wife's. Younger couples were most likely to have separate accounts, and the proportion of joint accounts increased with age.

Management is more concerned with spending the money that has been allocated to the general household budget. Jan Pahl's work in this area has been particularly influential and she has developed a typology that is used widely.[10] Broadly she identifies four systems of management:

- *The whole wage system,* in which one partner, usually the wife, is responsible for managing all the household expenses, except possibly the personal spending money of the other partner. This system was used by just over a quarter (26 per cent) of households. Most commonly it was the wife who was in charge (19 per cent compared with 7 per cent).
- *The allowance system,* where one partner has a set amount of money for day to day housekeeping. The other partner retains the rest of the money, often paying the larger bills. 16 per cent of households managed their money in this way; in half of them it was the wife who managed the housekeeping money; in the other half it was the husband.
- *The pooling system,* in which both partners have access to all the household money and they share responsibility for all household expenditure. This was by far the most common system, used by half of the couples surveyed.
- *The independent management system,* in which both partners have an income which they maintain separately. Each of them takes on responsibility for specific items of expenditure from their own money. This is by far the least common system, and was used by only 5 per cent of households.

There was a much weaker association between money management systems and household incomes than earlier qualitative research had suggested. Wife-managed whole wage systems were often operated by couples on state benefits or other low incomes; and independent management was sometimes preferred by better-off households. Otherwise there was no obvious link between the way couples chose to manage their money and the amount they had to live on.

There was, however, a clear division in the *types* of responsibility taken on by husbands and wives (Chart 2.5). Women were mainly responsible for buying food. Shopping for clothes was undertaken either by women on their own, or by couples jointly; men rarely did this themselves. Paying the bills – the rent or mortgage, fuel bills and HP or loan instalments – varied from couple to couple: about a third of husbands did this, a third of wives, and a third of couples shared it. Making large purchases was usually a shared decision.

Box E Married couples

Since the survey aimed to obtain information about both a husband's and a wife's use of credit, the best method of interviewing would have been to have asked each of them questions about their own transactions. Some people might have used credit without telling their partner, so these interviews should ideally be carried out in private.

If comparing husbands and wives had been the primary objective of the survey, separate interviews would have been essential. But the cost would have been prohibitive, given all the other complexities of the research. The procedure for interviewing married couples was as follows:

1. Ask either partner which one of them was mainly responsible for money matters.
2. The person named at 1 had to be interviewed.
3. If the answer to 1 was 'both', either could be interviewed.
4. Include both partners in the interview whenever possible.

The actual interviews carried out among married couples were as follows:

Husband alone	16%
Mainly husband, partly wife	7%
Wife alone	34%
Mainly wife, partly husband	7%
Both together	35%

Analysis of the credit commitments reported by different combinations of respondent suggested that husbands and wives did indeed tell us about more of their own transactions, and fewer of their partners', when the partner was not present. The survey method therefore led to an under-count of consumer credit, though in the context of the total market, the shortfall was not very large.

Average number of personal sources of credit recorded by husbands and wives, by whether present at interview.

	Husband's credits	Wife's credits
Interviewed alone	1.03	0.75
Interviewed with partner	0.68	0.58
Not present at interview	0.39	0.47

Chart 2.5 Responsibility for different aspects of household spending

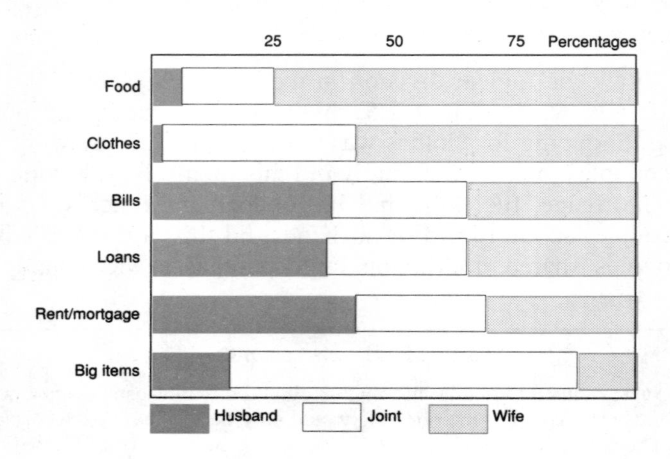

Source: PSI survey; analysis based on married couple householders

We are, of course, especially interested in whether husbands and wives used credit together or separately. Of all the commercial credit facilities recorded by married couples (see Chapter 4) one third were in the husband's name, one third in the wife's name, and one third in their joint names. But the allocation varied between different types of facility. Overdraft facilities were often on joint accounts. One-off instalment agreements and loans tended to be in men's names; women tended to be responsible for catalogues and store cards (Table 2.6).

Table 2.6 Couples' responsibility for use of credit

Percentages

	Husband	Wife	Joint	*Total (=100%)*
All active credit sources	35	33	32	*2685*
Overdrafts	27	16	58	*243*
Credit cards	42	24	34	*987*
Store cards	24	50	27	*331*
Mail order catalogues	3	66	30	*452*
Instalment agreements	58	30	12	*377*
Loans	46	16	37	*205*

Source: PSI survey; analysis based on active credit sources of married couple householders.
Note: Percentages run across the table. Thus, of all overdraft facilities, 27 per cent were in the husband's name, 16 per cent in the wife's and 58 per cent were joint accounts.

Consumerism

Chart 2.1 showed that while average disposable income increased in real terms between 1979 and 1988, the distribution was stretched: better-off households enjoyed the largest increases. This rapid rise in spending power has financed a boom in the sale of goods and services at the luxury end of the market, often referred to as 'consumer goods'. Official figures show that the amounts spent by households on cars, clothes, household appliances and leisure goods increased by three-quarters in real terms between 1979 and 1989 (Chart 2.7). Spending on other goods and services increased less than a third over the same period.

Chart 2.7 Total expenditure on consumer goods, 1979-1989

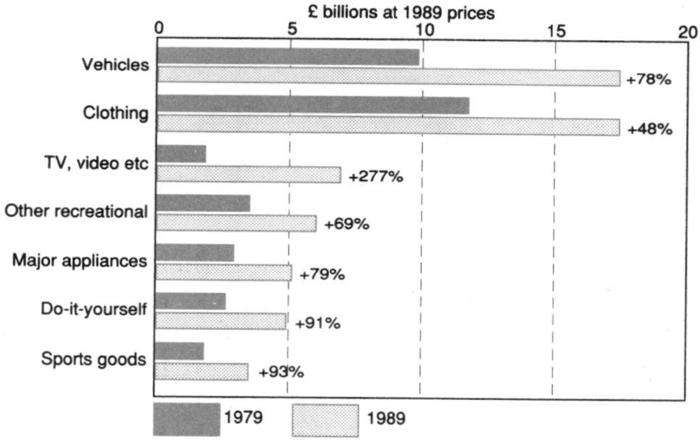

£ billions at 1989 prices
0 5 10 15 20
Vehicles +78%
Clothing +48%
TV, video etc +277%
Other recreational +69%
Major appliances +79%
Do-it-yourself +91%
Sports goods +93%
1979 1989

Source: Central Statistical Office [11]

These 'consumer' goods are frequently bought on credit: in fact they are more often bought on credit nowadays than they were ten years ago (Chart 2.8). The increase in 'consumerism' is clearly associated with the expansion of the credit market, to be described in Chapter 4.

It is therefore worth looking in more detail at the evidence about 'consumerism' from the current survey. Almost all households had a television, a fridge and a washing machine. There was little variation in the ownership of these 'necessities' by people at different ages or income levels or by different types of family. Some of the very poorest households – those with incomes below £100 a week – were managing without one or more of these items, but even in this group the majority of people had them.

Fewer households had a car or a video recorder and only a minority had a home computer. But the higher a household's income, the more of these 'luxuries' it had (Chart 2.9). Car ownership was especially closely associated with income.

Chart 2.8 Proportion of consumer items bought on credit

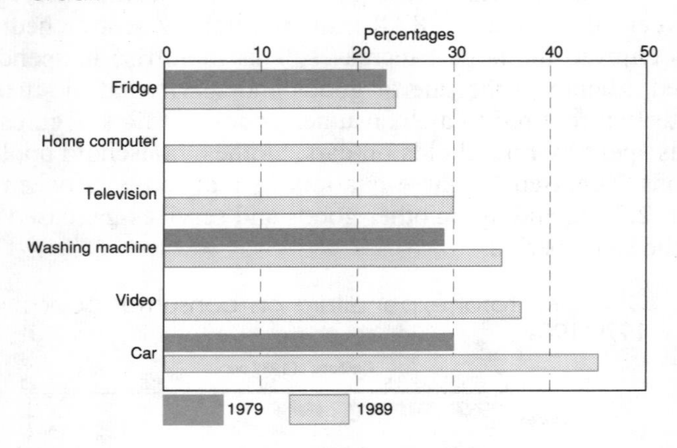

Sources: 1979 National Consumer Council;[12] 1989 PSI survey; analysis based on items bought by householders
Note: Directly comparable figures for videos, televisions and home computers are not available for 1979

Chart 2.9 Possession of six consumer durables, by household income

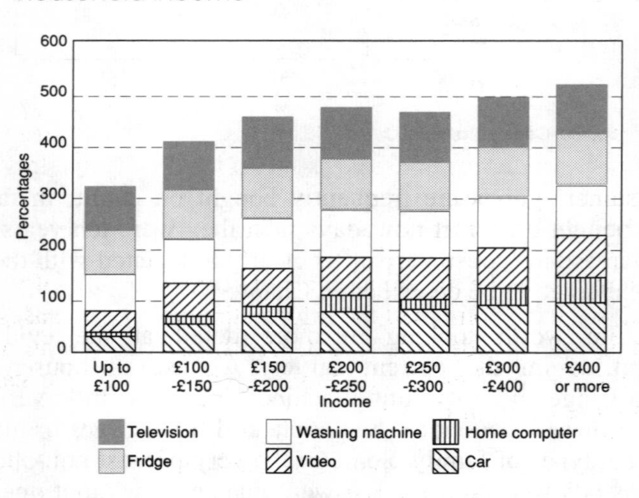

Source: PSI survey; analysis based on non-pensioner householders

Four households out of ten had bought one or more of these six consumer durables during the previous year, spending £600 on average. We had expected that the *number of items bought within the year* would show an even stronger link with income than the *number owned,* on the assumption

Box F Consumerism

The index of 'consumerism' was calculated by adding together the total amount spent by each household on the six durables in the past year. We then added £125 for each item owned, but not purchased in the past year; except for cars, where the valuation of existing vehicles was £1400 or £2600, depending on whether the household income was under or over £300 per week.

The average total score was just under £5k per household. Four groups were defined according to their position on the scale:

Low	Up to 0.5k	21%
Below average	0.5k to 5k	41%
Above average	5k to £10k	28%
High	Above £10k	10%

that poor people would have to keep their old equipment for years, while the rich could replace them frequently. But we were wrong: the frequency of replacement indicated by the ratio of ownership to purchase was about every seven years for most income bands, rising to every six years among the highest earners.

We had also expected poorer people to be paying less for each of the items they bought – cheaper models, perhaps, or second-hand goods. But again, the average cost of most items was similar for all income groups. The exception was cars: households with incomes in excess of £300 per week paid an average of £5,400 per car, compared with £2,800 spent by people with less than £300 per week.

One hypothesis was that poorer people might have had to turn to credit to finance their consumer purchases, while richer households could pay directly. Again, this expectation was unfounded. If anything, low income households were slightly more likely to pay cash.

In order to summarise the different levels of 'consumerism' of various kinds of household, we have combined the information about purchases and stocks of the six consumer goods shown in Chart 2.9 to provide an approximate measure of the value of each household's acquisitions. The calculation is described in more detail in Box F.

As the previous analysis of the individual consumer goods would lead us to expect, 'consumerism' was strongly associated with higher than average incomes (Table 2.10). In fact this way of analysing the data reveals an interesting pattern: households with incomes below £100 per week consumed very little, according to this measure; those above £300 per week were heavy consumers; but there was very little variation between households in the low- to middle-income ranges.

Table 2.10 Index of consumerism, by household income

Percentages

	Up to £100	£100 -£150	£150 -£200	£200 -£250	£250 -£300	£300 -£400	£400 plus
Total (=100%)	*255*	*176*	*255*	*201*	*177*	*284*	*206*
Low consumerism	35	9	5	7	5	1	1
Below average	48	66	67	59	56	4	3
Above average	14	21	22	30	31	63	59
High consumerism	3	4	5	4	7	32	37

Source: PSI survey; analysis based on non-pensioner householders

Income was not the only influence on consumerism. People in their thirties and forties were relatively heavy consumers; more so than those younger or older than them. This is a clear life cycle effect, with young people building up their stocks of goods, but still some way behind their elders. There was a sharp drop in consumerism at about retirement age. Pensioners had relatively low stocks, and made infrequent purchases – probably a combination of life-cycle and generation effects. Older people would be reluctant to replace worn-out goods out of their restricted and falling incomes; they would be unlikely to want to buy new-fangled inventions like videos and home computers. None of the over-seventies had a computer.

Chart 2.11 Level of consumerism, by type of household

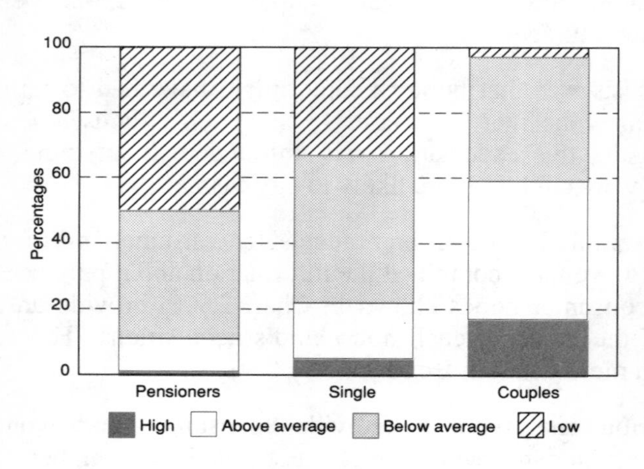

Source: PSI survey; analysis based on householders without children

The other notable point was that couples had far more consumer goods than single people. Whether there were children in the family made little difference (except for home computers – families with children owned two-thirds of all the computers in the sample). But among households below pensionable age, husbands and wives scored twice as high on this measure as householders without partners (Chart 2.11). It looks as if couples encourage each other to buy household goods to an extent that single people would not do on their own. One argument is that a washing machine (for example) is twice as valuable to a couple as to a single person, for the same price.

Hardship

While top incomes were climbing through the 1980s, bottom incomes stood still. After allowing for inflation, the average income of the poorest tenth of households hardly rose at all. They were not worse off in absolute terms, but the strain on their budgets increased as they saw their fellow citizens disappearing over the horizon. In 1979, fewer than one person in ten lived in a household with an income less than half the national average. By 1988 the figure had risen to more than one in five.[13]

Many researchers have described what it is like to try to budget on a low income.[14] One of the obvious difficulties is that a large proportion of a small budget has to be devoted to immediate necessities such as food and fuel. Although better-off households can spend more on these necessities, food, fuel and so on take up so small a share of high-income budgets that most of their additional income is available for luxury items such as cars or durables. The Family Expenditure Survey, for example, shows that two-thirds of the income of a two-child family on income support was spent on necessities. High-earning families spent about a quarter of their money on necessities; more than half of their budget was available for luxuries.[15]

We re-interviewed a small number of low-income families to see how their circumstances had changed a year after they had taken part in our main survey. Of the 18 families:

- two were appreciably better off because the husband or the wife had found work;
- two were slightly better off: their income had increased a bit, but so had their commitments;
- twelve were in virtually the same position they had been in the year before;
- two were worse off, because of reduced earnings.

For most people, therefore, lack of resources was a long-term problem, from which there was little prospect of relief:

> *The government say it's up to you, up to the individual themselves to make a better way for themselves. [But] if the opportunity's not there there's not much else you can do; you have to stay in the employment*

you've got. My husband has tried for other jobs... but he hasn't been very successful. But maybe one of these days. . . . .

I'm getting a bit tired of living on a limited budget. It's very difficult when you're always in debt all the time, because you just can't climb out of the hole. What I really need is a year when I have a good wage or a good amount coming in so that I can just clear everything and start from scratch.

Some put money aside for bills or birthdays, or saved child benefit payments so that they could afford to buy their children clothing. But for most it was a question of 'I would save if I could'.

I do actually believe in saving and would like to save. All the children have savings accounts, but there's only a couple of pounds in there. It's not that I don't want to save; it's that there's nothing **to** *save.*

Money and money management clearly assumes a much greater importance in low-income families where the budget has to be eked out. This was illustrated all too clearly by one young mother who was living on income support with her husband and three small children. Their total income was £96.75 a week, with their rent being paid in full.

I pick up the child benefit weekly and income support fortnightly. I think it would be easier if I got them both weekly. I pick up the child benefit, and put money aside for bus fares and lunches to take them to school – £5 a week. They have a little treat, usually a book or something; it is their money after all. The rest for day-to-day; milk and bread. I take my shopping out first – £55 for the fortnight. I buy two lots of nappies for £14 and tins of baby milk, £9.80. They don't quite last the fortnight. I pay the TV rental – £12.97 a month. I have to pay Mum if I've borrowed from her. I go to second-hand shops for clothes or ask my Mum; she bought them shoes. We've got to get beds for the boys. They've been 'top and tailing' in one bed. I've asked for a budgeting loan (from the Social Fund), but I haven't heard yet. Extras turn up and interfere with the budget... I can't save anything. I don't put anything by.

There has been a long debate in this country about whether the standard of living available to people who have to rely on social security benefits or low earnings constitutes 'poverty'.[16] One argument is that the steady increase in the purchasing power of benefits between 1948 and 1979 has taken claimants out of poverty – certainly as compared with the experience of millions barely surviving in the third world. The other argument is that levels of living have to be assessed within the context of current national standards;

claimants still cannot afford to participate in the social and economic activities which are normal in Britain today.

The poverty debate is concerned with whether people have enough money to live on. The current research does not bear directly on that set of issues. We are more concerned with the relationship between credit, debt and the money management problems which may be associated with low incomes. We use the word 'poor' in a general sense to refer to people with very little money, without on this occasion taking sides in the argument about where a poverty line might lie. The lowest income band used in the survey analysis is below £100 per week (net) at 1989 prices.

By the same token we say 'rich' when talking about households at the upper end of the distribution, without taking a view about the point at which prosperity becomes wealth. The top-income band used in the analysis starts at £400 per week after tax, or about £27,000 per year before tax.

We use the term 'hardship' to mean the kinds of week-to-week problem of budgeting just described. The full-scale survey contained several questions that can be used to indicate the extent of hardship in different groups. First, people were asked if there was anything they really needed but could not afford.

Decorating or home repairs	34%
Presents for the family	23%
A holiday or family outing	23%
Large items of home equipment	18%
Clothing	14%
Small items of home equipment	6%
Car repairs	6%
Food	4%
Things for a new baby	3%

Half of all households needed but had been unable to afford at least one of the items during the previous year. Some were short of two or even three. Although a few well-off households said that they could not afford some of these things, each item on the list was mentioned much more often by those at the other end of the income scale. People with less than £100 per week reported an average of three times as many unmet needs as people with more than £400.

Respondents were also asked how often they had money left over at the end of their budgeting period; and how often the opposite occurred, so that they ran out before the end of the week or month.

	Money left over	Runs out
Most weeks/months	19%	8%
More often than not	15%	10%
Sometimes	22%	20%
Hardly ever	19%	16%
Never	24%	44%

And how well did they feel they were managing on their money?

Managing well	43%
Just getting by	51%
Getting into difficulties	6%

Not surprisingly, the households getting into difficulties tended to be the same ones who said they ran out of money most weeks, never had money left over and had needed things which they could not afford. And those who seemed to be performing well according to one of these measures tended to score high on all four. All of them correlated with income in a similar way. Rather than analyse each of them separately, therefore, the four questions have been combined into a single score, which will be interpreted as an index of 'hardship'. The index is explained in Box G.

Table 2.12 shows that evidence of hardship was heavily concentrated among households with incomes below £100 per week. Nearly four out of ten people in that income bracket were in 'severe hardship'. Nearly eight out of ten faced at least some hardship. Above £100 per week, there were still some signs of a link between income and hardship, but it was nowhere near as strong as it was at the bottom of the income distribution.

Box G Hardship

The answers to each of the four questions described on this and the previous page were scored, so that the best possible answer counted zero, and the worst possible answer counted ten. For each household, the average of the these four scores was taken as an indicator of the extent of hardship.

We grouped the scores into three categories, as follows:

Low	Less than 5.0	53%
Medium	5.0 to 7.5	35%
Severe	Over 7.5	12%

People's control of their household budget depends as much on their income as on their natural skills. If Table 2.12 shows that hardship is primarily a problem for low-income families, the hardship is probably caused by lack of money. It should not be concluded that poor people are spendthrift. As we saw earlier, people's attitude to money (if I have money I spend it / I try to keep some in hand) was not related to income.

Table 2.12 Level of hardship, by household income

							Percentages
	Up to £100	£100 -£150	£150 -£200	£200 -£250	£250 -£300	£300 -£400	£400 plus
Total (=100%)	*255*	*176*	*255*	*201*	*177*	*284*	*206*
Low hardship	19	48	54	60	67	65	76
Medium	45	37	39	29	27	29	21
Severe hardship	36	15	8	10	7	6	3

Source: PSI survey; analysis based on non-pensioner householders

There was no clear pattern of increasing or decreasing hardship over the life cycle. This negative conclusion is nevertheless important. The fall in income associated with retirement did not seem to lead to an immediate increase in budgeting problems, presumably because it had been foreseen.

References

1. Department of Employment, *New Earnings Surveys,* 1979 to 1990, HMSO

2. Central Statistical Office, 'The effect of taxes and benefits on household income, 1979', *Economic Trends,* January 1981; 'The effect of taxes and benefits on household incomes, 1988', *Economic Trends,* March 1991. Note that the 'unadjusted' figures for 1988 are used, for comparison with the 1979 figures.

3. M. Friedman, *A Theory of the Consumption Function,* Princeton University Press, 1957; F. Modigliani and R. E. Brumberg, 'Utility analysis and the consumption function' in K.K. Kurihara (ed.), *Post-Keynesian Economics,* Rutgers University Press, 1954

4. Council of Mortgage Lenders, *Housing Finance,* 1991. 'Liquid assets' consist mainly of national savings and deposits with banks and building societies.

5. National Opinion Polls, *Consumer Credit,* Department of Trade and Industry, 1971

6. National Consumer Council, *Consumers and Credit,* NCC, 1981

7. See notes 5 and 6

8. M. Edwards, *Financial arrangements within the family,* National Women's Advisory Council, 1981; M. Edwards, 'Financial arrangements within families', *Social Security Journal,* December 1981, pp.1-16; J. Pahl, 'The allocation of money and the structuring of inequality within marriage', *Sociological Review,* 1983, 31(2), pp.237-262; L. Morris and S. Ruane, *Household finance, management and the labour market,* Gower, 1984; G. Wilson, *Money in the family,* Avebury, 1987; J. Pahl, *Money and marriage,* Macmillan, 1989

9. Pahl, 1989; see note 8

10. Pahl, 1989; see note 8

11. Central Statistical Office, *United Kingdom National Accounts,* HMSO, 1990

12. See note 6. The figures here are based on a PSI reanalysis of the NCC data.

13. Social Security Committee, *Low Income Statistics: Households Below Average Income Tables 1988,* House of Commons paper 401, HMSO 1991

14. eg. L. Burghes, *Living from Hand to Mouth*, Child Poverty Action Group, 1980; E. Evason, *Ends that Won't Meet*, CPAG, 1980; R. Berthoud, *The Reform of Supplementary Benefit*, Policy Studies Institute, 1984; J. Bradshaw and H. Holmes, *Living on the Edge*, CPAG, 1989

15. R. Berthoud, *Credit, Debt and Poverty*, HMSO, 1989

16. See, for example, a series of articles in the *Journal of Social Policy*, April 1987

3 Household Commitments

All households have certain basic commitments that must be met out of the family budget. The great majority have direct housing costs such as mortgage repayments or rent. Most pay local taxes and just about everybody has to pay for fuel. Each of these is a potential source of debt.

Mortgages

Public discussion of personal borrowing often overlooks the fact that for every £1 of consumer credit more than £5 is lent in mortgages for house purchase. Chart 3.1 shows that the volume of mortgage lending nearly trebled between 1980 and 1990. The current value of mortgages represents an average of £12,000 for every household in the country; it is equivalent to nine months of total personal income.

Chart 3.1 Volume of mortgages outstanding, 1979 to 1990

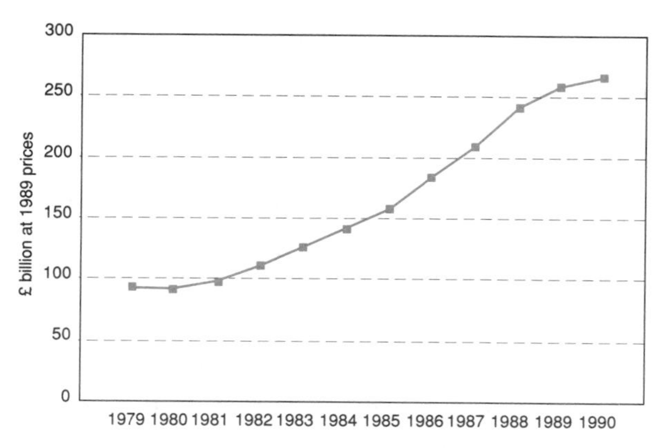

Source: Council of Mortgage Lenders [1]

A number of changes during the 1980s contributed to the continued growth of mortgage finance. The building societies were joined by the banks in the early 1980s, followed by specialist mortgage brokers in the late 1980s. Commercial sources accounted for only 9 per cent of mortgage capital in 1979, but for 39 per cent by 1989.[2] In the 1970s, humble couples had to queue for the privilege of borrowing from the building society with which they had saved regularly; by the end of the 1980s eager financial institutions competed with each other for the privilege of lending.

This relaxation in the supply combined with government policies encouraging home ownership to create a rapid expansion in the number of home buyers. The proportion of households buying their home with the help of a mortgage rose from 30 per cent in 1979 to 42 per cent in 1989.[3] Part of this expansion came from the sale of council houses under the Right-to-Buy scheme: 1.3 million tenants became owners between 1980 and 1989.

The combination of more people and more money in the market for a static supply of housing led to a rapid rise in house prices between 1982 and 1989. The increase every year was exciting for those who bought last year, but frustrating for those who wanted to buy next year, and the rush to buy ahead of the next rise may have helped to fuel the next round of increases. Naturally the rise in prices meant larger mortgages. The phasing of this cycle varied between different parts of the country, but Chart 3.2 shows how prices and mortgages changed over the country as a whole.

Chart 3.2 Average house prices, 1979 to 1990

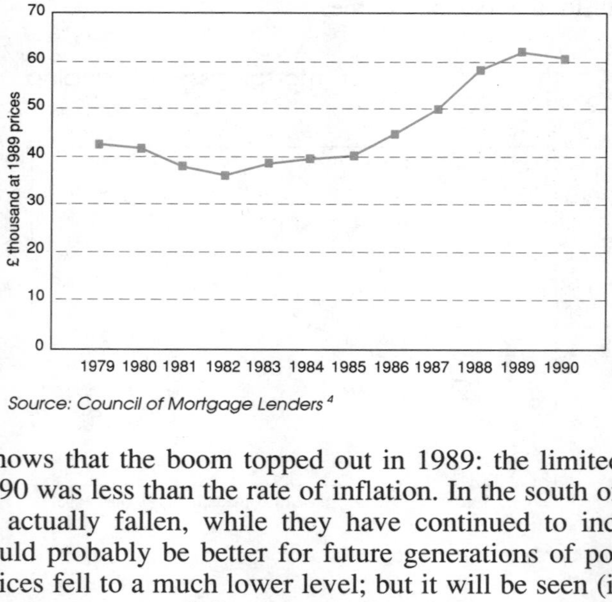

£ thousand at 1989 prices

0 10 20 30 40 50 60 70

1979 1980 1981 1982 1983 1984 1985 1986 1987 1988 1989 1990

Source: Council of Mortgage Lenders [4]

The chart shows that the boom topped out in 1989: the limited increase in values in 1990 was less than the rate of inflation. In the south of the country prices have actually fallen, while they have continued to increase in the north. It would probably be better for future generations of potential home owners if prices fell to a much lower level; but it will be seen (in Chapter 9) that a fall can have a potentially serious effect on the people who bought at the peak of the cycle.

The rapid rise in prices and advances had two consequences for borrowers. First, the price increase tended to be reflected in the size of the mortgage, rather than in the amount the buyers paid out of their savings or from other sources. In 1979, first-time buyers paid an average of £30,000 (at 1989 prices): they borrowed £23,000 and contributed £7,000 themselves. In 1989, first-time buyers were having to pay £40,000: borrowing £33,000, but still contributing only £7,000 directly.[5] This was potentially a riskier lending policy, especially when the underlying value of the properties against which the mortgages were secured started to fall at the end of the decade.

The second consequence of the rise in the average advance was that the ratio of mortgages to the borrowers' incomes grew larger: for first-time buyers, the average ratio increased from 1.7 to 2.2 between 1979 and 1989.[6] If the recent average has been 2.2, there must be many cases where the ratio was much higher than that - people with incomes barely adequate to sustain a mortgage, living in areas of high prices, dealing with lenders prepared to take higher risks. Again, this increase in the ratio of mortgages to incomes is a potentially risky policy, especially if interest rates rise rapidly soon after the agreement is concluded.

Since the standard period of repaying a mortgage is 25 years, and needs to be completed before retirement, there is strong pressure for people to take out mortgages in their twenties or thirties. The life-cycle theory predicts exactly the same pattern, young people borrowing against future earnings, with a reduction in commitments as income falls at retirement. Historically the growth in owner-occupation has tended to occur because each succeeding generation of young people was more likely to buy than their predecessors, rather than because there was an expansion among all age-groups simultaneously. The big increase over the past 10 years, however, has not worked out that way (Chart 3.3): the proportion of young people buying a property has hardly changed, and the biggest increase has been among people in the second half of their working lives, most of whom were sitting tenants buying their council homes under the government's Right-to-Buy scheme.[7]

Chart 3.3 Proportion of households in owner-occupied accommodation, by age, 1979 and 1988

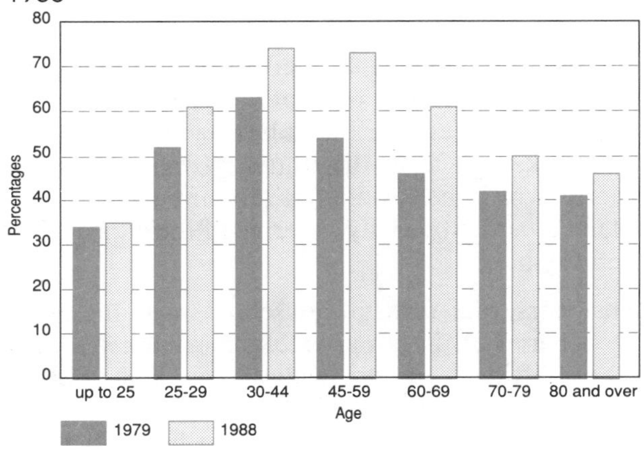

Source: General Household Survey [8]

Table 3.4 shows how these influences worked out for the members of the survey sample. As one would expect, borrowing behaviour was strongly related to the age of the householder. The people taking out mortgages for the first time over the past three years tended to be in their twenties. Some households had negotiated revised mortgage agreements in the past three years. This was most common for people in their thirties. The next group consists of people who held a mortgage, but had not borrowed recently. They were mainly in their forties and fifties. Finally, there were owner-occupiers with no outstanding mortgage. The great majority of them were over the age of sixty.

Table 3.4 Mortgage borrowing, by age

Percentages

	Up to 29	30 to 39	40 to 49	50 to 59	60 to 69	70 or more
Total (=100%)	*319*	*453*	*388*	*316*	*335*	*395*
First-time mortgage	21	6	5	5	1	1
Subsequent mortgage	15	23	12	6	*	*
Existing mortgage	13	36	45	41	10	5
All with a mortgage	47	65	62	51	11	5
Outright owners	1	4	7	26	49	46
Tenants	51	31	32	23	41	49
Average mortgage payments per week (incl insurance)	£74	£74	£59	£38	£33	£9

Source: PSI survey; analysis based on all householders
Note: 'First-time mortgage' means a loan taken out in the past three years by a first-time buyer. 'Subsequent mortgage' means a loan taken out in the past three years by an existing owner-occupier, either to move to a different home, or to raise additional money on the same property.

The relatively low level of owner-occupation among people now past retirement age is primarily a generation effect: home buying was much less common when current pensioners were at work. But there is also clearly a life-cycle pattern: the prime age for initial borrowing is in the twenties; some additional activity takes place in the thirties; by the fifties and sixties an increasing proportion of home-owners have completed their payments. All this can be explained perfectly easily in terms of the expected rise and fall in income over the life time.

Among non-pensioners, four-fifths of households with high levels of income had a mortgage (Chart 3.5). It can probably be assumed that the remainder would have had no difficulty in borrowing money if they had wanted to, so 80 per cent probably represents the ceiling on demand for mortgages. By the same token, four-fifths of people would like to buy a house if they could afford it.[9] But less than half of households with an income below £200 per

Chart 3.5 Mortgage holding, by income

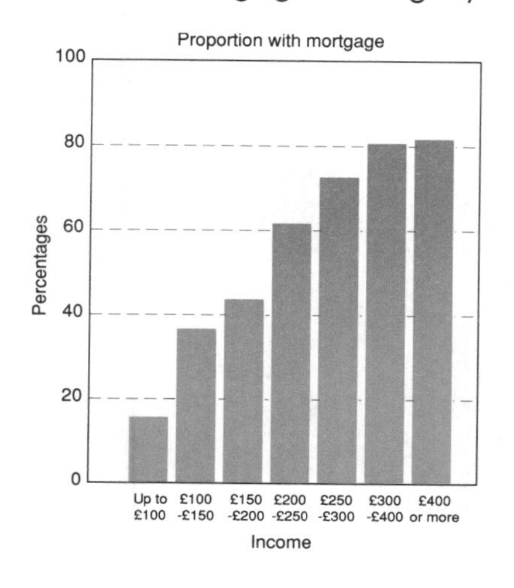

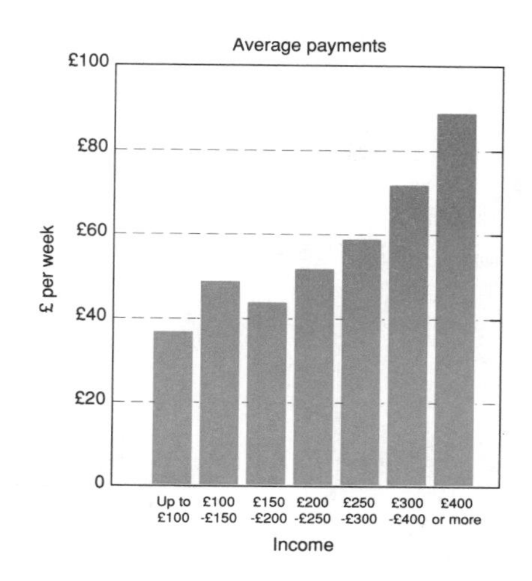

Source: PSI survey; analysis based on non-pensioners

week were buying a house on a mortgage, and only 15 per cent of those whose income was below £100 per week.

Chart 3.6 plots the estimated current value of each household's mortgage according to the date at which it was taken out. The more recent the transaction, the larger the amount, for three reasons.

- Repayments reduce the amount outstanding. During the early years the capital sum reduces very slowly indeed: half way through a 25 year contract the borrower still owes about four-fifths of the original loan. It is during the final years that the outstanding loan reduces rapidly. (The figures in Chart 3.6 are an estimate of the current value, based on data about the original value and the year of the contract.)
- Recent mortgages have a long-run tendency to be larger than those taken out many years earlier. House prices rise over the years because of inflation, and because a proportion of the increasing national income will tend to be spent on improved accommodation.
- House-price inflation was particularly steep in the late 1980s. This is a particular misfortune of the households who happened to enter the market at the time.

As a result of this combination of factors, the current value of a loan was far more strongly linked to the date it was agreed than it was to more obviously relevant aspects of a household's circumstances, such as its income. Because younger people tended to have borrowed more recently, it was they who

Chart 3.6 Average current value of mortgage, by date at which it was agreed

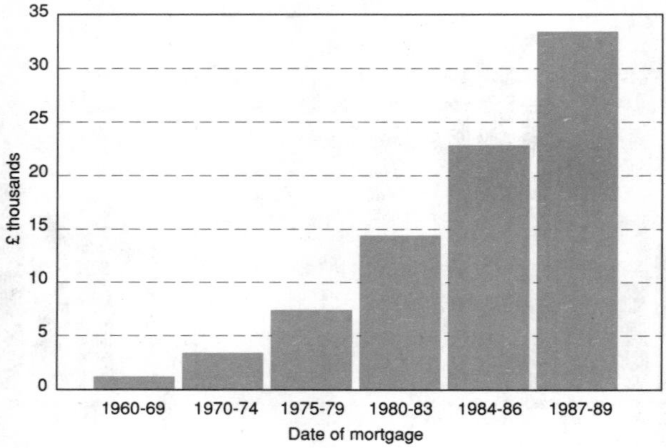

Source: PSI survey; analysis based on mortgage holders

generally owed the most. Borrowers in their twenties owed just under £30,000 on average. This represented two years of their net incomes. Those in their fifties currently owed just under £10,000, seven months of their net income. The survey suggests that 500,000 households currently owed more than their annual income. 400,000 of them were in their twenties or thirties.

The immediate issue for borrowers is not the size of the mortgage, but the amount of their regular repayments. The average mortgage holder was paying £53 per week. (Remember that all amounts are stated in weekly equivalents; £53 per week is £230 per month.) The bottom line of Table 3.4 showed that average commitments were about twice as high for borrowers in their twenties and thirties as for those in their fifties, mainly because the older people had borrowed so much longer ago. Chart 3.5 showed that commitments were as high as £91 per week for borrowers earning more than £400 per week, but that there was very little difference between middle- and low-income households. Poor households had little chance of getting a mortgage, because few mortgages could be had for less than £40 per week.

Monthly repayments are a function of the amount borrowed (determined at the date of purchase) and by the rate of interest (varying from year to year). There are three ways of looking at changes in interest rates over the past ten years (Chart 3.7).

- *Nominal interest rates* have fluctuated between 11 and 15 per cent. They have recently been at a particularly high level, though the 1991 figures have fallen below the 1990 peak. But is difficult to pick out an underlying trend towards either higher or lower interest rates.

- *Interest net of tax*. Few borrowers pay the full rate of interest, because of tax relief. The total cost of this subsidy has risen dramatically over the years, because of the growth in mortgage lending, but the rate of relief has tended to shrink. First, the government's policy of transferring revenue-raising from income tax to national insurance contributions and VAT has reduced the standard rate of relief from 33 per cent to 25 per cent. Second, the £30,000 per property limit for tax relief has had more effect as the average advance has grown. Third, relief will in future be limited to the standard rate of tax.

- *Real interest rate*. Inflation also reduces the real rate of interest below the apparent charge. High inflation is small comfort in the short term to borrowers facing high interest charges, but it is a boon in the medium term. If they can survive the first few years, the real cost of their loan should fall. During the late 1970s the reduction in the real value of a loan more than compensated for the interest charges: savers were effectively paying borrowers to take their money. During the 1980s there have been peaks and troughs in the real net interest rate, but it has usually been below 5 per cent.

Although the long-run cost of a mortgage is very low, short-run changes in interest rates can have an important effect on repayment commitments. The typical loan taken out in 1988 would have attracted net interest charges of £58 per week. This would have risen to £72 in 1989 – the year of the survey; and it rose again to £80 per week in 1990. Most people who had borrowed as

Chart 3.7 Mortgage interest rates, 1979-1990

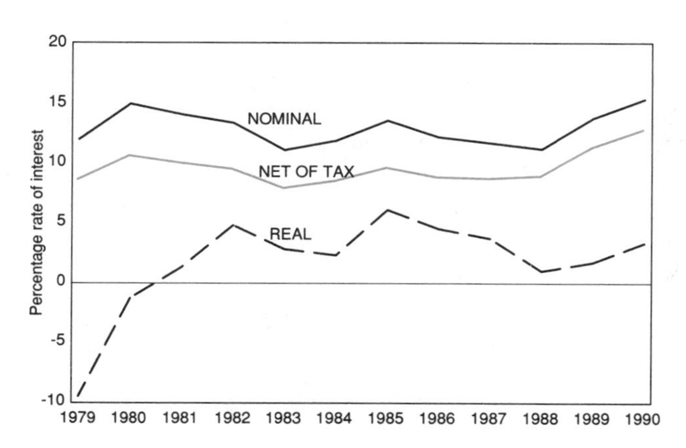

Source: Council of Mortgage Lenders [10]
Note: The top line shows actual average interest rates charged by lenders. The second line takes account of tax relief on an average new advance. The third also takes account of the rate of inflation over the following year.

much as they could afford in 1988 would have had to pay more than they could afford in 1990.

Rents

Most households who do not own their home have to pay rent. As the number of owners has expanded, the number of renters has declined. Whereas most of the growth in owner-occupation since the war has been at the expense of private rental, the recent council house sales have eaten into the stock of accommodation rented from local authorities. Increased activity by housing associations has been on too small a scale to make much difference to the overall ratio of owner-occupation to tenancies. Table 3.8 shows the pattern of tenure by age-group. There is a life-cycle effect: many young single people rent privately before buying their first home; and some elderly owner-occupiers move into rented sheltered housing.[11]

Table 3.8 Renting by age

Percentages

	Up to 29	30 to 39	40 to 49	50 to 59	60 to 69	70 or more
Total (=100%)	*319*	*453*	*388*	*316*	*335*	*395*
Council tenants	26	22	23	19	33	33
Private tenants	15	4	3	1	3	10
Housing association tenants	4	2	2	2	4	4
Other tenants	5	2	3	1	1	2

Source. PSI survey; analysis based on all householders

The recruitment of lower-middle-income households from renting to owning has the curious effect of making both tenures seem poorer. The new buyers have lower incomes than existing owner-occupiers, but higher incomes than the remaining tenants. Rented housing, and council housing in particular, has increasingly been reserved for poor families.[12] Chart 3.9 (left) shows that this is so, even if we leave out the concentration of pensioners in council housing. Remember that the income gap between rich and poor has also been stretched over the past decade (see Chart 2.1), so the polarisation of the housing market has been proceeding at double speed.

Over the same period there have been changes in the arrangements for supporting poor people's rents. During the heyday of council housing, a substantial proportion of the cost was met direct from the public purse, and not passed on to tenants in the form of economic rents. It is a matter of debate exactly how much the subsidy amounted to,[13] but recent governments have favoured reducing the general subsidy and increasing rents to market values. Average unrebated rents increased 60 per cent faster than the cost of living between 1979 and 1989.[14] Housing benefit meets the whole rent of claimants of income support, and they are effectively insulated from changes in the subsidies. People just above the income support level can claim a partial rebate, but these have become less generous over precisely the same period as rents have been increasing. It is therefore lower-middle-income households who have faced the rent squeeze – the same group that was being encouraged to look to owner-occupation.

Chart 3.9 Renting, by income

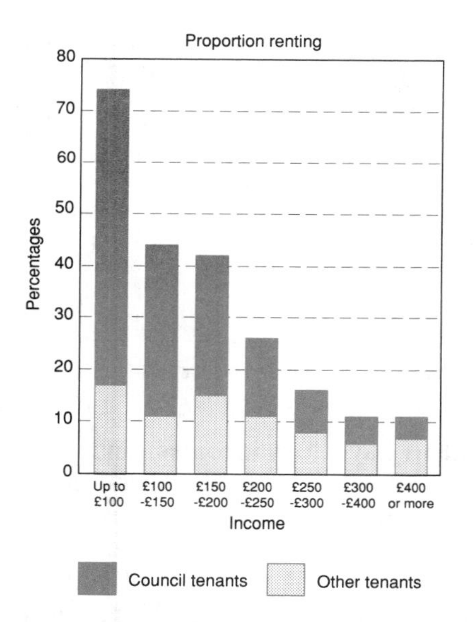

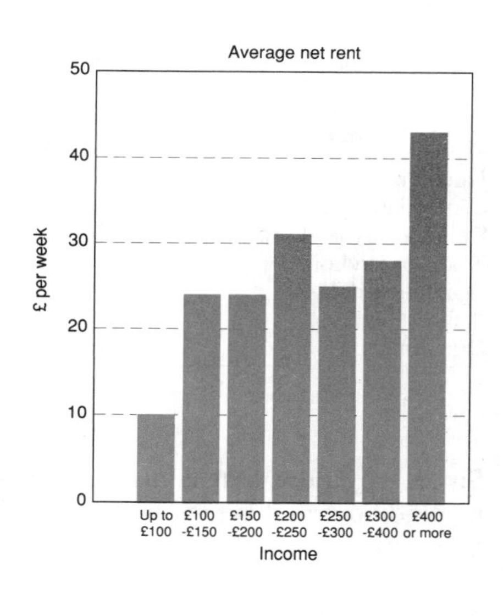

Source: PSI survey; analysis based on non-pensioner householders
Note: The average rent includes the rates of those tenants who paid them together.

The survey did not provide a very precise measure of rental commitments. Many tenants paid their rates, and sometimes fuel or service charges, together with the rent, and were not able to say how the total divided up. A large proportion of tenants claim rent rebates or allowances and some were not clear what their net rent came to. Chart 3.9 (right) showed the amounts of net rent recorded by people at different income levels. Housing benefit meant that people with very low incomes paid relatively low rents. Most of the high-income tenants rented in the private sector and paid high rents.

It is known that one of the factors associated with keeping up to date with rent payments is the method of collection.[15] Door-to-door collection tends to encourage prompt payment, while the least effective method, from the point of view of efficient collection, is payment at the post office. Avoidance of arrears is not, of course, the only consideration. Door-to-door collection is almost certainly the most expensive in terms of staff time, and so long as the collection is in cash it is also the method most exposed to the risk of theft and violence. The latter arguments appear to have predominated in the thinking of councils; the survey shows that doorstep rent collection was less prevalent at the end of the 1980s than at the beginning of the decade (Table 3.10). Giros paid through the post office had become the most widespread system.

Table 3.10 Rent collection for council tenants, 1981 and 1989.

Percentages

	1981	1989
Total (=100%)	*997*	*428*
Paid at post office	17	34
Sent to landlord	1	29
Collected by landlord	42	19
Taken to landlord	35	9
Standing order/ direct debit	2	7
Other methods	1	2

Sources: 1981 Department of the Environment;[16] 1989 PSI survey; analysis based on council tenants who have rent to pay.

Since we know that council tenants tend to have low incomes, and low-income households tend not to have bank accounts, it is not surprising that a large proportion of rent is paid by specific transactions, rather than by the standing orders or direct debit arrangements common for mortgage payments. On the other hand, although three-fifths (61 per cent) of council tenants with rent to pay had a current account with a bank or building society only 11 per cent of those who had accounts used an automated payment mechanism for their rent.

Local taxes

Local taxes are a household commitment over which families have little room for manoeuvre. At the time of the survey (late 1989) the old domestic rates remained the local tax in England, Wales and Northern Ireland; the community charge or poll tax had already been introduced in Scotland.

Three-quarters of tenants in England, Wales and Northern Ireland reported their rates as an inclusive amount with their rent, and did not record a separate amount. Just about all Scottish tenants paid their community charge separately from their rent. The change to separate local tax payments was likely to disrupt household budgets simply by introducing a new item of expenditure, even if the total amounts paid had been the same.

Chart 3.11 shows average amounts reported by rates payers and poll tax payers, after allowing for rebates.

Chart 3.11 Average net rates or poll tax payments, by household income

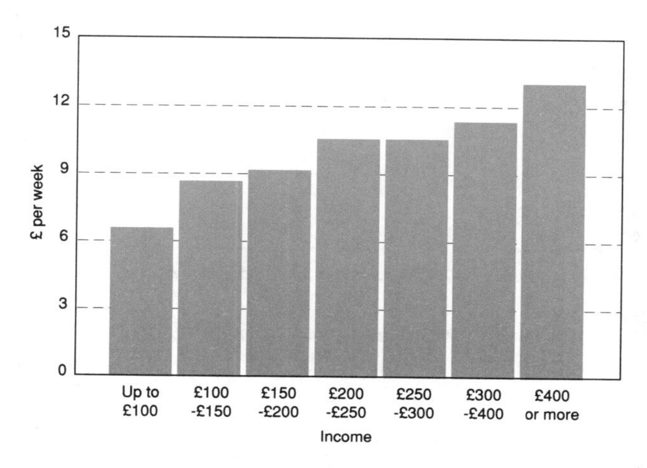

Source: PSI survey; analysis based on non-pensioners who paid rates or poll tax

Household services

Household services, such as fuel and telephones, also need to be included in this review of household commitments.

The two piped fuels, electricity and gas, can be paid for in a variety of ways.

- *Quarterly billing* has always been the most common arrangement.
- *Fixed monthly payment plans* have been encouraged by both industries. These schemes have been extended to about a quarter of all customers, with most of the growth occurring during the 1980s.
- *Prepayment meters* used to be common in poorer homes, especially in rented property. They are a costly and inconvenient method of collection for the supply industries and there were growing security problems. Consequently the number of slot meters has reduced over the years, even though low-income customers continued to prefer them.[17] This reduction has been offset to a certain extent by installing prepayment coin or token meters for customers with a history of arrears, although problems in the production of the meters has delayed their introduction. Table 3.12 shows that there has been a continued reduction in the number of gas meters over the past ten years, while the number of electricity meters (including non-cash token meters) has recovered slightly. Both types of meter were used predominantly by low-income customers.

Table 3.12 Methods of paying for electricity and gas, 1980 and 1989

Percentages

	1980	1989
Electricity		
Total (=100%)	*na*	*2106*
Quarterly credit	88	67
Regular fixed payments	5	23
Prepayment meter	7	9
Gas		
Total (=100%)	*na*	*1642*
Quarterly credit	77	66
Regular fixed payments	9	29
Prepayment meter	14	5

Sources: 1980 Fuel industry statistics;[18] 1989 PSI survey; analysis based on households using each fuel.

The two fuels usually delivered in bulk – coal and oil – have diminished in importance, though solid fuel remains the primary source of heat in Northern Ireland.

The other main domestic service is the telephone. The vast majority of private lines were paid for quarterly, although a tenth of the survey households belonged to monthly budget schemes.

The analysis of housing costs showed that mortgage, rent and rates/poll tax all tended to rise with income, although the slope of the increase was not very steep. For fuel and other household services, on the other hand, there

Chart 3.13 Average spending on fuel and telephone, by household income

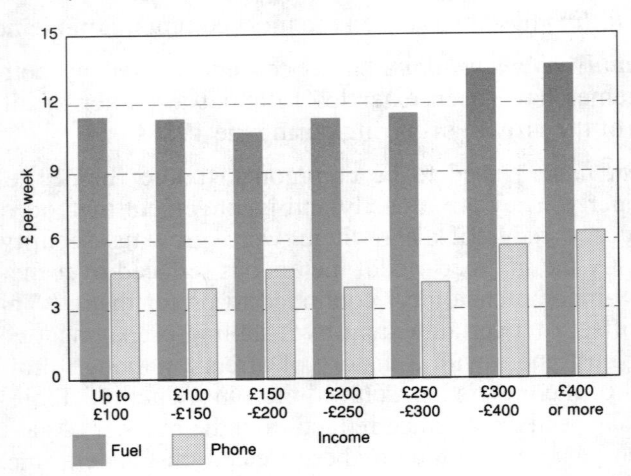

Source: PSI survey; analysis based on non-pensioners whose income was known

was very little variation in costs between rich and poor households (Chart 3.13).

References

1. Council of Mortgage Lenders, *Housing Finance*, no 11, August, 1991

2. See note 1

3. Office of Population Censuses and Surveys, *General Household Survey, 1989*, HMSO, 1991

4. See note 1

5. See note 1

6. See note 1

7. E. Kempson, S. McKay and L. Perkins, *Household Budgets and Housing Costs*, PSI, 1992, forthcoming

8. See note 3

9. British Market Research Bureau, *Housing and Saving*, BMRB, 1989

10. See note 1

11. P. Dodd and P. Hunter, *Trading Down and Moves out of Owner Occupation*, HMSO, 1990

12. A. Murie and P. Willmott, *Polarisation and Social Housing*, Policy Studies Institute, 1989; D. Maclennan, K. Gibb and A. More, *Paying for Britain's Housing*, Joseph Rowntree Foundation, 1990

13. J. Hills, *Thirty Nine Steps to Housing Finance Reform*, Joseph Rowntree Foundation, 1991

14. Department of the Environment, *Housing and Construction Statistics*, 1990, HMSO, 1991

15. S. Duncan and K. Kirby, *Preventing Rent Arrears*, HMSO, 1983

16. See note 15

17. R. Berthoud, *Fuel Debts and Hardship*, Policy Studies Institute, 1981

18. See note 17

Part II
CONSUMER CREDIT

4 Patterns of Borrowing

The increase in credit use over the past ten years might be taken as an indication that, as a nation, we have become more favourably disposed towards credit – more aware of the advantages, less worried about the potential problems. But people still tended to be cautious in their views about it.

Attitudes to credit

When they were asked a straight question, less than a fifth of adults were positively in favour of credit. Many people felt that it should be used only as a last resort. The most popular view – held by getting on for half the people interviewed – was that credit was never a good thing. Perhaps the most surprising conclusion was that people were more antagonistic to credit than they had been ten years earlier (Table 4.1). No one could use these figures to suggest that increased credit use had been caused by changing public attitudes. If anything, people seem to have reacted against the credit boom, fearing the consequences, even though many of them were active borrowers. In 1979, only 11 per cent of credit commitments were held by people who thought that credit was never a good thing (not shown in the table). By 1989, that proportion had nearly doubled, to 20 per cent. The extent to which households are borrowing against their better judgement is, perhaps, a measure of the state of public anxiety on this issue.

Table 4.1 Attitudes to credit, 1979 and 1989

Percentages

	1979	1989
Total (=100%)	*775*	*2843*
A sensible way of buying	7	6
A convenient way of buying	20	12
Occasionally necessary	42	37
Never a good thing	31	43

Sources: 1979 National Consumer Council;[1] 1989 PSI survey; analysis based on all householders and spouses present at the interview

Another way of probing people's attitudes was to ask them to say how far they agreed or disagreed with each of a series of statements. The answers are presented as a score out of 10, so that if everyone had agreed strongly with one of the statements, it would have scored 10; if everyone disagreed strongly, it would score zero.

Virtually everyone supported the self-evident statement that:

If you lose your job, having outstanding credit commitments can make the situation much worse score 9.7

But perhaps a more damning criticism was that the majority of people felt that:

Credit encourages you to buy things you don't really need score 7.9

On the plus side, many people recognised that:

Having a credit card saves you carrying round a lot of cash score 6.3

But on the whole the sample disagreed with the suggestion that:

Credit makes financial planning and budgeting easier score 3.9

Taken together with the direct question about whether credit was a good thing, the overwhelming impression is of a view of credit which is at best cautious, at worst antagonistic.

We used the combined answers to these questions to identify the quarter of the sample who were most 'in favour' of credit; and the quarter who were most 'against' (see Box H). Those who were relatively 'in favour' tended to be youngish – especially people in their thirties – and to have above-average incomes (Table 4.2). The people who took the strongest stand 'against' credit tended to be elderly; among people of working age, it was those with low incomes who were least in favour of credit.

Comparison with the budgeting characteristics analysed in Chapter 2 showed that 'consumers' took a favourable view of credit. People in 'hardship' did not stand out strongly as either for or against.

Box H Attitudes to credit

We scored each of the five questions reported in this section, so that the most unfavourable answers each scored zero, the most favourable answer scored 10. The household's overall attitude was calculated as the average of these scores. Where the householders were a married couple, both husband's and wife's opinions are included in the score.

The sample was divided into three groups, as follows:

'Against'	Up to 1.8 points	25% of households
Medium	1.9 to 4.4 points	51% of households
'In favour'	4.5 points or more	24% of households.

Note that these cut-off points were designed simply to identify the top and bottom quarters of the scores. The fact that a quarter of the sample were 'in favour' of credit is not a finding of the study. Many of the 'in favour' category scored less than half of the maximum points.

Table 4.2 Attitudes to credit, by age, household income, 'consumerism' and 'hardship'

Percentages

	'In favour'	'Against'	*Total (=100%)*
Age			
Up to 29	25	16	*319*
30 to 39	36	12	*453*
40 to 49	33	15	*388*
50 to 59	25	22	*316*
60 to 69	14	31	*335*
70 to 79	8	53	*395*
Household income (non-pensioners)			
up to £100	18	27	*255*
£100 to £150	21	18	*176*
£150 to £200	28	17	*255*
£200 to £250	24	18	*201*
£250 to £300	36	8	*177*
£300 to £400	38	12	*284*
£400 or more	42	8	*206*
'Consumerism'			
Low consumerism	12	45	*473*
Below average	21	24	*913*
Above average	33	16	*615*
High consumerism	39	9	*223*
'Hardship'			
Low hardship	26	23	*1,187*
Medium	23	27	*778*
Severe hardship	18	28	*259*

Source: PSI survey; analysis based on all householders. See Box H for the definition of attitudes to credit.
*Note: Percentages run **across** the table.*

The supply side

The growth in consumer credit over the 1980s has taken place in conjunction with major changes in the financial services industry.

Various forms of credit controls were used almost continuously in the 1950s and 1960s and for much of the 1970s. Successive governments restricted borrowing for 'non-priority' purposes in two ways: by regulating the balance sheets of financial institutions; and by controls on the down-payment and repayment conditions for hire purchase and other forms of instalment credit.

The most common form of balance sheet control was ceilings on bank lending. At times these were formal guidelines set for all banks, while at other times the guidelines were looser and covered only the clearing banks. In 1971 the Heath government lifted the balance sheet controls and, with the introduction of 'competition and credit control', relied on interest rates to regulate the market. The controls were, however, reintroduced in December 1973 when the government required banks whose lending rose above a specified rate to make interest-free supplementary deposits at the Bank of England. This system, known as the 'corset', continued until July 1980. Since then there have been no direct controls on the volume of credit advanced by the clearing banks, apart from the standard prudential regulation by the Bank of England.

Controls on the terms for consumer credit lending mainly operated on hire-purchase agreements – the main source of consumer credit in the 1960s and 1970s. These required customers to put down a minimum cash deposit (25 per cent of the purchase price for example) and to pay off the sum borrowed over a maximum repayment period (such as 24 months). Variations in deposits and repayment periods on hire purchase agreements were used by Chancellors of the Exchequer as the main short-term economic regulator for many years. But in 1982 these controls were also removed.

The third major change in the legislative framework was the 1986 Building Societies Act, allowing building societies to offer a wider range of financial services – personal loans, overdrafts and credit cards – in direct competition with the banks. The controls on building societies were further relaxed in 1988, when they were permitted to increase the proportion of funds raised from sources other than their investors.

So, by the end of the 1980s, traditional controls over the supply of credit had been removed; the credit supply was left to market forces. The level of consumer borrowing, and consequent changes in the money supply, could be adjusted only by raising and lowering interest rates. Interest has a potential effect over a wide range of economic sectors: not only on consumer credit but also on personal savings, on corporate cash-flow and investment, on public-sector borrowing and on the exchange rate. Government policy on all these aspects of the economy is subject to the same regulator, and there is no tool available to adjust consumer credit as such.

Historically, the credit industry was divided into clearly-defined sectors. Banks offered private customers overdrafts or personal loans; building societies offered mortgages; finance houses backed hire-purchase agreements. One effect of deregulation has been to encourage competition not only within each sector, but between sectors. Every type of financial institution has diversified its range of products, and has targeted those products at a wider range of customers.

The high-street banks began lending for house purchase, in direct competition with the building societies. They also developed personal loans with long repayment periods and revolving credit accounts, both secured on the value of property.

Credit cards have had the biggest impact, both financially and on public perceptions of credit. The first card was issued in 1966. Since then there has been a remarkable growth in the number in circulation. The number of credit cards nearly tripled, from 11.6 million in 1980 to 29.8 million at the end of 1990.[2]

Since the Building Societies Act lifted controls in 1986, building societies have been free to offer their customers a range of unsecured credit: personal loans, overdrafts and credit cards. Many societies have also introduced new types of secured loan as well as increasing the number of further advances against existing mortgages. Most of the largest societies are using their own funds for these new products; others, however, act as agents for a finance house. The Abbey National went one stage further and ceased to operate as a building society when, in 1989, it became a public limited company – effectively a bank.

Finance houses have also experienced a rapid growth in lending, especially since the lifting of hire-purchase controls in 1982. Many of the largest finance houses were set up originally in the 1920s and 1930s to provide loans for car purchase. While this remains a large part of their business, they, too, have diversified into personal loans as well as first and second mortgages.

There have also been new entrants to the credit market. A number of the large retail groups offer revolving credit facilities, such as budget accounts and store cards, to their customers. Most of these schemes are backed by a finance house; but the finance house is sometimes owned by the retailer, or is a member of the same group of companies. The Monopolies and Mergers Commission identified just under 9 million retail store cards in circulation in 1987; by early 1990 there were over 12 million.[3]

While each type of financial institution has broadened the range of its products so that they are all competing directly with each other, the distinctions have been further blurred by a process of mergers, take-overs and agency agreements so that it is no longer possible to make a clear distinction between categories of organisation.

The credit boom

Deregulation encouraged a boom in consumer credit in the 1980s, both because it lifted constraints on borrowers and lenders, and because it encouraged competition within the financial services industry. Banks and finance houses were obliged to develop more sophisticated marketing strategies in order to keep up with each other. Electronic technology provided systems to identify and target the promotion of specialist products on people who were likely to be receptive. Improved risk assessment was essential if the rapid expansion was to be controlled, and computer-based information systems were also developed during this period. None of this would have been effective if there had been no demand for credit, and the rapid rise in the incomes and expectations of a section of the population was therefore a key element in the rapid expansion of the market.

Chart 4.3 shows that the amount of money owed by consumers grew from £21 billion in 1981 (at 1989 prices) to £48 billion in 1989. The total nearly doubled in eight years – a compound growth rate of 11 per cent per year.

Chart 4.3 Volume of consumer credit outstanding, 1979 to 1990

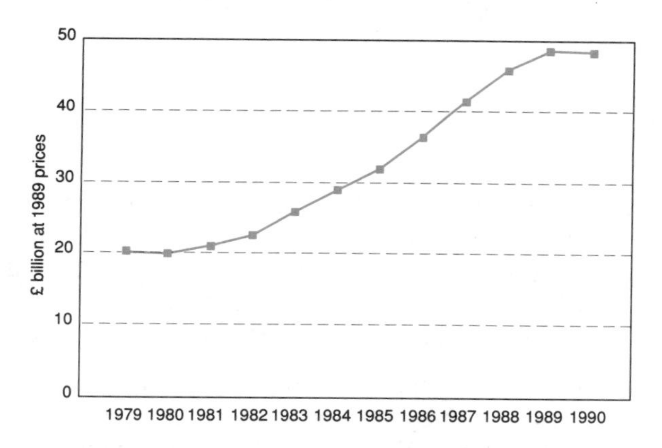

Source: Central Statistical Office [4]

This rate of increase was much faster than the growth in the economy over that period: the stock of outstanding credit grew from 8 per cent of annual consumers' expenditure in 1979 to 15 per cent in 1989. Another way of putting it is that at the beginning of the 1980s the average household owed just under £1,000 (at 1989 prices, excluding mortgages) – 4¼ weeks of its disposable income; by the end of the decade the average had risen to £2,250 per household, representing 7½ weeks of income.

The most recent statistics show that the expansion in consumer credit seems to have stopped: the increase in 1990 was less than the rate of inflation, and early 1991 figures show a small decline in the amount owed. It is too early to say whether this means that the long-run growth has reached a plateau, or whether the slow-down has been a temporary response to the exceptionally high interest rates imposed by macroeconomic policy.

Because of the rapid change in the organisational structure of the industry, it does not really make sense to use the statistics to compare the growth rates of different sources of credit. Chart 4.4 shows that the banks and specialist finance houses still dominate the market, accounting for three-quarters of all consumer credit.

Chart 4.4 Sources of consumer credit, 1990

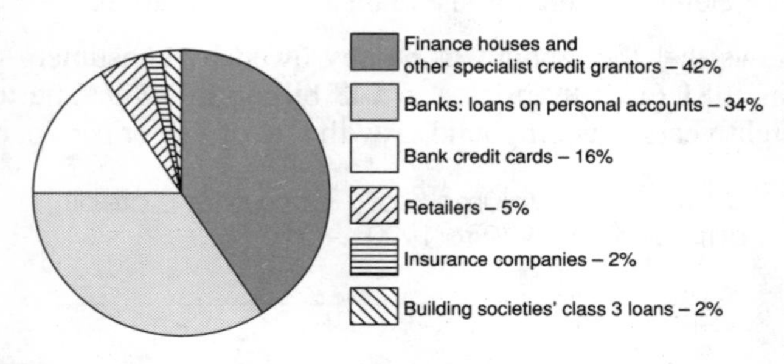

Source: Central Statistical Office [5]

Official figures show the huge growth in the total amount of consumer credit during the last decade. What they do not show is how the growth has been distributed between households. Has the increased credit use occurred because more people started to use credit, or because the existing pool of credit users increased their commitments? Or have both changes occurred?

To answer this question it is necessary to turn to information collected by sample surveys. The PSI survey provides information about the position in 1989. A survey of consumer credit was conducted by National Opinion Polls for the Crowther Commission in 1969; and another was undertaken by Social and Community Planning Research for the National Consumer Council in 1979. The three surveys each adopted their own research methods, and they do not form a strictly comparable time series. But it is useful to make some broad comparisons over, conveniently, two ten-year periods. Table 4.5 analyses current credit 'commitments' reported by each survey; the 1989 figures use a definition from our own survey adapted to be as close as possible to those used in the 1979 study, as explained in Box I.

Table 4.5 Credit facilities, 1969 to 1989

	Has any credit commitment	Has three or more commitments	Average number of commitments
1969	22%	3%	0.4
1979	48%	8%	0.8
1989	60%	16%	1.2

Sources: 1969 NOP; [6] *1979 National Consumer Council;* [7] *1989 PSI survey. See Box I.*

Box I Comparison with the 1979 NCC survey

The 1979 survey was of a sample of adults in two cities in England; the 1989 survey covered households in the United Kingdom. The most important difference between the surveys lies in the treatment of married couples. The PSI survey identified credit agreements held by the husband, by the wife and by the couple jointly. We assume that the adults in the NCC survey reported their own personal agreements, plus joint agreements, but not contracts held by their spouse in his or her own name. In order to compare the surveys, Table 4.5 is based on a reanalysis of both sets of data in which:

- non-householders are excluded from the 1979 survey;
- the 1989 survey is based on the sole and joint agreements reported by each adult, counting husbands and wives separately.

The NCC survey in 1979 identified which of 18 types of credit commitment people had at present. This would lead to some under-counting, to the extent that people had more than one commitment of a particular type. The PSI survey has been analysed to count active credit commitments currently outstanding. There are also likely to be some differences between the surveys in the interpretation of what a 'commitment' consists of – especially for credit cards which are paid off every month. We have excluded them from the count in this analysis, though we are not sure that they would not have been included in the answer to the 1979 question.

The results of the 1969 survey recorded in Table 4.5 are exactly as reported by NOP; no attempt has been made to adjust them to compare more directly with the other two sources.

The evidence suggests that there are now more people with credit commitments than there were 10 or 20 years ago, and that they tend to have a larger number of commitments than previously. In 1969, less than a quarter of the people surveyed had consumer credit commitments. By 1979 this had risen to half, and in 1989 to three-fifths (Table 4.5).

Even more striking has been the increase in the number of adults with multiple credit – a five-fold increase over twenty years. Indeed, the 1989 survey suggests that around 400,000 people may have had six or more credit commitments (not shown separately in Table 4.5). Only one respondent to the 1979 survey reported multiple credit on that scale; none at all in 1969. The total number of facilities reported in 1989 came to three times the number in 1969.

On the other hand, the growth in the number of commitments (50 per cent between 1979 and 1989) was not as great as the expansion in the overall volume of credit indicated by the official statistics. That implies that people have been borrowing larger amounts from each source.

Chart 4.6 compares types of credit commitment, as reported by members of the 1979 and 1989 samples. The comparisons are bound to be affected by differences in the way questions were asked. But there are signs of an increase in the number of standing credit facilities with banks, credit cards

Chart 4.6 Types of credit commitment, 1979 and 1989

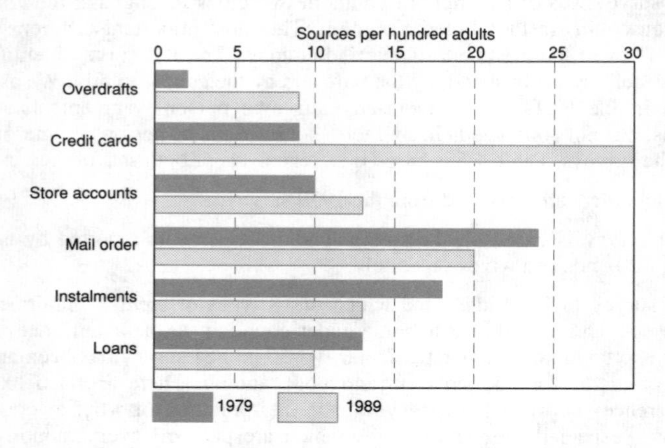

Source: 1979 National Consumer Council;[8] 1989 PSI survey. See Box I.

and retailers, while the number of people buying on credit from mail-order houses, one-off instalment agreements and loans has declined slightly.

Table 4.5 and Chart 4.6 used specially adapted definitions from the PSI survey for comparison with the earlier sources. Table 4.7 gives details for households in the United Kingdom based on what we regard as the most reliable definition.

- Three-quarters (73 per cent) of all households had *credit facilities* available to them over the course of the preceding year; the overall average was two facilities per household.
- A quarter of these were unused bank overdraft facilities or plastic cards which were not actually used for credit, because they were paid up-to-date every month. Three-fifths (60 per cent) of households had used one or more facilities as active sources of credit in the course of the preceding year. The overall average was 1½ sources per household. Since there are about 22 million households in the country, this implies about 33 million active credit sources over 12 months.
- Roughly a quarter of the credit used in the year was no longer outstanding at the end of the year, when the respondents were interviewed. Just over half (51 per cent) of all households had credit currently outstanding. The average current user had two commitments, so the overall average was just over one per household.
- We estimate that the *regular payments* required to service these outstanding credits averaged £14 per week. This represents nearly 7 per cent of net household income as recorded by the survey.

- These figures include some informal borrowings from family, friends and employers. Just under half (48 per cent) of households had an outstanding *commercial credit agreement*. Servicing commitments for commercial credit averaged £13 per household.

Table 4.7 Total consumer credit commitments

	Per cent of households	Average number of sources per household	Average weekly repayments
Credit facilities	73%	2.0	
subtract:			
current accounts, cards paid up every month		(0.5)	
Active credit sources	60%	1.5	
subtract:			
sources paid off at time of interview		(0.4)	
Current credits	51%	1.1	£14
subtract:			
informal borrowings		(0.1)	(£1)
Current commercial credits	48%	1.0	£13

Source: PSI survey; analysis based on all householders.
Note: The averages are calculated across all households, not just those with any commitments.

These various levels of definition of credit are potentially confusing. Wherever possible, we will stick to two concepts.

- Analysis of the number of users, and of frequency of use, will be based on active sources of credit used at any time during the previous year. People with facilities which they keep paid up-to-date do not count as 'users' for this purpose.
- The volume of credit in pounds will be analysed on the basis of the regular payments to service currently outstanding commitments. (See Box J for an explanation of how this was calculated.)

One consequence of this pair of definitions is that a household might be defined as a 'user', but because all their agreements had been paid off at the time of their interview they would be measured as having zero repayments.

Many credit users had used only one 'active' source over the year. Similarly, many of them had borrowed relatively small amounts, with repayments of less than £10 per week. We are particularly interested in 'heavy' commitments (Table 4.8). About a tenth of all households had used four or more active sources; about a tenth were paying in excess of £40 per week to service their credit commitments; about a tenth had committed more than 20 per cent of their total net income. These three groups of 'heavy users' were often the same people, though of course there were some households with a single large loan, and others with many small commitments.

Table 4.8 Extent of credit use

Percentages

Number of active sources		Weekly repayments		Repayments as proportion of income	
None	42	Nil	47	Nil	47
One	23	Up to £10	18	Up to 5%	15
Two	15	£10 to £20	12	5% to 10%	15
Three	10	£20 to £40	12	10% to 20%	13
Four or more	10	£40 plus	10	20% plus	9

Source: PSI survey; analysis based on all householders

Box J Calculating the amount of commitments

The majority of current credit commitments had an agreed weekly or monthly repayment. For those commitments for which a regular repayment agreement was not reported, we used the following formula to estimate how much the repayment would have been, if it had been agreed.

$$P = k_n \sqrt{A}$$

where k_n is a constant for commitment type n

No bank overdrafts were subject to regular payment agreements. For them we estimated repayment agreements on the assumption that the overdraft could have been converted to a loan.

Note that the amount of commitments includes both repayment of the capital, and interest or other service charges. It is a measure of the short-term impact of the commitment on the household budget, not of the 'cost' of the advance.

Box K 'Instalment agreements','loans' and 'borrowings'

One-off advances were allocated to three categories according to the borrower's method of approach.

Where the borrower negotiated with a retailer or supplier to buy an item on credit, we call this an 'instalment agreement'. The credit may actually have been provided by a finance house, but the borrower had no direct contact with it. This method of buying is often called hire purchase, or HP, and we sometimes use this term.

Where the borrower negotiated with a commercial financial institution for an advance which could be spent anywhere, we call this a 'loan'.

Where an advance was obtained from a non-commercial source – relatives, friends, an employer or the social fund – we call this 'borrowing'. The key distinction is that the lender does not usually charge interest.

Table 4.9 shows what sources were involved. Despite being joined by newcomers to the market, mail order was still the most common form of credit, used by three out of ten households. Instalment agreements and loans were the next most common, each of them being used by about a fifth of all households over the course of a year. But because loans tended to be used for the largest advances, they were the most important source of credit in terms of volume.

In many people's eyes, plastic cards epitomise the 'credit society', yet they were far from being the most commonly used source. It is true that nearly four out of 10 households had a credit card, but the majority of them said that they paid off the full amount owing each month. These cards are available as a credit facility, but were not used as an 'active' source of credit. About a sixth of households were using credit cards to defer payment beyond the end of the month.

Bank overdrafts, store cards and informal borrowing were the least common forms of credit, but each was used by about one tenth of households.

Table 4.9 Sources of active credit

	Per cent of households	Average number of active sources per h'hold	Average weekly repayments per h'hold
Revolving credit			
Mail order catalogues	31%	0.38	£1.9
Credit/charge cards	17%	0.21	£1.3
Bank/BS overdraft	13%	0.14	£1.0
Store cards	8%	0.09	£0.4
One-off credit			
Instalment agreements	22%	0.27	£3.0
Loans	19%	0.22	£5.4
Informal borrowings	10%	0.11	£0.9
Mortgage extensions	4%	0.04	na

Source: PSI survey; analysis based on all householders

Notes: 1. The total of the centre column of this table adds to the 1.5 active sources per household in Table 4.7. The total of the right hand column adds to the £14 per household per week in Table 4.7.

2. Repayments of mortgage extensions are included in the cost of mortgages analysed in Chapter 3. They are excluded here to avoid double counting.

Households with just one credit commitment most commonly used mail-order catalogues, the next most common source being goods bought by instalment payments. Together these accounted for six out of 10 single-credit households. Both these sources were also used by heavy credit users, but the types of credit most strongly associated with heavy credit use were credit cards, store cards and loans.

Consumer credit and the life cycle

Age was the single most important factor associated with households' use of credit (Table 4.10). Five out of six people in their thirties had entered the credit market. They used an average of 2.9 active sources in the course of a year. Use declined steadily with age, so that only a fifth of people who were aged over 70 had a credit commitment in the previous year, and those few had used only 1.2 sources apiece. So people in their thirties had 10 times as many active credit agreements per household as those in their seventies.

It seems reasonable to expect that, as people get older, they will have acquired most of the things that they need and will therefore buy fewer items. It might also be expected from the economic theory of the life cycle that older people will have accumulated greater savings and so have less need to use credit. We found that people in their seventies who had bought consumer goods had almost all (94 per cent) used cash or savings to pay for them.

Table 4.10 Credit use, by age

	Up to 29	30 -39	40 -49	50 -59	60 -69	70 plus
Total (=100%)	*319*	*453*	*388*	*316*	*335*	*395*
Percentage with any active use of credit	80%	83%	76%	65%	33%	20%
Average number of sources per user	2.7	2.9	2.6	2.0	1.9	1.2
Overall average	2.2	2.4	2.0	1.3	0.63	0.24

Source: PSI survey; analysis based on all householders

A constant problem in analysis by age across a cross-section of the population is that we cannot immediately tell whether the crucial difference between (say) 40 year-olds and 50 year-olds is that the latter are 10 years further on in their life cycle, or that they were brought up 10 years earlier. The difficulty is especially acute when we know that there has been a substantial change in attitudes and behaviour over recent decades. Is the greater extent of use of credit by younger people part of a permanent tendency for people to borrow early in life? Or does the rapid growth in credit mean that recent generations are borrowing more than their predecessors?

Fortunately, we can compare the findings of the 1969, 1979 and 1989 surveys. Chart 4.11 compares adults' credit use by age at each date. Each curve has been smoothed to show the pattern from age to age (Box L). The dashed lines linking the three curves follows the credit careers of the same cohorts of people as they grew 10 and 20 years older.

Box L Credit use by age

The curves in Chart 4.11 take the form:

$$\text{Credits} = a(\log\text{Age}) - b(\text{Age}) - c$$

Such a curve explains 75 per cent of the variance between single-year ages in the 1989 survey.

For the 1969 and 1979 surveys, a curve of the same form was fitted as close as possible to data for age bands.

The data from the 1979 and 1989 surveys have been reanalysed as described in Box I.

The three surveys show that the pattern of credit between age groups has not changed in the past 20 years. But all age groups were more likely to have credit commitments in 1989 than people of the same age did 10 or 20 years ago. The surveys can also be used to show what happened to the same groups of people as they grew 10 years older. In 1969, 20 year-olds were estimated to have about 0.3 credit commitments each; they had 1.1 in 1979 when they were 30; and 1.5 in 1989 when they were 40. People aged 60 in 1969 also had 0.3 credits; but this increased to only 0.5 when they were 70; and had fallen to 0.2 by the time they were 80. For them, they ageing effect had become more important than the overall change in the use of credit.

Chart 4.11 Credit commitments by age; 1969, 1979 and 1989

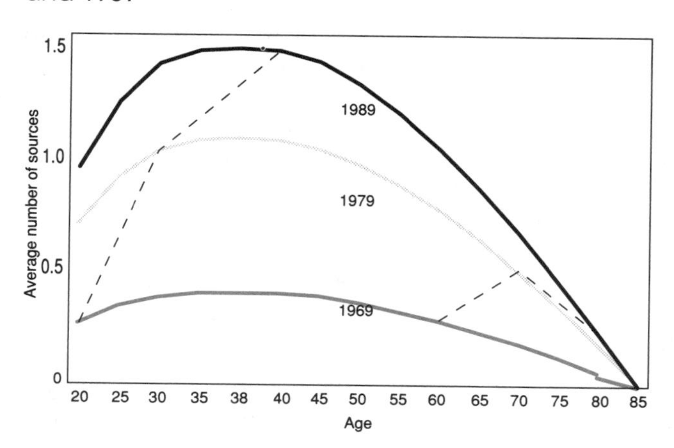

Sources: 1969 NOP;[9] 1979 National Consumer Council;[10] 1989 PSI survey. See Box L.

These comparisons cannot be used to support the suggestion that the current distribution of credit between age groups was simply a reflection of different levels of activity by successive generations, determined by the state of public opinion and of the market at the time they reached adulthood. If that had been true, each cohort's activity would be fixed; the dashed lines in the chart would be horizontal. A more convincing explanation is that an individual's activities are the product of two independent factors:

- the overall level of supply and/or demand at any point of time has been rising. This affects all age groups; hence each curve of credit use by age lies vertically above its predecessor;

- people's personal propensity to make use of the opportunities in the market falls as they grow older. This affects each cohort as it ages: hence the new level of credit use by each cohort is lower than that of the people 10 years their junior.

This suggests that the life-cycle theory outlined in Chapter 2 has a strong influence on the use of consumer credit, just as it did on mortgage borrowing.

There is, however, a serious flaw in the life-cycle theory as an explanation for the detailed patterns of activity revealed in Table 4.10 and Chart 4.11. People in their twenties were slightly less likely to use credit than those in their thirties. The difference is not very great, but the simplest statement of the life-cycle theory would have predicted the highest level of use among the youngest people – at the start of their life-cycle, with low but rapidly rising earnings. (Remember that the comparison so far is between *householders* at different ages; the position of young people living with their parents will be considered later.)

There are three possible explanations for the relatively low level of credit activity among householders in their twenties. One would be to look at an individual's demand for credit as something which builds up cumulatively over a period. The raw theory states that you want to spend (say) £100 above your current annual income at age 20 and another £90 at age 21, £80 at age 22 and so on. Since you do not want to start repaying until age 30, you need a total credit of £190 at age 21, £280 at age 22 and so on, to maintain your planned pattern of spending. This could provide a good explanation of why credit users might build up their level of commitments over their twenties and thirties; but it is harder to use cumulating need to explain why people should delay their entry into the arena.

A second hypothesis is that although people might enjoy a long-term expectation of increasing incomes, the twenties is a period of short-term uncertainties. Each individual is not yet clear how his or her career will work out. Changes of job are frequent, and while most of them may have positive effects, that is not certain in advance. People do not know whether or when they will marry; what the state of the housing market will be when they need to buy; whether they will have children or what effect that would have on the family income. It is also a time when people are most likely to live in furnished accommodation and want mobility and freedom from the burden of possessions. These uncertainties could depress credit use below the very high levels that would be expected on the basis of a confident growth in resources.

The third possibility may be connected to the second. We will show (in Chapter 8) that householders in their twenties have the highest risk of debt. Whatever the reason for that, younger people may use less credit because they are aware of the risk. Certainly creditors know that lending to people in their twenties is potentially risky, and are more cautious about lending to them. One way or another, a high level of risk might exercise a constraint on borrowing. Evidence of a constraint on the supply side appears later in this chapter.

None of this suggests that people in their twenties had a low use of credit; simply that it was lower than the life-cycle hypothesis might have predicted.

Up to this point in the analysis, the life cycle has been associated with the build-up and run-down of earnings and pensions – the income life cycle. Another, parallel, life cycle affects the formation and dissolution of families. Given the importance of the income life cycle to the use of credit, it would be natural to assume that the family life cycle would also play a big role. Indeed, one possible explanation for the rise and fall of credit use either side of the thirties might have been the rise and fall of family responsibilities. Family structure did influence credit use, but it was much less important than age. Rather than present the findings for all family types at once, it is easier to make a series of comparisons.

Non-householders compared with single householders. Almost all of the results of the survey quoted in this report are based on householders; any income, expenditure, credit or debt of adults living as part of another person's household are not counted at all. The survey did, however, include a sample of 160 non-householders aged 18 or over. The great majority of the non-householders were unmarried and without children; most of them were below the age of 30. The young single non-householders reported an average of 1.5 active credit sources over the year; single householders below the age of 30 also reported 1.5 sources. So people living with another household (often their parents) used neither more nor less credit than members of their age group who had set up home on their own.

Among the single young people, a relatively high proportion of the non-householders' credit consisted of informal borrowings (from their parents). So they used rather less commercial credit than other young people. Since both groups of single people used less credit than couples and families (see below), these figures do not really substantiate the view that young people as a group tend to borrow 'too much'.[11]

Box M Single people and couples

The categories are defined according to household structure rather than marital status. 'Single' includes separated, divorced and widowed people living without a partner. 'Couples' include people living with a partner they are not married to.

Single householders compared with couples without children. The left-hand side of Chart 4.12 plots the average number of active credit facilities used by childless single householders and householder couples. In every age group, couples used more credit than single people. The averages for all non-pensioners were 1.7 active sources for couples, 1.3 for single people.

It will be remembered that couples scored substantially higher than single people on our measure of 'consumerism', based on purchases and stocks of durable goods. This additional use of credit is consistent with that finding.

Chart 4.12 Credit use by family type

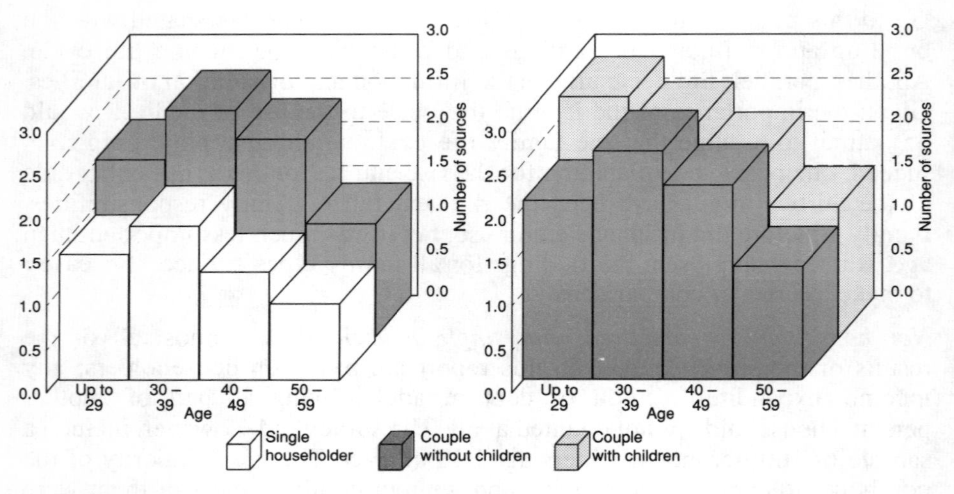

Source: PSI survey; analysis based on non-pensioner householders

Couples with children compared with those without. The group with the largest number of credit commitments was couples with children: 2.4 active sources on average, compared with 1.7 for non-pensioner couples without children. But a large proportion of couples with children were in their thirties, while many couples without dependent children were in their fifties. The right-hand side of Chart 4.12 shows that for most groups, age was important in influencing credit use, but having children was not. The exception was among people in their twenties. Young couples with children used more credit than those who had not started a family. Having children projected a young couple into a pattern of behaviour more typical of people in their thirties.

The number of *lone parents* in each age group was too small for detailed comparison with single people without children. But the findings (not shown in the chart) are consistent with the analysis of couples, suggesting that children added to credit use in the twenties, but not at later ages.

Children turn out to have less effect on credit behaviour than appeared at first sight. While it may be concluded that having children does not usually lead people to take out more credit than they would if they had decided not to have a family, the fact remains that families with children had a large number of commitments. They accounted, in fact, for almost exactly half of all the active sources identified by the survey, principally because they were in the peak borrowing age group. That will be an important point to bear in mind when the discussion turns to arrears and debt; having children *did* seem to influence people's ability to keep up their payments. The extent of borrowing among families therefore has a bearing on the extent of debt.

Recent changes in household structure appeared to have had some influence on some people's credit use. We were surprised to find that households formed in the past three years reported rather fewer sources than others of similar age and income; we had expected them to use a lot of credit to buy furniture, furnishings and equipment. There are some signs of credit being associated with the beginning and end of child-rearing; Chart 4.13 indicates that both a new baby and a child leaving home seemed to add to the number of commitments. These analyses add interesting detail to the picture, but they do not really help to explain the overall pattern of household behaviour.

Chart 4.13 Credit use by changes in household structure over the past three years

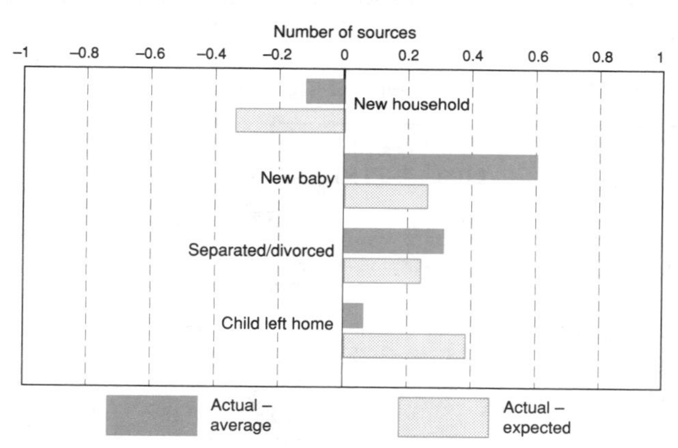

Source: PSI survey; analysis based on non-pensioner households
Note: The chart shows how far the average number of active sources of credit was above (+) or below (-) the overall average (green) and what would have been expected, for households with the same age and income (green shading). See Box N.

Economic influences

There has never been any clear explanation of the relationship between income and the use of credit. At first sight, the survey appeared to show that there was only a weak link – rich and poor both had a similar probability of entering the credit market. But it turned out that this balance was the result of two opposing forces: people at opposite ends of the spectrum borrowed in different ways for different purposes.

The single most important change in people's income occurs at retirement. It has already been established that pensioners had a low use of credit – not because they were poor as such, but because they were in a period of declining income. They are also at a time in their life when they tend to need fewer consumer goods. It helps to leave them out of the argument altogether from now on: the analysis of the economic influences on credit will be confined to people below pensionable age.

Frequency of use of credit

Three-quarters of non-pensioners used some source of active credit. The proportion was 68 per cent among households with incomes below £150 per week; it was 77 per cent where the income was above £150 per week. So there was not much difference in the likelihood of credit being used between the poorest and the richest households. This negative finding is nevertheless important. Households with low incomes were almost as likely as others to make use of credit facilities in the course of a year.

But households with relatively high incomes reported a larger number of sources than those at the other end of the scale. So, as Table 4.14 shows, overall use of credit was linked to income levels; but income was much less important than age in explaining people's activity.

Table 4.14 Use of credit, by household income

	Up to £100	£100 -£150	£150 -£200	£200 -£250	£250 -£300	£300 -£400	Over £400
Total (=100%)	*255*	*176*	*255*	*201*	*177*	*284*	*206*
Percentage using any source	67%	69%	75%	77%	77%	78%	76%
Average number of sources among users	2.14	2.25	2.45	2.71	2.77	2.84	2.96
Average number of sources overall	1.43	1.55	1.85	2.08	2.13	2.21	2.25

Source: PSI survey; analysis based on non-pensioner householders

Other indicators of current or changing levels of resources within the household were, for the most part, similarly unhelpful in distinguishing between credit users and non-users. Variations in earnings through changing levels of bonus or overtime payments, for example, did not affect the level of credit use. People who had changed jobs in the past three years were more likely to use credit than other people of the same age and at the same income level, but this was equally true whether the new job paid better or worse than the previous one.

The level of credit use by people currently in work was similar, whether they had been unemployed in the past three years or not. We found fewer credit users among the unemployed than among those in work, but when age and other factors were taken into account unemployment did not have a significant effect. People in work were especially likely to be in the peak borrowing age group, while unemployed people were more likely to be in their twenties, fifties or sixties.

Self-employed people used substantially more credit than employees. But it was not people running their own businesses who were most active: it was those who worked on a self-employed basis for one or more larger organisations. The additional credit may have been used to maintain continuity of spending between busy and slack periods of work.

Savings are usually thought of as the opposite of credit, and in that light it looks odd that anyone with money put aside would want or need to borrow. On the other hand, people with long-term savings and investments might prefer to use short-term credit facilities to deal with immediate requirements, rather than disturb their nest egg. The survey suggested that credit use was most common among households with small to moderate levels of savings (Chart 4.15, left panel). It might be argued that those with big balances had no need for credit, while those with no savings at all might find it risky, or difficult to obtain.

The right hand panel of Chart 4.15 suggests that people with high housing costs used more credit sources than those who paid little for their accommodation. High housing costs limit available income, and might have been expected to reduce credit use. The indications are that the influence is

Chart 4.15 Use of credit, by savings and housing costs

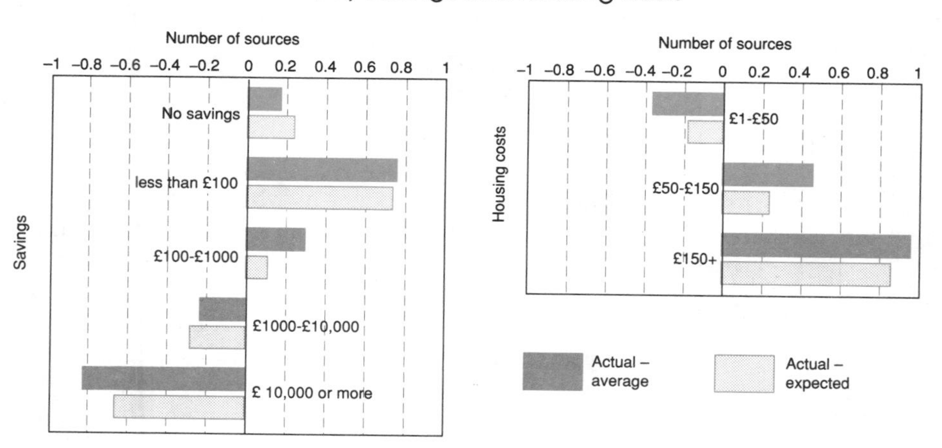

Source: PSI survey; analysis based on non-pensioner householders. See Box N.

the other way round: that people who have to spend a large proportion of their income on housing tend to use extra credit in an attempt to keep up the lifestyle which they would have expected on the basis of their total income.

Consumerism and hardship

The analysis in Chapter 2 identified two distinct features of household budgets which we labelled 'consumerism' and 'hardship'. Each of these is no doubt a highly complex social and economic phenomenon that would require detailed measurements to describe precisely. The survey data offers no more than 'indicators' of the position of each household on these two dimensions.

Consumerism was indicated by the value of durables purchased in the past year, plus the number of other durables in the household, from a list of six: televisions, washing machine, fridge, car, video and home computer. As expected, the dimension was closely associated with income, with high-income households buying and owning many consumer durables. It was also associated with age, with younger families, especially those in their thirties, scoring higher than older people.

Most households scoring high on the 'consumerism' index were credit users, while 'non-consumers' borrowed much less often. This is not quite as tautological as it seems at first sight: the index includes ownership of durables, as well as those bought within the previous year; purchases did not necessarily involve credit; and credit facilities may have been used for other purposes.

Box N Controlling for age and income

Several analyses in this chapter show the use of credit by particular categories of household, after taking account of their age and income. This is done by calculating, for each member of the sample, the 'expected' use of credit, based on all households in the same age group and income range. To the extent that the 'actual' use of credit was greater or less than expected, we can conclude that any difference (between, say, 'consumers' and 'non-consumers') was not simply explained by the ages and incomes of the two groups.

Chart 4.16 (left) shows two measures of the extent to which people scoring high on 'consumerism' used more credit than those at the other end of the scale. The grey bars on the graph show the actual difference in credit use between each group and the overall average (for non-pensioners); the green bars show the difference between the number of sources actually used, and the number of sources they would have used if respondents had been behaving just like other people of the same age and income. 'Consumer' households used twice as many credit sources as non-consumers. And more than half of this difference remains after age and income have been taken into account.

Bearing in mind that consumerism and credit use are both associated with high incomes, and also associated with each other, a path of cause and effect can be suggested:

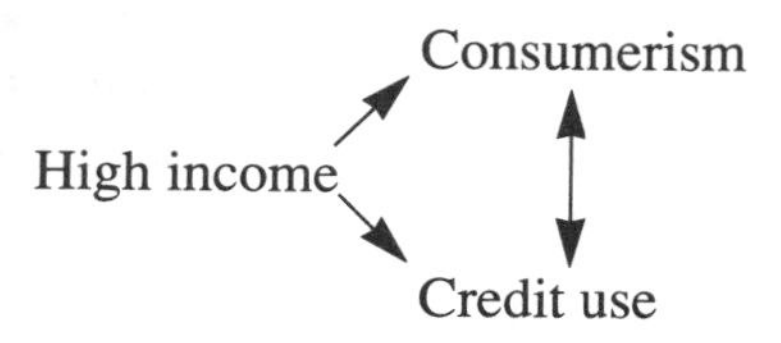

Chart 4.16 Use of credit, by 'consumerism' and 'hardship'

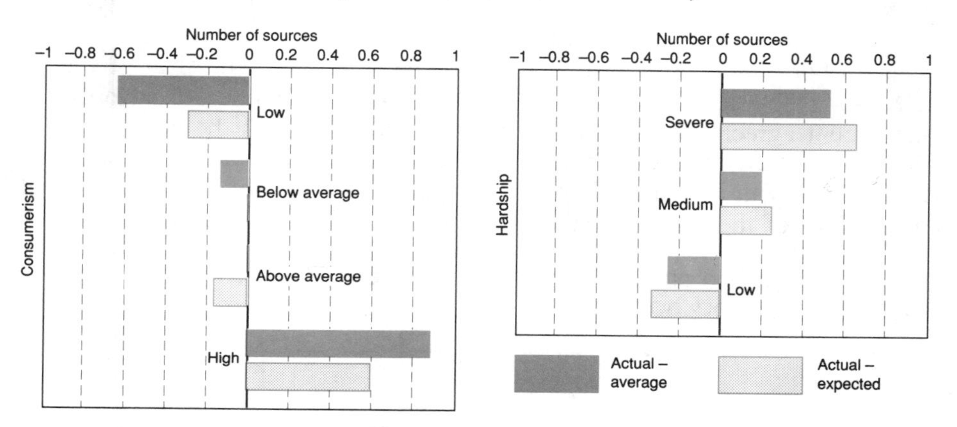

Source: PSI survey; analysis based on non-pensioner householders. See Box N.

'Hardship' was indicated by a series of questions about difficulties with the weekly or monthly budget. As expected, the dimension was closely associated with income, with low-income households experiencing most hardship.

Since low-income households scored low on consumerism, you might expect hardship to be associated with a low use of credit. On the contrary, people scoring high on the hardship index used more sources of credit than those with low scores (Chart 4.16, right). A path of cause and effect can be suggested:

Low income ⟶ Hardship ⟶ Credit use.

This pair of conclusions about the roles of consumerism and hardship in mediating a link between income levels and credit use was already indicated by secondary analysis of the 1979 survey of consumer credit commissioned by the National Consumer Council.[12] It therefore appears to be a stable feature of the market. It helps to explain why credit use varied so little between households at different levels of income: there were two opposite influences which tended to balance each other out. The findings suggest that high- and low-income households have a broadly similar need for credit, but for different reasons. In other words, credit fulfils two different roles in household budgets. Poorer families, on the whole, use credit to ease financial difficulties; those who are better-off take on credit commitments to finance a consumer life-style. Both would use it to improve their lot: one to reduce their poverty; the other to increase their prosperity.

Scale of commitments

If this hypothesis about a different role for credit in rich and poor households is correct, we would expect the details of credit use to split into two types of activity. This immediately becomes apparent when the analysis turns to the scale of borrowing at opposite ends of the income scale. The clearest way to see this is by looking at the amounts borrowed in one-off advances – instalment agreements, loans and borrowings. These will be considered in detail in Chapter 6 (Table 6.3). Over half of all the advances reported by households with incomes of up to £100 per week were for £250 or less; but nearly half of the advances secured by households earning more than £400

Chart 4.17 Median amount of one-off advances, by income, 'consumerism' and 'hardship'

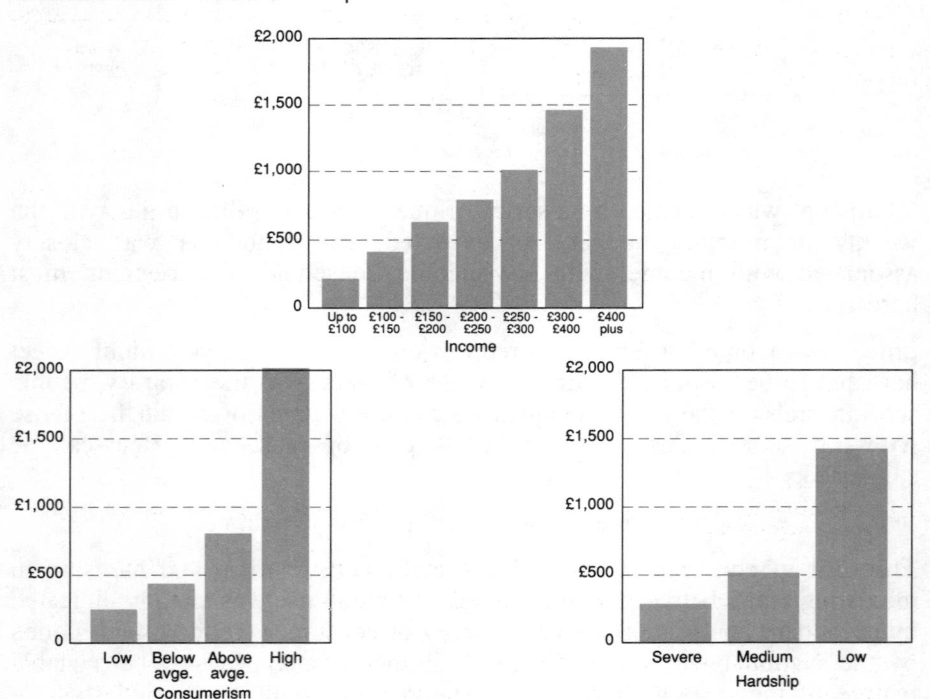

Source: PSI survey; analysis based on one-off advances.

per week exceeded £2,000. The first panel of Chart 4.17 shows that the median amount borrowed by households at these extremes of income ranged from £200 to £1,900.

The second and third panels of Chart 4.17 compare the one-off advances taken out by households who scored high and low on our 'consumerism' and 'hardship' scales. As one would expect, people with a strong consumer orientation, with their heavy use of credit and relatively high incomes, tended to have borrowed quite large sums. Households in hardship, on the other hand, were frequent credit users but had low incomes; their one-off advances were on the low side. This seems to confirm the idea that the two different pressures to use credit at opposite ends of the social scale operated in different ways: one to borrow large sums to support consumerism; the other to draw relatively modest amounts to meet short-term requirements.

Chart 4.17 covered the (capital) amount borrowed in one-off advances. We cannot treat revolving credit in the same way, and the overall measure of households' commitments consists of an estimate of the regular repayments required to service all sources of credit. Table 4.18 analyses the total repayment commitments of people at different levels of income. Households with incomes in excess of £400 were paying nearly three times as much as those with less than £100 a week; £35 per week on average, compared with £7 (Chart 4.19, left). Three in 10 households at the top of the income range were paying more than £40 per week; only 2 per cent of people with low incomes were paying at that rate.

Table 4.18 Repayment commitments, by income

Percentages

	Up to £100	£100 -£150	£150 -£200	£200 -£250	£250 -£300	£300 -£400	£400 or more
Total (=100)	*255*	*176*	*255*	*201*	*177*	*284*	*206*
Nil	41	38	32	31	26	28	32
Up to £10 pw	35	25	19	22	21	20	11
£10 to £40 pw	22	31	35	32	36	31	28
More than £40 pw	2	6	13	14	16	20	29
Average	£6.80	£10.30	£14.20	£17.50	£19.80	£30.70	£39.50
Average as a proportion of income	11%	8%	8%	8%	7%	9%	7%

Source: PSI survey, analysis based on non-pensioner householders. See Box J for an explanation of how repayments were calculated.

From this perspective, it looks as if credit behaves just like other types of goods or service; the higher your income, the greater your expenditure. Of course only a proportion of credit repayments count as expenditure in the full sense; much of the money is simply repaying the capital, and it is the interest that represents the true cost. But repayments measured in pounds per week look equitable.

Looked at as a proportion of income, on the other hand, rather a different picture emerges. Over most of the income range, repayment commitments averaged about 8 per cent of income. But while the best-off households were spending a little less than that, the worst-off had committed a higher proportion of their limited income (Chart 4.19, right).

Chart 4.19 Repayment commitments, by income

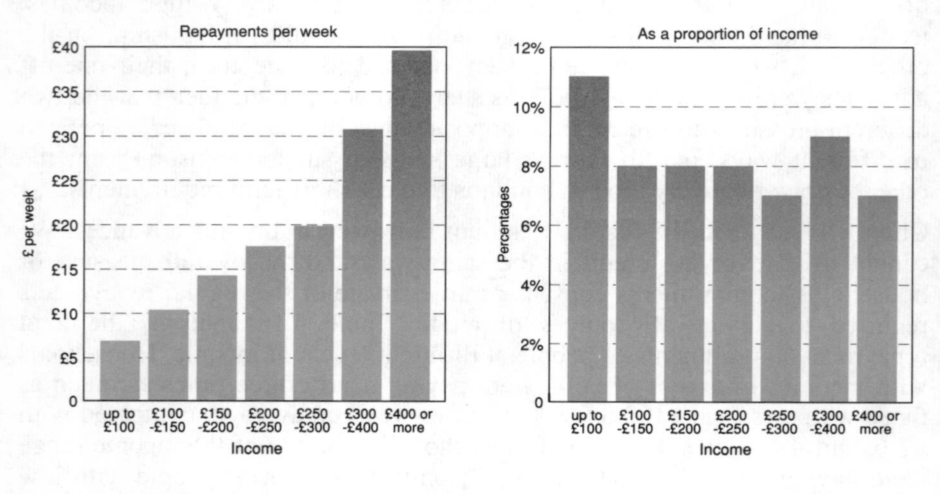

Source: PSI survey, analysis based on non-pensioner householders

The distinction between the credit needs and opportunities of rich and poor will be an important consideration throughout the remainder of this report. We will find, in the next two chapters, that the differences are not just of scale: high and low income families used different types of credit, from different sources for different purposes. Credit is by no means the only market which has been found to operate in distinct ways at opposite ends of the social scale. Dual market theories are common explanations for the polarisation of housing and jobs, for example.[13]

It would, on the other hand, be a mistake to exaggerate the depth of the cleavage. For one thing, a distinction between the top and the bottom of the range can ignore the people in the middle, who appeared to be participating in both markets. And even at the extremes the separation was not complete. Some rich people were behaving in the manner typical of the poor and borrowing because they were hard up. More worryingly, some poor people were adopting the consumer-spending behaviour of the rich.

Personal and social influences

We have been trying to explain why households at different stages of their life cycle and with varying resources use credit in particular ways. But borrowing is also a matter of choice, influenced by individual perceptions and lifestyles, as well as by the economic circumstances in which people find themselves. We therefore want to explore how far the extent and scale of credit use can be explained by householders' budgeting habits and attitudes, as described in Chapter 2. Throughout this section the influences of age and income will be taken as given; the analysis will show the extent to which personal and social factors play an additional role in increasing or decreasing credit use, above or below what might have been expected for a household of a given age and income. The method has been described in Box N.

Some of the budgeting habits which might have been expected to affect credit turned out not to be linked in any meaningful way. There was little variation, for example, between people with or without a current account; nor according to whether the household budgeted by the week or the month. Among married couples, the allocation of responsibility between husband and wife did not seem to have any systematic influence.

Chart 4.20 Use of credit, by attitudes to money, and to credit

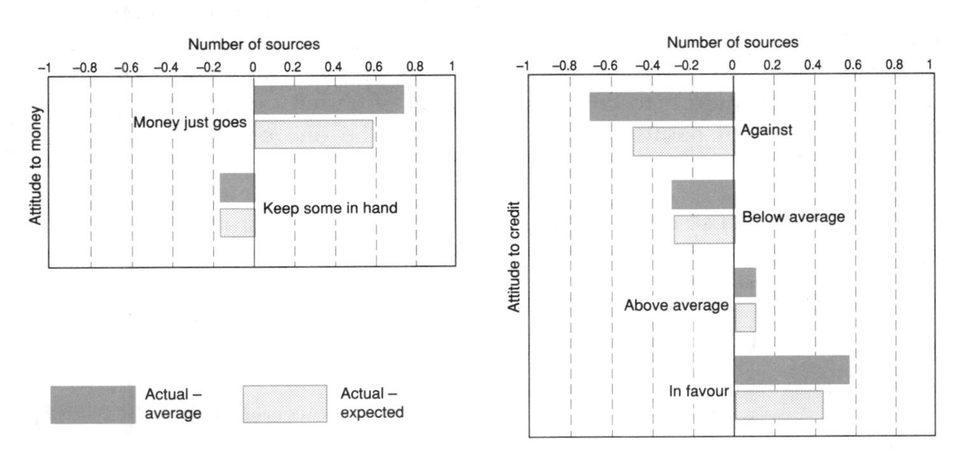

Source: PSI survey; analysis based on non-pensioner householders. See Box H and Box N.

Attitudes to spending did, however, seem to make a difference. First, people who said that 'if the money is there, I find it just goes' reported more active sources than those whose attitude was 'I always try to keep some money in hand for an emergency' (Chart 4.20, left).

Second, people with a relatively favourable attitude to credit used more of it. At the beginning of this chapter we used the combined answers to five questions about credit to identify the quarter of households who were most 'in favour' of credit, and the quarter who were most 'against'. The people with more favourable views used nearly 2½ sources, on average, compared with only 1¼ by those who were more worried about borrowing. Chart 4.20 (right) shows that part of the difference can be explained in terms of age and income, but variation remains even after these have been taken into account. It may seem perfectly obvious that people who approve of credit will be the main users, but the analysis is useful in confirming three things:

- that personal attitudes do have an influence on behaviour, which is not conditioned solely by the circumstances in which people find themselves;
- that personal attitudes do not explain all of the variation in behaviour – circumstances are important too;
- that although most credit is used by people who approve of it in principle, some people find themselves drawn into the market even though they think that credit is, in the words of one of our questions, 'never a good thing'.

Attitudes to credit are a source of variation between individuals and households, but everyone is no doubt influenced, one way or another, by the views and experiences of other people: their family, friends and neighbours; the messages conveyed by newspapers and television and by advertisements in those media. We have no direct measures of social influences on credit use, but it is of interest to compare the level of activity in different parts of the country. Local habits and opinions might be one of the influences at work.

Chart 4.21 Credit use and repayments, by affluence of area

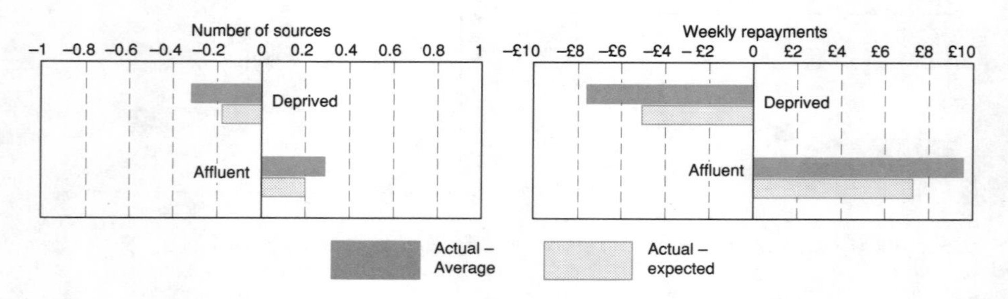

Source: PSI survey; analysis based on non-pensioner householders. See Box N.

Households in Scotland (averaging 1.5 sources) and Northern Ireland (1.5) used rather less credit than those elsewhere in the UK (1.9 sources). Within England and Wales, we were not able to detect variations between regions with any confidence. That does not mean that there are no differences, but they did not seem to be large enough to be picked up by a sample which averaged only eight local districts in each region.

We rather expected households living in urban areas to use more credit than people living in the country, but this was not the case.

The most substantial source of local variation was between 'affluent' and 'deprived' areas. Each of the postal districts from which the sample was selected were allocated an 'affluence index' on the basis of census and other information – data, for example, about the number of owner-occupied homes, size of houses, car ownership, the occupations of the residents and so on. If the 94 districts (in Great Britain) are divided into a top quarter and a bottom quarter according to this index, we find households in the 'affluent' areas using 2.2 sources of credit and spending £28 per week on their commitments; while those in 'deprived' areas used 1.6 sources, and spent £11 per week (Chart 4.21). We assumed at first that this was simply because higher-income households lived in the affluent areas. But more detailed analysis showed that most of the difference held up even after correcting for the influence of age and income. The results lead to the interesting and plausible suggestion that credit use is influenced as much by your neighbour's income as your own.

Constrained supply

The discussion so far in this chapter has assumed that it is simply up to the customer to decide how much money to borrow. But credit is not a commodity like fruit and vegetables which everyone can buy if they pay for it. Lenders can refuse advances if they are not satisfied that the money will be repaid. These refusals, and potential customers' expectation of refusal, may act as a constraint on the supply of credit.

There was overwhelming agreement that the supply of credit should be limited in some way. Most people thought that:

> *The amount of credit that you can get should be linked to the amount that you earn* score 9.0

> *Credit limits on credit cards should only be increased at the customer's request, not automatically* score 9.1

> *There should be tighter controls on advertising credit* score 9.0

And a majority of people also agreed that:

> *A deposit should be required before you can enter any credit agreement* score 7.8

although this view was not as strongly endorsed as the other three.

The replies people gave to these four statements were not substantially affected by the extent to which they used credit. Non-users and heavy users alike thought that there needed to be controls on credit.

Advances in information technology have enabled financial institutions to develop more sophisticated ways of assessing the credit-worthiness of potential borrowers. The old system of taking up references was too slow in the new competitive market in which credit-granters were operating. They needed a system that would allow them to make rapid checks and to lend to a wider range of people without an unacceptable level of default. So there has been a rapid development of a range of methods of risk assessment. These include credit referencing, and various kinds of credit scoring. The methods of screening have become more sophisticated with improved computer equipment and software and as the volume of consumer lending increased.

Credit referencing enables lenders to check information about the candidate in a central data base. These systems are operated by specialist agencies on a subscription basis, and are usually accessed by an on-line computer network or by telephone. A reference typically involves three checks. First the borrower's name and address are verified against the appropriate electoral register. Then a search is made for county court judgements recorded against the borrower in the past six years. Finally, a search is made for information on the borrower's record of repayment of other credit commitments, using arrears information contributed to the pool by many of the subscribers to the service. Until recently checks were made against the address at which the borrower lived, at three levels: same surname and same initials; same surname but different initials; same address but different surname. The Data Protection Registrar is currently in dispute with the industry about the use of information about someone other than the candidate, who happened to live at the same address, possibly a previous owner or tenant.[14]

Credit scoring was developed in the United States and introduced in Britain in the mid 1970s. It is a statistical technique to assess the probability of a given borrower repaying an advance, which enables lenders to lend to the maximum number of people within the limits set by their own risk criteria. There are two types of credit scoring.

Application scoring, as its name suggests, is used to assess the risk attached to lending to a particular applicant for credit. It is essentially an actuarial exercise. Credit scorecards are built upon a statistical analysis of the characteristics of previous borrowers. Characteristics which are associated with good chances of timely repayments are given high scores; those associated with bad paying are assigned low scores. A total score is calculated, by adding up the characteristic scores for a particular applicant, and compared with a 'pass mark', above which the application will be accepted and below which it will be refused. This pass mark is determined by the lender and will represent the highest risk they are prepared to take.

Behavioural or performance scoring in contrast helps the management of existing accounts by updating the risk assessment. It is based on the borrower's own behaviour and uses indicators such as the number of payments missed during the last six months. Behavioural scores are updated regularly and enable credit limits to be adjusted accordingly. They therefore allow lenders to accept applications from people whose credit score is on the borderline, because they will be able to monitor subsequent behaviour closely. Banks and building societies have the added advantage that they can pick up the early signs of financial difficulties by monitoring their customers' performance on their current accounts as well as their credit facilities.

In principle, more accurate risk assessment should have two benefits for the credit industry and its customers. It should reduce the number of advances made to bad risks. And it should reduce the number of good risks turned away in error. Taking the same process a stage further, the industry can target advertising and new products on types of customer, and on individual customers, who are good risks and who are not borrowing as much as they might. The industry argues, therefore, that the development of risk assessment methods has enabled the rapid expansion in the supply of credit without increasing the risk of bad debt.

On the other hand, every scorecard is based on a conscious decision about the appropriate balance between minimising risks and maximising opportunities. Representatives of consumer interests have argued that too many lenders are accepting high levels of risk in order to advance as much money as possible at high rates of return. Clearly different lenders adopt different policies. A social/political judgement of an acceptable level of risk might not coincide with a decision based on purely commercial criteria.

Only 2 per cent of the householders in our survey said that they had applications for credit turned down during the preceding year. Refusals were most commonly reported for plastic cards, bank loans and HP. Some people had been turned down more than once; there were three refusals reported for every 100 households.

The credit industry tends to report a refusal rate of about a quarter of all applications. The number of rejections recorded in the survey is estimated to be about a tenth of the number of new commercial credit facilities taken out in the previous year, so there seems to have been under-reporting of rejections by potential customers or over-reporting by lenders.

Before we analyse what sorts of people were being turned down, it is interesting to compare the number of rejections with two other indicators of the level of supply available to individual borrowers. Many people's activity in the credit 'market' consisted largely of what we refer to as informal 'borrowings', not from commercial sources but from family, friends or organisations motivated by a desire to assist. One interpretation of informal borrowing is that an additional source of credit is available to these people which is cheaper than, and therefore preferable to, commercial facilities. But most of the households who borrowed informally had low incomes and (probably) restricted access in the commercial market; people who were in a position to exercise choice tended to borrow in the formal sector. So informal borrowings might be interpreted as an indication of constraint in the supply of commercial credit. For the sample as a whole, there were about 11 'borrowings' for every 100 households, compared with 136 commercial agreements.

The third indicator of supply consists of credit facilities that were available to households, but which they did not use. These consist of bank accounts with an overdraft facility, but which were not overdrawn, and credit and store cards which were paid off in full every month. This is by no means a complete measure of unused credit opportunities: there is no count of the mail-order catalogues that could have been used, of goods which might have been bought on hire purchase, or of personal loan offers that were thrown in the waste paper basket. But the unused revolving credit facilities can indicate who had more opportunities than they wanted, in contrast to those who had less than they needed. There were 57 'extra' credit facilities, in this sense, for every 100 households.

Taking the three indicators together, an overall measure of the availability of credit might consist of:

		per 100 households
	the number of unused facilities	57
minus	the number of informal borrowings	11
minus	the number of rejections	3
divided by	the number of active commercial sources	136
equals	supply ratio	32%

Over the population as a whole, therefore, the survey suggested that there were more credit opportunities than constraints. That does not, in itself, mean that there is 'too much' credit about, any more than a plentiful supply of goods in shop windows implies a glut. It does, however, suggest that most people's use of credit is not restricted.

You would not, of course, expect the same people to report both unused facilities and rejections. Table 4.22 shows that, on the whole, the supply of credit to individuals was distributed along expected lines. The better-off households had many unused facilities, and their use of credit appeared not to be constrained by its supply. The worse-off households had few unused facilities; on the contrary, they were being rejected relatively often, and turning to informal sources such a family and friends. So they made relatively little use of the standard commercial sources. This low level of use may partly have been caused by *con*straints – the experience or prospect of being refused by commercial lenders; but it is also no doubt a consequence of *re*straint – people not borrowing money they knew they could not repay.

Table 4.22 Supply of credit, by income

Numbers per hundred households

	Up to £100	£100 -£150	£150 -£200	£200 -£250	£250 -£300	£300 -£400	£400 or more
Total (=100)	*255*	*176*	*255*	*201*	*177*	*284*	*206*
Unused facilities	11	41	36	39	61	117	170
Refusals	7	9	5	2	3	3	*
Borrowings	31	19	12	11	9	10	9
Active commercial	112	136	173	198	204	211	217
Supply ratio	–25%	10%	11%	13%	24%	50%	74%

Source: PSI survey; analysis based on non-pensioner householders

Chart 4.23 Supply of credit, by age

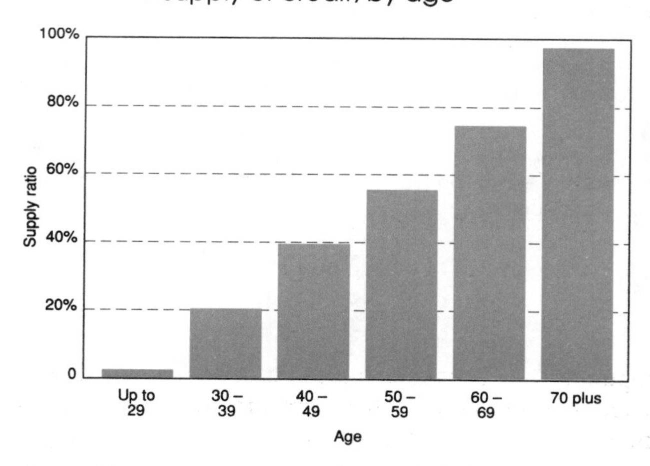

Source: PSI survey; analysis based on all householders. See previous page for definition of supply ratio.

It will be seen in Chapter 8 that younger people had a relatively high risk of arrears. Chart 4.23 suggests a rather restricted supply of credit to people in their twenties, and this helps to explain why they were borrowing less than might have been expected. Constraints were less and less as people grew older, and this strongly implies that the low use of credit by people in the later stages of the life cycle derives from a low level of demand.

References

1. National Consumer Council, *Consumers and Credit,* NCC, 1981

2. British Bankers Association, *Annual Abstract of Banking Statistics. Section 14 Bank Credit Cards,* Volume 8, May 1991

3. Estimates supplied by the Retail Credit Group

4. Central Statistical Office, *Financial Statistics,* HMSO, August 1991, Table 9.5 and equivalent tables in previous editions

5. Central Statistical Office, *Financial Statistics,* August 1991, Table 7.5

6. NOP Market Research Ltd, *Consumer Credit,* Department of Trade and Industry, 1971

7. See note 1

8. See note 6

9. See note 6

10. See note 1

11. For a more detailed look at the borrowing behaviour of young people living at home, see J. Ford, *Young Adults' Socialisation to Credit Use and Credit Management,* End of Award Report to the ESRC, Grant number R000231645, 1991

12. R. Berthoud, *Credit, Debt and Poverty,* HMSO, 1989

13. See, for example, D. Maclennan, K. Gibb and A. More, *Paying for Britain's Housing,* Joseph Rowntree Foundation, 1990; C. Craig, J. Rubery, R. Tarung and F. Wilkinson, *Labour Market Structure, Individual Organisation and Low Pay,* Cambridge University Press, 1982; F. Wilkinson (ed.), *The Dynamics of Labour Market Segmentation,* Academic Press, 1981

14. E.J. Howe, *Credit and the Assessment of Individuals,* Office of the Data Protection Registrar, 1989; Industry Forum on Data Protection, *Striking the Balance,* IFDP, 1988; and subsequent Tribunal decisions

5 Revolving Credit

Consumer credit arrangements can be allocated to two broad categories. This chapter will describe standing credit facilities such as bank overdrafts, credit cards, store cards and mail-order catalogues. Their common feature is that account holders can continuously run up larger commitments (subject to a limit) as they buy goods and services; and reduce the amount outstanding as they repay. These revolving facilities operate differently from the one-off agreements described in the next chapter.

Of course, the distinction between revolving facilities and one-off agreements is not perfect. Some people use mail-order catalogues so rarely that each purchase could be seen as an independent contract; other people borrow so often from check traders, tallymen or their family that the arrangement could be interpreted as a standing facility. But for most purposes it is convenient to distinguish between the two classes of credit along the lines adopted in these two chapters.

Although they are used in different ways, credit cards and store cards have many points in common and the two types of account can at least be compared directly with each other. It is very difficult to draw comparisons between them and either bank overdrafts on the one hand, or mail-order accounts on the other. Each type of service has its own set of parameters. Most of the detailed description in this chapter will, therefore, take each type separately.

Extent of use

Despite their differences, it is possible to make at least some broad comparisons between the four sources of revolving credit in terms of their frequency of use and the levels of repayment required. Table 5.1 shows the level of active use of these sources, excluding accounts that were paid off in full every month.

Mail-order catalogues were much the most common source of revolving credit. Although they often have rather a working-class market image, they were used to about the same extent across most of the income range, with only the highest income group using them less often than others. We looked for signs that different catalogues catered for widely different sectors of the market, but a clear pattern did not emerge.

Another feature of mail order (not shown in the table) was that it was a relatively common source of credit among elderly people, used by 23 per cent of households in their sixties and 15 per cent in their seventies. This was

Table 5.1 Active use of revolving credit, by income

Sources per hundred households

	Up to £100	£100 -£150	£150 -£200	£200 -£250	£250 -£300	£300 -£400	£400 plus
Total (=100%)	*255*	*176*	*255*	*201*	*177*	*284*	*206*
Mail order	45	39	60	51	47	44	30
Credit cards	10	15	20	33	40	39	43
Overdrafts	9	12	13	20	23	28	27
Store cards	6	8	14	11	18	16	16

Source: PSI survey; analysis based on non-pensioner households

below the rate of use among younger and middle-aged people, but far more common than any other source of credit for the older age groups.

Credit cards, overdrafts and store cards were more commonly used by households in the middle- and upper-income ranges. This leaves mail order the dominant source of revolving credit for low-income households.

Mail-order accounts, and most store cards, are paid in fixed weekly or monthly instalments imposed by, or agreed with, the creditor. Overdrafts, and most credit cards, have no fixed rate of repayment; the customer decides how much to pay each month depending either on the amount outstanding or on the availability of funds. We have converted all current credit commitments to a weekly equivalent (as described in Chapter 4, Box J). In so far as the four sources can be compared, overdrafts were the largest commitments, with repayments averaging £7.60 per week (Chart 5.2). Store card commitments were half this size.

Chart 5.2 Repayment commitments on revolving credit facilities

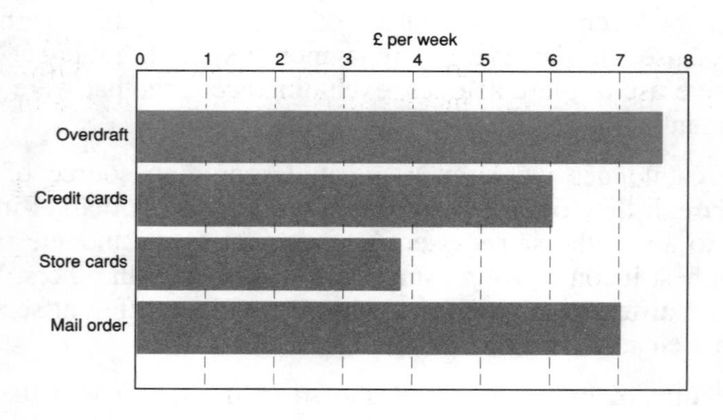

Source: PSI survey; analysis based on current commitments for revolving credit

Current account overdrafts

We have already seen in Chapter 2 that the majority of households held a current account with a bank, or sometimes with a building society. Pensioners, other people without employment, and weekly paid workers had relatively few current accounts, but most people with middle to high incomes had one.

Box O Units of analysis

In previous chapters, most percentages and averages were based on counting households as the unit of analysis. In this and the next chapter, many calculations use credit commitments as the unit of analysis.

Suppose a couple had three loans, of £1,000, £2,000 and £3,000. Counting households, we would say they owed £6,000. Counting credit commitments, we would say the loans averaged £2,000 each.

Nearly a quarter of the current bank accounts offered an agreed overdraft facility, but only 12 per cent of current building society accounts did so. Bank accounts were also far more common, so that they accounted for the great majority of overdraft facilities. The average agreed credit limit was £1,800.

In fact, 14 per cent of current bank accounts were overdrawn, to an average of £1,200, at the time of the survey. This includes account holders who were overdrawn, even though they did not report an agreement with their bank that they could go into the red. Current account overdrafts with building societies were again less common. 6 per cent of them were overdrawn and the average overdraft was £600. Building societies accounted for a small proportion of this form of credit – about 8 per cent by volume.

Accounts were more often overdrawn where there was a prior overdraft agreement than where there was none (Table 5.3). Even so, more than a quarter of overdrawn accounts were unauthorised. But the unauthorised overdrafts were usually rather small and accounted for only 1 per cent of overdrafts by volume.

Accounts with below-average limits on their overdraft facility were least likely to be overdrawn. A quarter of accounts with limits below £250 were overdrawn but the proportion increased to half of those with a limit of more

Table 5.3 Current account overdrafts, by whether an overdraft facility had been agreed.

	Agreed facility	No agreement
Total (=100%)	*534*	*2,154*
Per cent overdrawn	40%	4%
Average overdraft	£1520	£60

Source: PSI survey; analysis based on all current accounts

than £250. Very few (7 per cent) accounts with an overdraft facility had gone over the agreed limit, but at the same time few were well under the limit. This would seem to suggest that people either make no use of their overdraft facility or else use it almost in full. Another interpretation is that authorised limits may be set in response to requests from customers, rather than determined by the bank in isolation.

The more prosperous households were, the more likely they were both to have a current account, and to have an agreed overdraft facility (Chart 5.4). Although better-off households also had more actual overdrafts than poorer families, they used fewer than half of the facilities available to them. The most distinctive characteristic of a high income household, therefore, was an unused overdraft facility.

Chart 5.4 Facilities on current accounts, by income

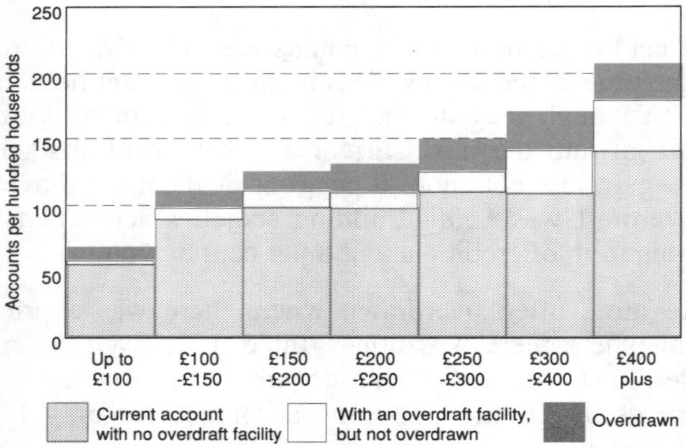

Source: PSI survey; analysis based on non-pensioner householders

■ Credit cards and store cards

There has been a huge growth in the number and range of plastic cards available to the public in recent years. Almost 40 per cent of households in the survey held a credit or charge card. Store cards were a good deal less common: only 15 per cent of households had any. The majority of cardholding households had only a single account, but some had several cards – 1 per cent held five or more. This may not seem a lot; on the other hand, five-card families held an estimated total of 1 million accounts between them. (Husbands' and wives' cards are counted separately for this purpose if they each held separate accounts; an account used by both is treated as a single facility.)

Table 5.5 Numbers of credit and store cards

Percentages

	Credit/charge cards	Store cards	Either type
Total (=100%)	*2,224*	*2,224*	*2,224*
None	62	85	58
One	25	12	24
Two	10	2	11
Three	3	1	5
Four			2
Five or more			1

Source: PSI survey, analysis based on all householders

Table 5.6 Credit cards and store cards compared

Percentages

		Credit cards	Store cards
Total (=100%)		*1,191*	*404*
Cards used at least monthly		49	25
Main items bought	Clothing	54	76
	Motoring	53	
	Household goods	41	27
	Entertainments	29	
	Holidays	24	
	Leisure goods	22	
Facilities used as active source of credit		39	52
Average credit limit		£1170	£550
Increase in limit in past year		31	11
Fixed monthly repayment (as % of cards used for active credit)		17	54
Average weekly commitment (among cards used for active credit)		£6.00	£3.80

Source: PSI survey; analysis based on all credit and store cards
*Note: hardly any **charge cards** were used as active sources of credit, and they are not shown in the table.*

Table 5.6 summarises some of the differences between credit cards and store cards. Credit cards tended to be used frequently, to pay for a wide range of goods and services, especially clothes and shoes, motoring costs (including petrol) and household goods. Store cards were used more occasionally, and tended to be concentrated on the purchase of clothes and shoes.

Figures about the number of credit and store cards in circulation tend to overstate the use of plastic as a source of credit. A significant proportion of card holders do not use them for revolving credit, but pay off the full amount owing each month. 61 per cent of credit cards, 48 per cent of store cards and just about all charge cards were reported to be paid off in this way. These cards may be described as credit *facilities* which were being used as a convenient method of payment; we use the word *active* to refer to those which were actually used to defer payment beyond the end of the monthly accounting period.

Plastic cards were the credit facility with the strongest link with income levels. Only one sixth of the poorest non-pensioner households had a credit or charge card, and even fewer had a store card (Table 5.7). The number of cards rose steeply with rising income. But the better-off households tended to repay their credit and store card bills in full: two-thirds of the richest customers compared with one-third of the poorest. This means that the use of cards as an active source of credit was much less strongly linked with income than appeared at first sight.

Table 5.7 Facilities on credit and store cards, by income

Accounts per hundred households

	Up to £100	£100 -£150	£150 -£200	£200 -£250	£250 -£300	£300 -£400	£400 plus
Total (=100%)	*255*	*176*	*255*	*201*	*177*	*284*	*206*
Credit cards							
Not used for credit	8	23	22	22	42	71	95
Used for credit	10	15	20	33	40	39	43
Store cards							
Not used for credit	1	1	3	2	5	16	36
Used for credit	6	8	14	11	18	16	16

Source: PSI survey; analysis based on non-pensioner householders

Credit limits

The average credit limit for all cards was just over £1000. Credit cards allowed their customers to borrow twice as much as store cards (Table 5.6).

Of course the limit is not necessarily a reflection of the amount borrowed. Many of the accounts with high limits were paid off in full every month, so they were not 'active' sources at all according to the survey definition. Those with limits of less than £500 were most frequently used as an active source of credit.

The higher a household's income the greater was the credit limit on their card. Households with less than £100 net income a week had average credit limits of £750 compared with £1,250 for those with incomes over £400. This difference is not, however, as great as might have been expected. Limits averaged about 2½ weeks income for the better-off families, while for those on the lowest incomes they represented 13 weeks income.

The majority of credit limits had remained unchanged during the previous year. A third of credit card limits and a tenth of store card limits had been increased (Table 5.6) and only a handful decreased. The higher the credit limit on an account the greater the likelihood that it had been increased. Just over one in seven (14 per cent) cards with a limit below £500 had been increased, compared with half (50 per cent) of those over £2,000.

Credit card companies have been criticised for encouraging overspending through automatic increases in credit limits. In fact there was a great deal of support among respondents for the view that credit limits should only be increased at the customer's request (see Chapter 4). But the great majority (84 per cent) of the credit increases *had* been made automatically by the creditor. Most accounts were within the previous credit limit when it was increased, but, even so, one in 10 were at the limit and a small proportion (3 per cent) were actually over the limit.

We have seen that accounts with higher credit limits were more likely to have had the limit increased in the previous year. There was, however, no link between the size of credit limit and either who changed the limit or the state of the account at the time of the change.

Younger customers tended to ask for the limit to be increased, quite often when the account was up to the previous credit limit. More than a quarter of the increases awarded to householders aged under 29 had been at their own request; and over a quarter of their accounts were at or over the limit at the time of the increase.

Methods of repayment

More than half of the store cards used as an active source of credit involved an arrangement for the customer to repay a fixed instalment every month. But the great majority of credit cards could be repaid as and when the customer preferred (Table 5.6). Most of those without a fixed repayment arrangement said that they paid off as much as they could each month, depending on how much money was available. A handful paid a fixed amount each month as part of their own budgeting plan, while a few others paid the minimum allowed by their credit agreement.

Fixed repayment agreements were rather more common among customers with incomes below £200 (40 per cent) than in the upper income ranges (21 per cent).

Credit commitments

Our summary measure of the extent of people's credit use is based on converting all amounts borrowed to the equivalent of a weekly repayment commitment. The average commitment for actively-used credit cards was £6.00 per week; for actively-used store cards it was £3.80 (Table 5.6). Neither of these figures varied systematically with income. Rich and poor differed in the number of cards they used, but once in use, the extent of their commitments were rather similar.

Mail-order catalogues

As we have seen, mail-order catalogues were the most widely-used form of consumer credit. Three out of 10 of the households in the survey had bought on instalments from them in 1989. Most users had only one catalogue, but one household in 20 used two, and a few more than two. A quarter of catalogues (24 per cent) were used by people with no other source of credit. They therefore formed a sector of the market distinct from other forms of credit.

Catalogues were often used by families with children, more than half of whom had bought items on mail-order instalments in the course of the year. These families made up over half (55 per cent) of all catalogue-users. Table 5.1 at the beginning of this chapter showed that all income groups bought by mail order to about the same extent, while other sources were more strongly related to income. So mail-order catalogues formed a high proportion of revolving credit in low-income households.

Catalogues were a source of credit used predominantly by women (see Chapter 2). Among married couples, two-thirds of the catalogues were used by the wife alone; three catalogues out of 10 were used by both the man and the woman; and only a very small number (3 per cent) were used by the man alone.

Most catalogues were used to buy clothing and footwear. The only other significant purchases were general household goods and household electrical and gas appliances.

The use of agents

A quarter of catalogue-users acted as an agent for others as well as buying items for themselves. About a third used an agent to order goods on their behalf. The remainder sent off for things themselves. People who were agents for others were often regular catalogue users.

There was an interesting difference in the way that catalogues were used by households at different income levels. Half of the poorest mail-order customers used an agent to order goods and only a quarter sent off for goods on their own account. In contrast, only a fifth of better-off households bought through an agent while a half of them sent off for items themselves.

Credit commitments

Three-quarters of catalogue customers had some outstanding repayment commitments at the time they were interviewed. They averaged £7.00 per catalogue per week. People who bought through an agent spent rather less (£4.90) than those who acted as agents (£6.90) or who sent off for things themselves (£8.60). But the level of commitment was very similar across all income groups.

6 One-off Credit

Most credit is advanced in lump sums subject to a specific contract, rather than under a standing agreement. In the survey interview, we distinguished between three kinds of one-off arrangement: 'instalment agreements', 'loans' and informal 'borrowings' (see Chapter 4, Box K). While in some respects it is important to retain the distinction between these three types of advance, they have many things in common, and it is possible to combine them to examine variations in, say, the size of the advance, what it was used for, and so on. On other occasions, it is appropriate to combine the instalment agreements and the loans, but not the borrowings, to look at advances in what we refer to as the 'commercial' sector.

40 per cent of households had owed money on at least one advance in the course of the year. The majority of them (25 per cent of all households) had only one, but 10 per cent had two, and smaller numbers had used three or even more. Households reporting four or more advances had, between them, more than a million agreements in the course of the year. People who were continuously renewing or topping up credit agreements with the same money lender were counted as having only a single advance for this purpose.

There was not much variation between income groups in the number of advances in the year. The average rose from 73 per hundred households with incomes below £100 per week, to 83 per hundred with incomes between £300 and £400 per week. The best-off group of all – with incomes above £400 – did, however, use rather more sources: an average of almost exactly 100 per hundred households.

Source of money

People had borrowed from a wide range of sources. Bank loans were the most common, accounting for a quarter of advances. Other common contracts were instalment ('HP') agreements negotiated through specialist dealers – most often car dealers – and high street or department stores. But informal borrowing within the family was the fourth most common means of obtaining money, about as important as HP offered by electricity and gas showrooms. Many of the HP agreements will have been contracted with a finance house, but direct loans from finance houses accounted for only 6 per cent of the total.

Loan from bank	25%
HP from specialist dealer	18%
HP from store	13%
Borrow from relative	11%
HP from fuel board	10%
Loan from finance house	6%
Borrow from social fund	3%
Loan from building society	3%
HP from other source	3%
Loan from check company	3%
Borrow from employer	2%
Borrow from friend	2%
Loan from moneylender	2%
Loan from credit union	0.1%

So there is an extended range of relatively rarely used sources of money. But each of them may be important to a particular clientele. The government's social fund, for example, accounted for 18 per cent of the advances reported by claimants of income support. Credit unions provided a negligible proportion of loans from a United Kingdom perspective; but in Northern Ireland, where these mutual associations flourish, they accounted for 8 per cent of all advances, 14 per cent of advances taken out by catholics, and 31 per cent of the one-off commitments reported by credit union members.

Even though there was not much variation in the number of advances, it was in the use of one-off credit agreements that the two distinct markets for credit showed up most clearly. Chart 6.1 reorders the sources used according to the level of income of their clientele. Even among the primary sources

Box P Minority lenders

While the survey identified several hundred examples of advances provided by the main sources, there were naturally fewer cases from lenders with only a small share of the market. Some of these minority lenders are particularly interesting, and we quote a number of ways in which, for example, building societies on the one hand or money lenders on the other differed from typical lenders. Because of the small samples involved, the conclusions should be treated with caution. The actual (unweighted) number of interviews on which these analyses are based are as follows:

Finance house	96	Social fund	81
Check trader	54	Building society	52
Moneylender	42	Friend	37
Employer	22	Credit union	22

The category described in the text and tables as 'moneylenders' is a combination of four small groups:

Loans from a moneylender or tallyman	20
Loans from a pawnbroker	8
HP from a doorstep salesman or tallyman	12
Loans from 'other' sources	2

Chart 6.1 Median income of borrowers from each source

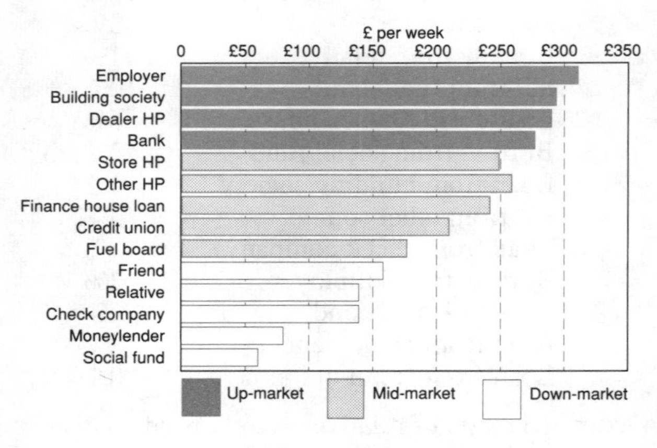

Source: PSI survey; analysis based on all one-off advances

there was a big gap between loans from specialist dealers (half of whose customers had an income in excess of £289), and fuel boards (for whom the half-way cut-off point was £176). Then there are niche lenders ranging from employers (£310) to the social fund (£60).

The colouring in Chart 6.1 has been used to divide the 14 sources into three groups, which we label 'up-market', 'mid-market' and 'down-market'. Table 6.2 shows how different the patterns of credit use were at opposite ends of the scale.

Table 6.2 Market sector of one-off advances, by income

Percentages

	Up to £100	£100 -£150	£150 -£200	£200 -£250	£250 -£300	£300 -£400	£400 plus
Total (=100%)	*185*	*139*	*189*	*167*	*141*	*236*	*209*
Up-market	15	32	52	53	55	58	70
Mid-market	27	38	32	33	30	33	25
Down-market	58	31	15	14	15	8	4

Source: PSI survey; analysis based on non-pensioners' one-off advances

Some institutions provided most of the credit for customers with plenty of money – principally banks and specialist dealers. They hardly penetrated into the low-income market. This might be because the up-market lenders do not offer services which poor people find attractive; or it might be because their lending policies exclude poor people, either by accident or by design. Elements of both these explanations will be recognisable in the following pages. Other lenders specialise in meeting poor people's credit needs – the family, the social fund, check companies and money lenders. There are problems associated with many of these sources, which will also appear later in this chapter. On the other hand, some of these sources, despite specialising in lending to the poor, command a very small proportion even of the low-income market. So middle-market sources such as finance house loans and high-street hire-purchase agreements make an essential contribution to the credit needs of benefit claimants and the low paid.

The variation between income groups was so strong that it is difficult to identify other influences on people's choice of source. Getting on for half of those borrowing from relatives were single people, early or late in their life cycle. Of the few pensioners who had borrowed at all, a third used hire purchase from an electricity or gas showroom. Virtually all of those borrowing from a building society were owner-occupiers, though by no means all of them secured the loan on their property.

Amount of advance

Unlike the revolving credit analysed in the previous chapter, the amount borrowed on one-off agreements can be analysed as a capital sum, making allowance for deposits put down on instalment agreements.

The average (median) advance was £600 (see Box Q).

Up to £250	26%
£250 to £1,000	29%
£1,000 to £2,000	10%
£2,000 to £5,000	24%
More than £5,000	10%

Not surprisingly, the amount borrowed was closely related to household incomes. Chart 6.3 shows that more than half of the poorest households borrowed less than £250 at a time. More than half of the loans taken out by the richest group exceeded £2,000 – indeed a quarter of these top-of-the-market advances were for more than £5,000. The medians ranged from £200 for the poorest households to £1,900 for the richest.

Box Q Average advances

The usual method of calculating average money figures, used through most of this report, is the 'mean'. This involves adding up the total number of pounds and dividing by the total number of households. But one-off advances have a strongly 'skewed' distribution; most are in the hundreds of pounds, but the relatively small number of loans of many thousands can exercise an undue influence on the mean.

Instead, we use the 'median', defined as the mid point of the list of advances. Half were for more than £600; half for less than £600.

Chart 6.3 Amount of one-off advances, by income

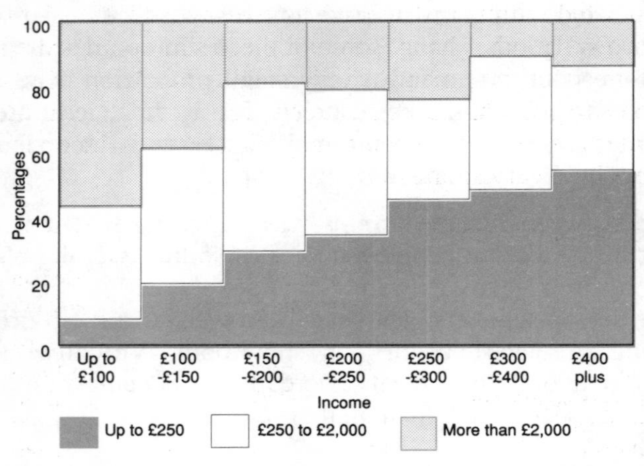

Source: PSI survey; analysis based on non-pensioners' one-off advances

The amounts borrowed also varied enormously from source to source: from an average (median) of £3,600 on building society loans, to £100 borrowed from a moneylender or tallyman. As Chart 6.4 shows, the amounts lent by different types of organisation followed roughly the same pattern as the incomes of their customers, and this no doubt goes some of the way to explaining each lender's position in the market. Since banks hardly ever (1 per cent) lent less than £250 on a personal loan, it is not surprising that poor people, who usually needed to borrow a few hundred pounds, went elsewhere: to a moneylender, for example, almost all (86 per cent) of whose advances were for less than £250.

Chart 6.4 Median amount of advance from each source

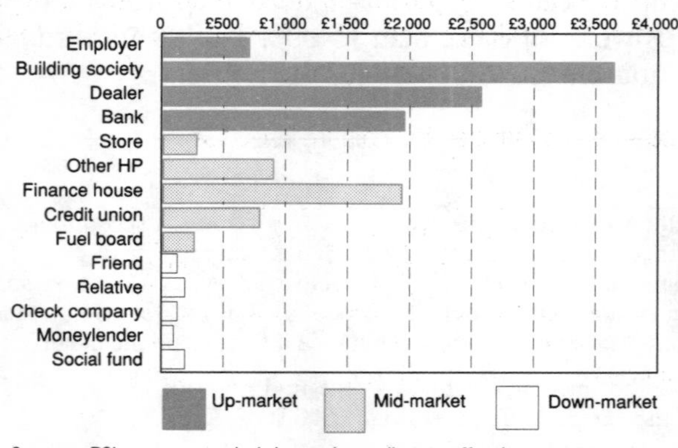

Source: PSI survey; analysis based on all one-off advances

Reasons for borrowing

Most one-off advances were used to buy a specified article. Cars were the most common single item, and tended to cost several thousand pounds. A range of household goods, led by gas and electrical appliances like cookers and fridges, tended to cost a few hundred pounds. But a number of loans were not to pay for purchases as such, but for more general purposes: to finance a business, to pay off debts, to pay bills or to make ends meet. Most of the latter involved very small sums.

Table 6.5 Purpose of advance

	Per cent of advances	Median amount
Purchases		
Car or motor cycle	29%	£2,800
Household electric/gas appliances	27%	£320
Electrical leisure goods	10%	£290
Others household items	6%	£380
Other purchases	9%	£560
Other purposes		
Business uses	4%	£1,530
Pay off debts	3%	£670
Pay bills	5%	£350
To make ends meet	8%	£100

Source: PSI survey; analysis based on all one-off advances

The different sources of credit were used for markedly different purposes. Table 6.6 summarises this in terms of the three broad categories of lender identified earlier. The great majority of cars were financed by the up-market institutions, especially banks and HP arrangements negotiated though dealers. The mid-market – especially fuel boards and high street retailers – dominated the supply of credit to buy other types of goods. Down-market lenders, including relatives as well as check companies and moneylenders, provided most of the loans for purposes other than a specific purchase. This was especially true of 'making ends meet': five out of six loans under this heading came from the down-market group.

Table 6.6 Purpose of advance, by market sector

Percentages

	Up-market	Mid-market	Down-market
Total (=100%)	*648*	*427*	*280*
To buy a car	49	12	6
Purchases other than cars	38	84	37
Other purposes	13	4	57

Source: PSI survey; analysis based on all one-off advances

About half of the small number of one-off credit agreements taken out by pensioners were to buy major household appliances. This suggests that older people overcame their reluctance to borrow only when their essential items – cooker, fridge and washing machine – needed replacing.

As we would expect from the diversity of borrowing behaviour at opposite ends of the income scale, there were big differences between rich and poor:

- 44 per cent of advances negotiated by households with more than £400 per week were used to buy cars. Below £100 per week, the proportion was 7 per cent;
- 22 per cent of the poorest group's transactions were to make ends meet, compared with 3 per cent of those of the richest. Getting on for half of the loans for this purpose went to people in the lowest income band. Poorer people also had a tendency to borrow to pay bills, but the link with income was much weaker here;
- purchases of cars, and 'making ends meet', were also strongly associated with 'consumerism' and 'hardship', as defined in Chapter 2 (Chart 6.7).

The survey clearly shows that the reasons poorer households and people in hardship had for using credit were different from those of better-off consumers. Making ends meet, and perhaps paying bills and/or debts, are the distinctive purposes associated with low income and hardship. On the other hand it is important to remember that the low-income group, like everyone else, also borrowed to buy specific items such as cookers, furniture or furnishings. Fewer than half of their advances were used for the purposes specifically associated with their budgeting needs.

Chart 6.7 Purpose of advance (selected answers), by 'consumerism' and 'hardship'

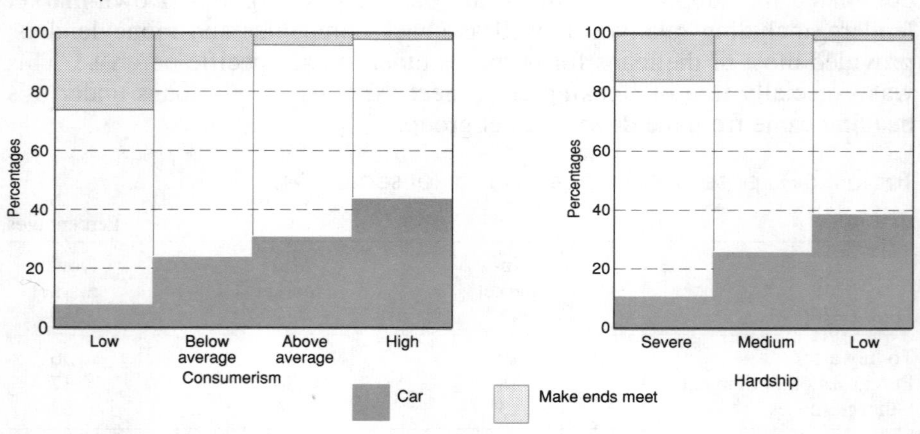

Source: PSI survey; analysis based on all one-off advances

'Responsible credit'

Much of the anxiety about consumer credit is caused by fears that people might borrow more than they can afford to repay. This is called 'irresponsible borrowing' when it is alleged that the customer does not think carefully before signing a contract, or takes a cavalier attitude to repayments. It is called 'irresponsible lending' when attention is being drawn to the possibility that retailers or financial institutions might persuade gullible customers to take out loans or instalment agreements, or fail to check on the credit-worthiness of those who ask for an advance. High-street signs offering instant credit have fostered a belief that instalment credit is obtained too easily and that people are encouraged to take on more credit than they can afford.

The main purpose of the survey was to obtain a complete record of each household's obligations. A full assessment of the extent of 'irresponsible' transactions would require a more narrowly-focussed investigation of the respective roles of borrowers and lenders in the run-up to each agreement. But a number of questions shed some light on the extent of the problem. These referred to instalment agreements and/or commercial loans, but not to informal borrowings.

Security on loans

13 per cent of all loans negotiated direct with the lender were secured against the borrower's home, meaning that about 3 per cent of households had taken out secured loans. The 650,000 households accounted for 5 per cent of owner-occupiers. Since these loans averaged nearly 5 years to repay, we can estimate that roughly 130,000 houses are being offered as security each year. Nearly half of building society cash loans were secured in this way, and 19 per cent of finance house loans, but only 11 per cent of bank loans.

Half of the secured loans were for amounts in excess of £5,000. Hardly any were for less than £1,000.

There has been a great deal of public concern about companies that advertise secured loans to consolidate other credit commitments or to pay debts.[1] Secured loans from building societies and finance houses were slightly more likely than unsecured loans to have been used to pay debts, to make ends meet or for business purposes, but the same was not true of bank loans. About a third of all the secured loans were to meet existing commitments of this sort, but the majority were taken out to support household or motoring expenditure.

As many as half of the finance-house secured loans had been taken out as the result of an advertisement sent to the customer's home.

Deposits on instalment agreements

The majority of hire-purchase and other instalment agreements required the borrower to pay a proportion of the cost immediately. But one third (35 per cent) did not.

Where the goods cost more than £1,000, 80 per cent of customers paid a deposit, averaging a quarter of the total price. For smaller items, 55 per cent had to make an immediate payment, averaging one fifth of the original price.

Lenders adopted varying practices which can be explained only partly in terms of variations in the amounts they advanced. Of the three main HP outlets, only 19 per cent of specialist dealers advanced the whole of the cost compared with 37 per cent of high-street stores and 58 per cent of gas and electricity showrooms.

Marketing

Another concern is that credit may be promoted so vigorously as to persuade people to borrow money they did not really want or could not afford. We asked householders who had taken out a commercial loan how they had decided to borrow from a particular creditor.

- Two-thirds (69 per cent) said that they had already done business with that organisation.
- One fifth reported some kind of direct influence in the marketplace:

from a shop or supplier of the goods or service	9 per cent
from advertisements sent to home	5 per cent
from advertisements on TV or in the paper	4 per cent
from advertisements in the lender's office	3 per cent
from a salesman who called	2 per cent

- About a tenth of borrowers said that they had heard about the lender through family and friends.

Table 6.8 shows that each of the three sectors of the market again had a distinctive characteristic. Banks and building societies relied mainly on their existing customers for business. Finance houses tended to recruit through the marketplace. Check companies and moneylenders used both of these sources, but benefited largely from local grapevines.

Table 6.8 Source of information about lender, by market sector

Percentages

	Up-market	Mid-market	Down-market
Total (=100%)	*370*	*77*	*50*
Already done business with them	81	34	30
Marketplace	15	57	21
Friend/relatives	4	9	49

Source: PSI survey; analysis based on all loans

Impulse buying

For instalment agreements, and for loans that were used to buy something, we asked whether the borrower had thought about it in advance. The majority (58 per cent) said that they had planned the purchase all along; another 15 per cent said that they had been thinking of buying the item for some time, although they had made up their minds at the last minute. These premeditated transactions seem unlikely to cause many problems.

But a quarter were not premeditated. 18 per cent were taken out 'in an emergency'; 8 per cent were purchases decided 'on the spur of the moment'.

'Emergency' credit showed a distinctive pattern. Half of all the advances under this heading were used to buy household electrical or gas appliances such as cookers, washing machines and so on. One third of all fuel-board HP agreements were reported to have been emergencies. The people concerned were commonly pensioners, or non-pensioners with below-average incomes. All of these findings are consistent with a genuine emergency, of an item of basic household equipment breaking down and needing replacement out of a limited income.

Spur-of-the-moment purchases did not have such a strong profile. We looked for evidence that these were luxury goods such as videos; or that the customers were poorer than average; but neither of these conclusions was strongly indicated. The two commercial creditors specialising in the lower end of the market – check companies and money lenders – were associated with impulse decisions more often than others (21 per cent of their advances) but they still accounted for only a small proportion of the total.

Checking ability to pay

A quarter (27 per cent) of the customers said that their loans or instalment agreements were arranged without them being asked any questions to assess their ability to repay the money borrowed. In these cases respondents believed that credit would have been given to anyone who asked for it, though it is possible that checks were being made behind the scenes.

Hardly any building society loans were offered without visible vetting (2 per cent), and this was rare for banks (10 per cent) and not very common for finance houses (18 per cent). But getting on for half of agreements negotiated through a check company or money lender (49 per cent), a high street store (46 per cent) or a fuel-board showroom (43 per cent) appeared to be offered without scrutiny.

The level of checks increased with the size of the loan – nearly half of people borrowing under £500 had not been checked, compared with less than a tenth of people borrowing more than £5,000. Loans taken out on the spur of the moment (44 per cent), or in response to an emergency (34 per cent), were particularly likely to have been granted without any checks being made.

Knowledge of interest rate

When people with instalment agreements or loans were asked what rate of interest was being charged on the advance, just over half of them did not know. Ten years earlier six out of 10 respondents to a similar survey had not known about the rate of interest,[2] so ignorance remains a long-term problem. The earlier research suggests that consumers are more concerned about the level of repayments on credit commitments than they are about either the interest rate or the total cost of the loan.

The actual level of interest will be dealt with later. At this stage, we are concerned that so many people had borrowed without knowing the rate; and that so many organisations had lent without making sure that interest was fully understood.

The oldest borrowers and those with below-average incomes were rather more likely than others to report ignorance of the rate of interest, but neither of these relationships helped to explain why some people did and others did not know this important piece of information. We thought that there might be variations between the customers of different types of creditor; or that people who borrowed large amounts would have taken more care on this subject; but neither hypothesis was substantiated.

Feelings about repayments

Another way of identifying potential problem advances was to ask respondents whether they expected to be able to keep up the repayments at the time the credit was arranged. Of course the question was being asked after they had had time to discover whether they actually could maintain their schedule, so there may be an element of hindsight in some of the answers. By far the majority of customers (80 per cent) expected to be able to repay without difficulty. However, 14 per cent said that they had expected that it would sometimes be hard to find the money and a further 2 per cent took out the agreement expecting that it would always be hard to make the payments. Another 2 per cent said that they had given the matter no thought at all.

There was a clear relationship with the degree to which the purchase had been planned. Only 10 per cent of planned purchases were expected to lead to repayment difficulties, compared with 19 per cent of items bought after a last minute decision, 16 per cent of spur of the moment purchases, and 28 per cent of goods bought as a result of an emergency.

A third of households with incomes below £100 per week had expected difficulty, but there was little variation across the rest of the income range. Another group expressing anxiety on this score was the small number of pensioners who had borrowed – often in an emergency.

A third (36 per cent) of those who had borrowed from finance houses had thought that it would sometimes or always be difficult to find the money to repay, and a similar proportion (32 per cent) of people who took loans from the two types of commercial creditor in the down-market sector. If borrowers' perceptions about the level of checks made were accurate, then a significant number of these loans were being made injudiciously.

It is not surprising that we found that people who had borrowed to make ends meet (50 per cent) or to pay off debts (33 per cent) were most likely to have expected difficulties making the repayments.

Box R Index of responsible lending

In order to identify the one-off advances which might be potential problems, we counted one point for each of the following answers:

No deposit (HP only)
Attracted by advertising (loans only)
Spur of the moment or emergency
No checks made
Don't know interest rate
Expected difficulty in repaying.

The scores were grouped in three bands:

No worry	0 points	21%
Moderate	1-2 points	64%
High worry	3-5 points	15 %

The maximum score is five, because the first two items covered different categories of advance. The score does not apply to informal borrowings.

Problem advances

This brief review of some of the aspects of credit which cause anxiety among consumers' representatives has identified a number of ways in which different types of instalment agreement or loan fall short of the ideal which is sometimes set for them. Evidence about whether these factors are actually associated with arrears will be presented in Chapter 9.

One possibility was that particular types of lender, or particular types of borrower, might be falling short in most of these ways, while other categories of loan earned a clean sheet on every count. It will have been noticed that four groups of creditor have each been mentioned more than once in the preceding pages – finance houses, fuel boards, check companies and moneylenders. But when we looked at all six potential criticisms together, the great majority of advances figured once or twice. Only one fifth (21 per cent) were squeaky clean; even fewer (15 per cent) were at high risk, with three, four or five worrying answers.

Chart 6.9 illustrates a batch of analyses to suggest that:

- it was small advances, rather than large ones, which were most likely to exhibit problems of this sort (top left);
- as already indicated, fuel boards, moneylenders and check companies were most involved in potentially worrying practices. Building societies had a very low problem score, measured in this way (top right);

Chart 6.9 'Responsible credit', by size of advance, source of credit, income, 'hardship' and 'consumerism'

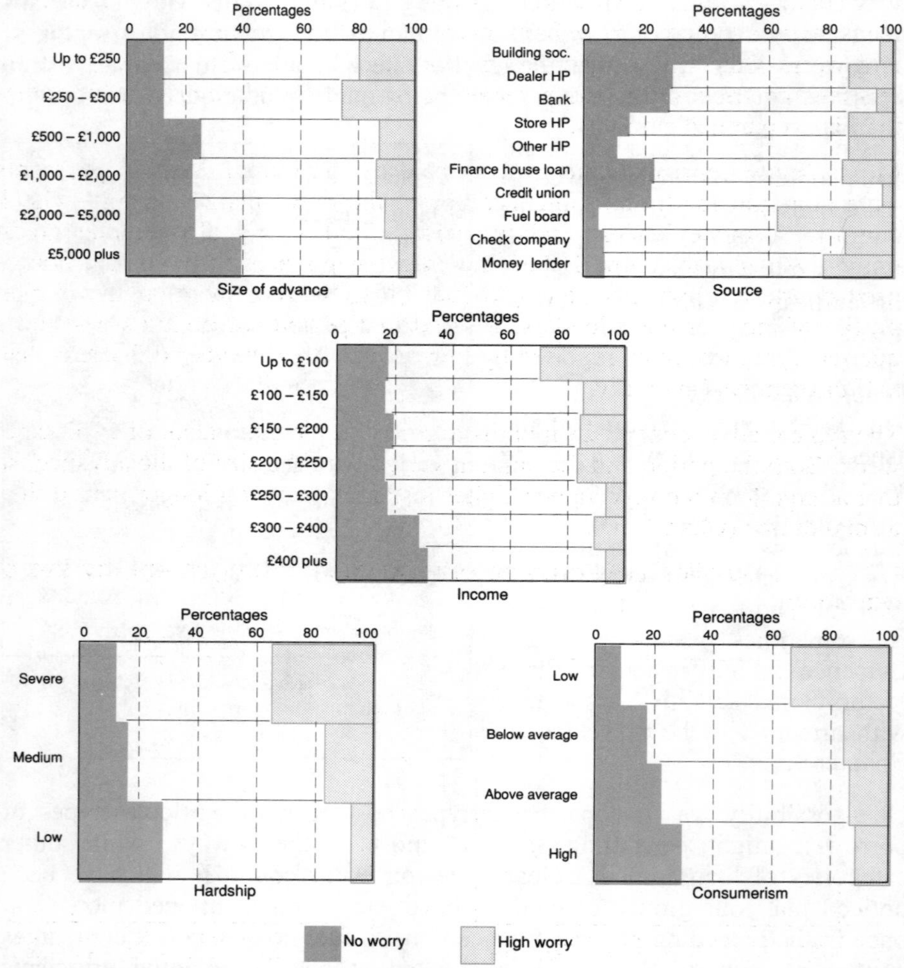

Source: PSI survey; analysis based on commercial advances. See Box R.

- there was a clear, but not particularly strong, tendency for potential problem advances to be associated with below-average incomes (centre);
- problems were also associated with high levels of budgeting hardship (bottom left), but with *low* levels of consumerism (bottom right). This tends to refute the argument that it is heavy consumers who get 'trapped' into taking out high risk credit.

Repayments and charges

All of the hire-purchase advances negotiated through suppliers were repaid by instalments; so, too, were the overwhelming majority of the formal loans from commercial or mutual organisations (96 per cent). The only exception was advances from pawnbrokers. Among informal borrowings, social fund loans were all repaid by regular instalments. Most money borrowed from employers was also subject to an agreed schedule. But money lent by relatives or friends was often repaid at the borrower's convenience rather than in preplanned amounts.

Most (78 per cent) instalments were paid by the month. Weekly payments were common for formal organisations in the down-market sector – check companies, moneylenders and the social fund – and also among credit unions. About half of the HP arrangements negotiated through fuel boards used quarterly payments added to fuel bills. Bearing in mind the market profile of most of these lenders, we find that periods of both a week and a quarter were most often reported by low income households, so that less than half of them paid monthly.

The typical advance took 28 months to repay, at the equivalent of £16.60 per week. Both the period and the amount varied with the size of the advance, so that a large loan required rather higher instalments over a longer period than a smaller one (Chart 6.10).

Chart 6.10 Duration and amount of repayment arrangement, by size of advance

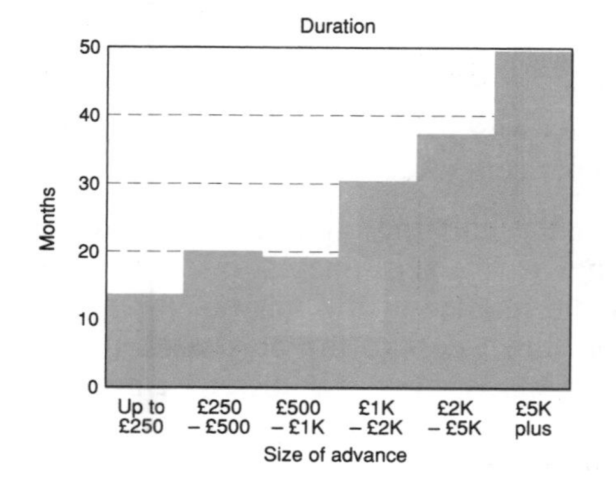

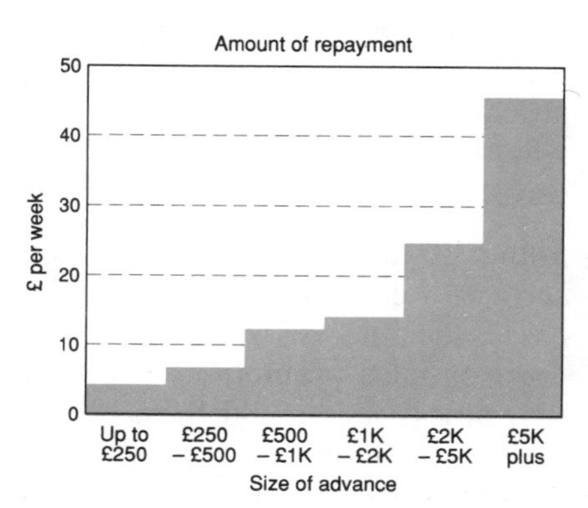

Source: PSI survey; analysis based on all one-off advances

The size of the advance was the most important factor in determining the length of the repayment period, and hence the repayment instalments. Since the amount borrowed varied so strongly with income, it follows that higher income households repaid over longer periods (Table 6.11). But because of the interaction between household income and the size of the advance, there was much less variation in the repayments made by households at different income levels than there was in the amount they had borrowed in the first place. The top income group had borrowed, on average, six times as much as the bottom group; but their repayments were only 3 times as great. Another way of putting it is that rich people paid about 60p per week for each hundred pounds they borrowed, while poor people paid about £1 per week per £100. This does not, in itself, mean that credit is more expensive for poor people but it does limit the amount that can be raised by people who can afford only a few pounds a week.

Table 6.11 Duration and amount of repayments arrangements, by income

	Up to £100	£100 -£150	£150 -£200	£200 -£250	£250 -£300	£300 -£400	£400 plus
Total (=100%)	*185*	*139*	*189*	*167*	*141*	*236*	*209*
Average duration (months)	19.8	22.6	28.7	27.4	26.5	33.1	30.3
Average instalment	£7.3	£11.20	£13.80	£15.70	£16.20	£ 21.00	£30.30

Source: PSI survey; analysis based on non-pensioners' one-off advances

The cost of an advance can be assessed in two ways. First, we have the information about interest rates reported by the half of householders in the survey who knew what they were. Second, we can use the information about the number and size of instalments to calculate what the effective cost was, expressed in terms of an annual rate. We confine both of these analyses to commercial advances, that is, HP instalment agreements and commercial loans. They exclude informal borrowings, which were defined by the absence of interest charges. At the time of the survey, the bank base rate which represents the floor of interest rates was 14 per cent. The main credit cards were charging between 25 and 30 per cent (APR).

Some of those who arranged their credit with the supplier of goods or services said that they had taken advantage of a zero-interest offer. In these cases, the interest was paid either by the retailer or the manufacturer as a form of sales promotion. There was no direct cost to the purchaser, unless the same goods could have been bought elsewhere for a lower cash price. These zero-interest advances represented 20 per cent of HP agreements, or 11 per cent of all commercial advances. The majority of them concerned purchases costing less than £500, and were repayable within 12 months. But the advantages of free credit were spread fairly evenly across all income groups, and the poorest borrowers did not benefit as much as might have been expected from the proportion of small advances they took.

Where interest was both charged and known, most borrowers thought that they were paying between 15 and 30 per cent. Hardly anyone said the cost exceeded 50 per cent. The average was 19 per cent, but Table 6.12 shows that interest rates tended to be higher for small advances than for large ones.

Table 6.12 Two estimates of the costs of advances, by size of advance

Percentages

	Up to £250	£250 -£500	£500 -£1,000	£1,000 -£2,000	£2,000 -£5,000	£5,000 plus
Reported interest rates						
Proportion with zero interest	24	21	11	1	3	1
Average interest (where paid)	24%	27%	20%	18%	15%	13%
Calculated charges						
Proportion with zero charge	29	19	8	3	5	12
Proportion above 100%	31	17	11	13	1	3
Median charge (where paid)	35%	32%	37%	33%	25%	19%

Source: PSI survey; analysis based on instalment agreements and loans where the relevant information was known

Since so many people did not know the rate of interest, we also estimated the rate of charge from information about the repayments, as explained in Box S. The results should be treated with caution, but shed a valuable alternative light on annual rates of charge. We get a much wider spread of figures than were provided in answer to the direct question. Many people apparently paid less than 10 per cent while some paid much more. If these exceptionally high and low rates of charge were spread about the sample in an unsystematic way, we might put them down to people not recalling the details of their arrangements accurately. But Table 6.12 shows a clear pattern. Using medians – the measure of typical charges least sensitive to exceptionally high or low figures – the table suggests that that true charges were similar to the reported figures at amounts above £2,000, but that the calculated costs of small advances were substantially higher than reported interest rates for smaller transactions.

There were a few extreme cases. The Director General of Fair Trading has cited examples of charges which he clearly regards as extortionate – at an annual percentage rate (APR) in excess of 1,000 per cent.[3] Money advisers in poor communities have also complained about occasional transactions above 1,000 per cent. It is clear that such rates are sometimes charged, but it has never been established whether they are rare or very rare. The evidence based on examples described by the OFT and debt counsellors receives some support from the survey: eight of the advances identified appeared to have rates of charge in excess of 1,000 per cent. A lone parent, for instance, had borrowed £100, and was paying £6.50 per week for a year – an annual rate of charge of nearly 2,200 per cent. Six of the eight super-charged loans were for amounts of £250 or less. Six were being repaid in weekly instalments. Three were from moneylenders; two from sources described by the borrower as a finance house; one each from a check company, a fuel board and a high-street store.

Box S Estimating annual charges

The calculation of the rate of charge is based on four items of information: the size of the advance, the number of instalments, the frequency of payment, and the amount of each payment. The estimates were made only when all four of those questions were clearly answered, and where the total amount repaid exceeded the amount borrowed. 62 per cent of commercial advances repayable by instalments met all these conditions.

Repayments at a given rate of interest are calculated by the formula:

$$P_f = \frac{A*I*(1+I_f)^N}{(1+I_f)^N - 1}$$

where P_f is the payment per week, per month etc.
A is the amount of the advance
I_f is the rate of interest over each payment period (per week, per month etc)
N is the number of instalments

The rate of interest per month (or per week etc) is calculated from this formula, and then has to be converted to an annual rate as follows:

$$APR = (1+I_f)^F$$

where F is the number of instalments per year (52, 12 etc).

Note that this calculation is based on total costs, and makes no attempt to distinguish between nominal interest charges, administration fees, insurance costs and so on. Obviously, the answers are only as accurate as the data provided to us by the respondents, which may not have been checked against written records. We have presented the results in terms of medians, rather than averages, in order to discount the extremely high rates of interest apparently being paid by a small number of people.

Because of the difficulties of collecting reliable data about complicated financial arrangements, the survey cannot be regarded as having provided conclusive proof of these very high rates of charge; we have simply added a further item of evidence to the reports coming from the OFT and advice agencies.

A separate point is that, leaving aside the super-charges, many of the small transactions cost in excess of 100 per cent per annum. There is much more solid evidence about charges in this range. The Birmingham Settlement, for example, has reported 14 examples, of which 12 were between 128 and 318 per cent.[4] The Consumer Credit Association, representing companies in the weekly collected credit market, gives a typical example of a £100 loan repayable over 26 weeks at £5.40 per week – which works out at 298 per cent (or 233 per cent if the repayments spread over 30 weeks in practice).[5] Table 6.12 suggests that as many as a third of all small advances may have been subject to charges in excess of 100 per cent. They were in evidence from all commercial sources except building societies. But check companies stood out – four-fifths of their loans were at this level.

Another way of calculating the cost of borrowing is simply to add up the total cost of repayments as a proportion of the original advance. For those instalment agreements and loans providing complete data, the average cost in this sense was £48 per £100.

According to this measure, the credit charges were closely related to the duration of the repayment period (Chart 6.13, left). The total cost of advances repaid within a year was one third of the amount borrowed (33 per cent); if the repayment period exceeded five years, the total cost was two thirds of the advance (69 per cent). That is as it should be: borrowers are buying time, so the more time allowed for repayment, the more they should be expected to pay.

Chart 6.13 Total cost of borrowing as a proportion of the amount advanced, by duration of repayment period and amount of advance

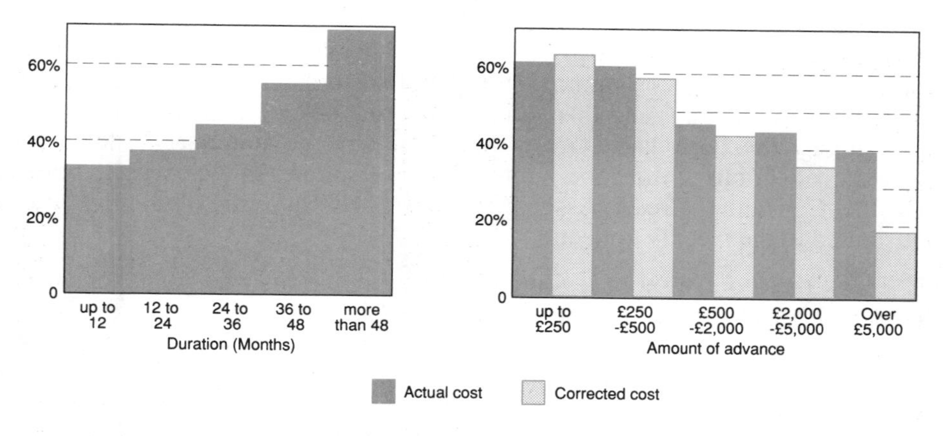

Source: PSI survey; analysis based on instalment agreements and loans where the relevant information was known.

Since small advances tended to be repaid over shorter periods, their total cost 'ought' to be less than large loans. In fact, they cost rather more. The dark-shaded columns of Chart 6.13 (right) show that the charge rose from an average of 38 per cent for loans exceeding £5,000, to 61 per cent for advances of less than £500. The light-shaded columns correct for the variation in the repayment periods, by showing what the total cost of each type of advance would be if it was repaid over two years. This correction shows the relatively high cost of smaller transactions, even more clearly than the APR calculation shown in Table 6.12. An advance of less than £250 costs nearly four times as much as a loan of £5,000 or more.

There are three factors affecting the costs of providing credit which should be taken into account in evaluating the charges paid by customers.

Proportional costs are those which would be expected to be ten times as great for a £1,000 loan as for £100. These include the cost to the lender of borrowing the money wholesale, plus an acceptable profit margin on the transaction. Small companies operating in risky markets might be expected to pay higher wholesale prices, and to plan a higher margin, but these costs should be roughly proportional to the size of the loan.

Fixed costs of making the advance – mainly administration. Lenders of large sums would be expected to invest more in checks on the repayment prospects, but set-up costs would usually represent a much larger proportion of a small loan than of a large one.

Collection costs include the administration of the repayment system, plus the administrative and capital costs of debts. These costs are not directly determined by the size of the loan so much as by the market in which it is offered. Small loans are repaid more quickly than large ones, but the number of instalments per pound is higher. Many poor people, borrowing small sums, prefer to pay in cash by the week, rather than by monthly standing order. This naturally costs more. Poor people also have relatively high rates of arrears and default, and this adds to the costs of creditors, which have to be paid by the borrowers. One way of reducing default rates is to make weekly collections at the door, but this also costs more. In the example given by the Consumer Credit Association, just over half the total cost was attributed to the weekly collection service.

There is, therefore, a set of legitimate economic reasons why small advances cost the lender more, and would be expected to lead to higher charges. Since we do not have direct data about each element of these costs, it is not possible for the research to draw the line precisely between genuinely high costs and excessive profits. But whatever the costs to the lender, the fact remains that many small advances cost a lot to the borrower.

References

1. Director General of Fair Trading, *Unjust Credit Transactions*, OFT, 1991; National Consumer Council, *Security Risks: loans secured on houses*, NCC, 1987

2. National Consumer Council, *Consumers and Credit*, NCC, 1981

3. OFT, 1991, see note 1

4. Janet Ford, *Consuming Credit: Debt and Poverty in the UK*, Child Poverty Action Group, 1991

5. *Memorandum submitted on behalf of the Consumer Credit Association of the United Kingdom in relation to Consumer Credit Act 1974: extortionate credit*, May 1991

7 The Impact of Credit on Household Budgets

We have looked at households' income and their spending both on regular household expenses and on consumer credit commitments. Bringing all this information together we can begin to draw an overall picture of household budgets at different levels of income.

The average household has a net income, after tax, national insurance and other deductions, of just over £200 a week. Table 2.1 breaks this down into three main components.

- Basic household costs includes the housing and household services commitments described in Chapter 3, plus a minimum allowance for personal needs. The average household was committed to spending £96 per week on these household costs, accounting for 46 per cent of their income. The remaining £111, 54 per cent of the total, is available to be spent on other things.
- Consumer credit commitments took up another £15 per week – 7 per cent of starting income, or 14 per cent of the money available after household costs had been met.
- That left £96 per household for discretionary expenditure: 46 per cent of the original amount.

Table 7.1 Analysis of income and commitments

	Amount	As proportion of: Net income	Discretionary income
Average net income:	£207	100%	
Basic household costs			
Housing costs: mortgage, rent and associated charges, local taxes	£40	19%	
Household services: electricity, gas and telephone	£17	8%	
Minimum personal needs: an allowance of £20 per adult, £15 per teenager and £10 per child for basic food, clothing and so on at income support levels	£39	19%	
Total	£96	46%	
Available income	£111	54%	100%
Consumer credit: total repayment commitments	£15	7%	14%
Discretionary income	£96	46%	86%

Source: PSI survey; analysis based on all householders.

Box T Comparing commitments with income

Comparison between income and a series of items of spending is very sensitive to oddball errors in the data. We have checked each case and excluded it from the analysis in this chapter if any one of the elements was right out of line – if consumer credit commitments exceeded income on their own, for example. For this reason some of the figures are slightly different from those reported in other chapters.

While we can check for absurdly high costs, we have not screened for absurdly low ones. The estimates of commitments may, therefore, err on the low side.

Basic personal needs

The income support basic rate in 1989 was £35 for a single person (over 25) and £55 for a couple. We have interpreted that as meaning £20 per adult; the extra £15 per household is assumed to be spent on household commitments such as fuel. Again, the estimate is on the conservative side.

Of course it can be argued that some of the commitments need not have been entered into, or that others might be reduced. In the short run, however, they are unavoidable. Moving house takes time to arrange, and may cost money. Existing credit commitments have to be repaid, even if no further commitments are taken on. Other areas of spending, like feeding the children, offer even less room for manoeuvre.

The crucial question is how the balance of spending varies between households with different circumstances. Table 7.2 shows typical household budgets at different levels of income; Chart 7.3 gives the same information as a graph.

People's housing expenditure was quite strongly affected by their income – at the top of the scale, by big mortgages; at the bottom, by rent rebates and local tax rebates. The other household costs – services and basic minimum personal expenditure – were very similar at all income levels. As a result, basic household costs accounted for a higher and higher proportion of people's budgets, the lower their income was. Among the poorest group, 92 pence in every pound was committed in this way: only £5 of their income remained available for other spending.

We discovered, in Chapter 4, that the average number and size of consumer credit commitments increased with household income. In fact our estimate of the costs of servicing credit was roughly constant as a proportion of total income – about 8 per cent. Table 7.2 and Chart 7.3 show that credit commitments represent only a small proportion of the *available* income of rich families, but the proportion rises with lower incomes. At the extreme, the modest £6 per week spent in the poorest group actually exceeded the tiny £5 per week of available income. The whole of their budgets has now been accounted for, with no leeway at all. Households with less than £100 per

Table 7.2 Income and commitments, by income

£s per week

	Up to £100	£100 -£150	£150 -£200	£200 -£250	£250 -£300	£300 -£400	£400 plus
Total (=100%)	*229*	*171*	*253*	*201*	*177*	*279*	*204*
Average income	£65	£123	£173	£224	£280	£342	£527
Basic household costs							
Housing costs	£13	£31	£38	£48	£58	£68	£87
Household services	£14	£16	£17	£16	£17	£24	£23
Basic personal needs	£33	£39	£44	£45	£43	£49	£46
Total	£60	£86	£99	£109	£118	£141	£156
(as % of total income)	92%	70%	57%	49%	42%	41%	30%
Available income	£5	£37	£74	£115	£162	£201	£371
Consumer credit	£6	£10	£14	£18	£20	£31	£35
(as % of total income)	9%	8%	8%	8%	7%	9%	7%
(as % of available income)	120%	27%	19%	16%	12%	15%	9%
Discretionary expenditure	–£1	£27	£60	£97	£142	£170	£336

Source: PSI survey; analysis based on non-pensioner householders

Chart 7.3 Income and commitments, by income

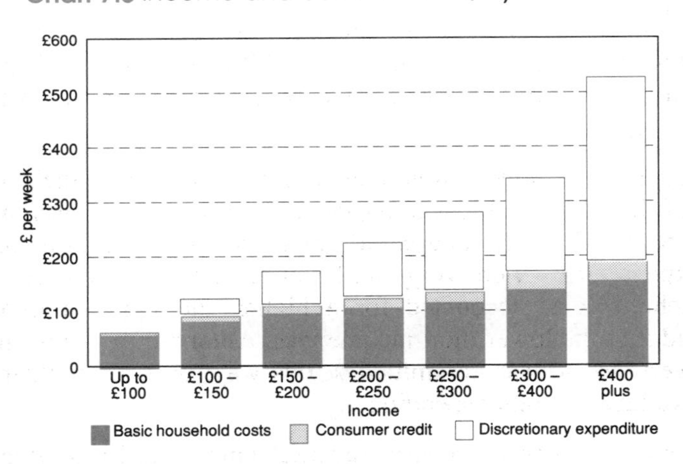

Source: PSI survey; analysis based on non-pensioner householders

week were evidently under pressure, not just from time to time, but week in, week out, until their income improved. This is not the only source of information that suggests that significant numbers of poor households spend more than their income every week. The highly detailed Family Expenditure Survey,[1] for example, indicates a regular deficit at the foot of the income ladder.

Since this relationship with income is observed for whole groups of people, we conclude that it is the variations in income that cause the precarious balance at the lower end of the scale, rather than personal variations in people's spending patterns. Nevertheless, some people with broadly similar levels of resource had more commitments than others. If the average discretionary income was zero, about half of the poor households showed a weekly surplus, and half a regular deficit. In fact 8 per cent of them were estimated to have £25 per week clear; while 10 per cent were overcommitted to the tune of at least £25 per week. This might also have been caused by circumstances – loss of income following unemployment, for example; variations in the availability of support within the family; sudden unforeseen expenses. It might also have been caused by differences in people's personal approach to budgeting.

While tables and charts provide important evidence about the extent of overcommitment, they do not show how the problem arises, or is avoided, in individual families. We conclude our analysis of the use of credit by turning to eighteen low-income households who were interviewed in much more detail.

Almost all of these families were using credit. But for the majority it was not for buying consumer goods such as microwaves, stereos or home computers. They were using credit for living expenses and necessities.

Three families had no credit commitments. All had used credit in the past, but had given it up for different reasons.

One woman's husband had lost his job through disability:

> *We have done so in the past, but not now. It's the best way. Well, you can't afford it now. I don't think they'd take Sam on now. We've never asked, but since he's been disabled and finished work, we tend not to bother.*

Another woman had been widowed with three young children:

> *I don't use credit since my husband died. I've had to adapt myself to the situation. It's no good having credit; I can't pay it.*

In the third instance, a single mother had used a mail-order catalogue and got into difficulties with the payments.

> *It's so easy to look at a catalogue, you don't realise how it builds up. I can't afford it in my position. I can't get credit anyway and if I could it wouldn't be worth it. I only used it for Christmas that time. I shan't use it again.*

Most families felt it was a case of *having* to use credit. Ten of the eighteen families used it sparingly – one or two commitments. Where they used commercial credit it was most often mail-order catalogues. One had a loan from the Provident check company; one used a store card and two had finance house loans. These families had all used credit for essentials such as shoes, clothing, beds, decorating and to pay bills. The two finance house loans were for second-hand vehicles that were needed by people who were self-employed.

Those who had a relative they could turn to for a loan did so with some regularity, to tide them over until they received their next benefit payment. One young divorced woman with three children, for example, borrowed £2 to £3 most weeks to enable her to buy food for the weekend. When the children needed clothes, other relatives helped out.

> *I don't get into debt. Recently I've had to borrow from my sister or my auntie – she's marvellous. I've got an auntie who practically clothes my youngest or I couldn't cope at all.*

But five of the 18 households were heavy credit users, with at least three current credit commitments and others that had been paid off during the previous year. Like others they used credit out of financial hardship, but three households had bought consumer goods: a video, a washing machine and a three piece suite.

A case study illustrates the predicament of those whose commitments had got out of hand. The household consisted of a couple with four children: one of school age, one working and two unemployed. The husband had been out of work for five years. The parents' income was £91.25 a week – £84 from income support and £7.25 child benefit – plus full housing benefit. The older children contributed £10 a week each to the housekeeping. They had the following credit commitments.

- One HP agreement – £480 for a washing machine which was being paid back through their electric slot meter.
- Three outstanding loans from a check company – one of £300 and two at £100 – taken out to buy clothes and to pay bills, with repayments of £26 per week.
- A social fund loan of £190 to meet the costs of decorating, the repayments deducted from their income support at source.
- A £382 loan from a finance house for a carpet, being repaid at £14 a month.
- Repayments of £15 a week to a mail-order catalogue for clothing.
- And they owed £40 to the wife's mother.

We do not have all the details of repayments on each item, but the total is estimated at £54 per week – more than half of their cash income. By using consumer credit to pay bills, the family was in a vicious circle. They needed to borrow because they had not got the money to pay a bill. When the next bill arrived they had even less money because of the repayments on the loan to the check company, so they needed to top up the loan.

> *There's nothing left by the time I pay my way... I'm only on £84 a week so you can imagine how much I've got to spend on food for the rest of the week, plus my electricity, my gas, this, that and the other. Sometimes I only have a tenner left out of my giro; sometimes I don't even have that. We don't like [to borrow] but we've got to do it, haven't we? Yes, it's the only way people can get by – continuously borrowing.*

Reference

1. Department of Employment, *Family Expenditure Survey 1989*, HMSO, 1991

Part III
DEBT

8 Patterns of Indebtedness

Debt has been a matter of public concern for many years. Rent arrears, mortgage repossessions, fuel disconnections and consumer debts have each been the focus for national attention from time to time. Citizens advice bureaux report half a million requests for help with debt problems every year. Specialist debt counselling services have been set up to help multiple debtors. Yet this is the first attempt to obtain a systematic measure of the extent of debt, and of its impact on households.

The origins of debt

Every commentator has a view about whether debt arises when people 'can't pay', or whether it is people who 'won't pay'. Actually, the issues are much more complex than such a simple distinction implies. There are at least six important potential explanations.

One argument is that debt is primarily caused by *poverty;* that debtors simply do not have enough money to meet their normal commitments. Another explanation is that people get into debt because there has been a major *change in their circumstances* which reduces their income, or increases their spending needs, unexpectedly; redundancy or illness are obvious examples. There is also a growing belief that debtors have *over-committed* themselves – borrowing more than they could afford to repay. Linked to this is the view that, while the majority of us are good at handling our financial affairs, there is a group of people who do not know how to *manage their money* and get into debt as a result. Then there is a strongly held belief, particularly in the credit industry, that a sizeable group of people *'won't pay'* – they have the money, but deliberately delay or avoid meeting their obligations.

All of these hypotheses focus on the actions or inactions of the debtor. Another set of explanations looks at the *creditor,* who may have encouraged overcommitment, levied excessive charges, or made inappropriate arrangements for collecting payments. Third parties (such as the DSS or employers) might also play a part.

The analysis of the prevalence of debt throughout this chapter contributes to our understanding of the problem, but does not provide a simple explanation of its causes. It is tempting to ask which one of the six explanations is true. But that is not helpful, because all of them might be, in different measure on different occasions. The six explanations may be conceptually distinct, but they are not logically incompatible. There are poor families who cannot manage their money. (There are also rich families who are poor managers; the main difference is that those with more money to play with can usually muddle through.) Similarly, there are people who take on heavy credit or mortgage commitments, and are then made redundant and cannot keep up the payments. Individuals' reluctance to pay might be compounded by organisations' inefficiency. It is appropriate to assess the relative importance of these explanations, without necessarily distinguishing between them case by case.

One approach was to ask the debtors themselves. For each 'problem debt' reported, the respondent was asked what the difficulty was. We could not expect them to give explanations critical of themselves – some did say that they deliberately withheld payment, but this was usually on an issue of principle like refusing to pay their poll tax. But all of the types of explanation were in evidence:

Insufficient income	25%
Reduced income	26%
Other changes in circumstances	7%
Overcommitment	24%
Unexpected bills	10%
Overlooked payment	8%
Withheld payment	4%
Creditor action	7%
Benefit problems	5%

So, as one would have expected, debtors themselves tended to explain their arrears in terms of the difficulties they faced, rather than failures on their own part. Another approach was to ask everyone, debtors or not, what the main reasons for debt were. The answers are presented, as before, as scores: ten means complete agreement, zero means complete rejection. Opinions varied on this subject, but on balance, respondents accepted that most debtors faced problems which were not necessarily of their own making. People get into debt, they thought:

... because their circumstances have changed	score 7.1
... because they don't have enough money to live on	score 6.8

Both of these explanations suggest that debtors can't pay because of circumstances out of their direct control. Many people also ascribe the problem to lack of budgeting skills:

... because they haven't managed their money sensibly	score 6.9

That view is at best understanding, at worst patronising. On the other hand, there was little support for the claim that debtors won't pay. Most respondents *disagreed* that people got into debt:

... because they are dishonest	score 3.0

The extent of debt

The survey identified debts at three levels. They are summarised in Table 8.1.

- One household in five (19 per cent) had been in *arrears* in the course of the previous year with payments on either a regular household expense, like the rent, mortgage or gas bill, or a consumer credit commitment. Many of them reported more than one item in arrears; there were 0.37 arrears per household.
- But about a third of these arrears do not appear to have been serious: they were not at all worrying and there was no problem over paying the money owed. One household in eight (12 per cent) had one or more *problem debts* during the year. They represent 2.6 million householders in debt. Taking multiple debt into account, there were 0.22 problem debts per household: 5.0 million debts in the UK over a year.
- About a third of these problem debts had been paid off by the time of the interview. 8 per cent of households were in debt at the time of the survey; 0.15 *current debts* per household. In terms of the total population, there were 1.8 million households currently in debt, owing money to 3.3 million creditors. The average amount of current arrears – £90 for every household in the country – represented a total of £2 billion.

Table 8.1 Total arrears and debts

	Per cent of h'holds	Average no. of debts per h'hold	Average arrears per h'hold
Arrears	19%	0.37	
subtract:			
not a problem		(0.15)	
Problem debts	12%	0.22	
subtract			
debts paid off at time of interview		(0.07)	
Current debts	8%	0.15	£90

Source: PSI survey; analysis based on all householders.
Note: the averages are calculated across all households, not just those with any debts.

So there are various ways of defining debt, just as there were a number of definitions of credit. For simplicity, two concepts will be used through most of the analysis. In identifying debtors and describing the number of debts, we will refer to problem debts reported over the course of a year – the centre line of Table 8.1. When the volume of debt in pounds is under consideration, it is the current amount outstanding which is important: the bottom right hand figure of the table.

Box U What is a 'debt'?

The interview identified each household expense or consumer credit agreement, and respondents were asked whether they had fallen behind or had any difficulty with that payment during the previous year. These difficulties have been referred to as *'arrears'*. The commitments covered in this way and the precise definition of arrears for each item were:

Rent – Mortgage – Rates/poll tax – Water rates – Service charge – Ground rent – Electricity – Gas – Other fuels – Phone – Rented TV/video – Maintenance
*Have you been behind or owed any *** payments at any time during the past 12 months?*

Overdraft
Have you had any difficulty paying off your overdraft at any time during the past 12 months?

Credit/Store cards
*Have you been unable to meet the minimum payment on your *** account at any time during the past 12 months?*

*Have you gone over the credit limit of the *** account for more than a short period at any time during the past 12 months?*

Catalogues – Instalment agreements – Loans – Borrowings
*Have you fallen behind with the payments for the *** at any time during the past 12 months?*

After all these arrears had been identified, the interviewer went through each in turn, and asked 'How worried are you?' about each item. If the arrears were 'not at all' worrying, the interviewer checked whether there had been any problem over paying the arrears. No further questions were asked about items where the respondent had no problem after all; they have been removed from the analysis of debt. The arrears that remained have been called *'problem debts'* or sometimes just *'debts'*. Households with three or more such problem debts have been considered to be in *multiple debt*.

The majority of debtor households owed money to only one creditor. But, even so, more than half a million households – that is getting on for 3 per cent – had been in debt to three or more creditors over the year. For more than 150,000 households, with five or more debts over the year, the problem was very serious indeed:

	per cent of all households	per cent of all debtors
One debt	6.4%	55%
Two	2.5%	22%
Three	1.2%	10%
Four	0.7%	6%
Five or more	0.7%	6%

The majority of debts were amounts of less than £500, though some stretched up to £2000 or more. It must be stressed that these figures do not include the original amount borrowed by these families as mortgages or consumer credit commitments – only the *missed payments*. Nor do they include the majority of mortgages and consumer credit commitments which were not causing any problem.

	per cent of all current debts
Up to £100	31%
£100 to £500	49%
£500 to £1000	12%
£1000 to £2000	5%
More than £2000	4%
Median amount of each debt	£200
Mean amount of each debt	£610

Media attention has focussed on consumer credit debt and on credit cards in particular. Such debts need to be set in context. Many more people were in debt on their regular household expenses than on consumer credit commitments. Rent arrears were easily the most common problem. Mortgage arrears tended to be the most substantial in terms of the amount owed. Household commitments accounted for about two-thirds of all debts – about 3 million in total. But there were still about 1 million consumer credit debts.

	per cent of all debts over year	median amount currently owed
Household commitments		
Mortgage	6%	£710
Rent	22%	£200
Local taxes	10%	£130
Household services	18%	£160
Other commitments	9%	£110
Consumer credit		
Overdraft	10%	£530
Credit/store cards	6%	£340
Mail order	6%	£60
One-off advances	12%	£240

It is frequently argued that the level of debt is increasing. But there are no official statistics covering all types of debt to enable trends to be monitored. Some detailed series of figures (examined in Chapter 9) show an increase; others do not; there is no series at all covering consumer debt. Nor is there a previous national survey of all types of debt with which to compare our 1989 figures.

There were, however, several studies of specific types of debt at the beginning of the 1980s. Combining these with some of the published statistics, we concluded that there may have been about 1.3 million households with current arrears in 1981.[1] Our own survey suggests that there were 2.8 million households with current arrears in 1989 – double the earlier figure. (Note that the comparison is based on 'arrears' because no questions about 'problem debts' were asked in 1981.)

The 1981 analysis suggested that roughly 130,000 households may have been in multiple arrears, defined as owing money to three or more creditors at the same time. We estimate that some 530,000 households were in that position in 1989.

The earlier figures are broad estimates and need to be viewed with caution. The comparison seems to indicate, however, that indebtedness grew over the 1980s; and that multiple debt in particular increased at a worrying rate.

Debt and the life cycle

Debt was more common among young people than in older age groups (Table 8.2). A quarter of householders in their twenties reported at least one problem debt. The incidence fell steeply with age, so that it was extremely rare among people aged over 70. Very similar findings were observed in 1981,[2] and it seems likely that the gradient is a permanent feature of ageing. Looked at another way, nearly two-thirds of all debts belonged to people in their twenties or thirties – twice their proportion in the population.

At first sight, we might try to explain the pattern of debt in terms of credit commitments, since the use of consumer credit was also strongly related to age. But the fall in the number of debts with advancing age was far more rapid than the decrease in the number of commitments. Moreover, people in their twenties, had rather *fewer* commitments, but *more* debts, than those in their thirties. In fact our measure of 'risk' – debts as a proportion of commitments – fell from 7.1 per cent in the twenties to 0.4 per cent in the seventies.

Table 8.2 Problem debts, by age

	Up to 29	30 to 39	40 to 49	50 to 59	60 to 69	70 plus
Total (=100%)	*319*	*453*	*388*	*316*	*335*	*395*
Proportion with						
any problem debts	24%	17%	14%	6%	5%	1%
three or more debts	6%	4%	3%	1%	*	*
Average number of debts	0.49	0.35	0.26	0.12	0.07	0.02
Risk: debts per 100 commitments	7.1	4.5	3.7	1.8	1.4	0.4

Source: PSI Survey; analysis based on all householders

The standard theory of the income life cycle is not particularly helpful in explaining this pattern. It would have predicted that people with rising incomes – in their twenties and thirties – would have been in a better position to meet their commitments, while those with falling incomes – in their sixties and seventies – would have had most difficulty. Considerations of uncertainty might, however, provide a better explanation. Young people have a general expectation of increasing incomes, but a proportion of them will be disappointed. During periods of low income, they might hope for an improvement. Older people can predict their retirement income well in advance, and know that it will not improve. According to this hypothesis debt would arise when actual income fell short of what had been expected.

Chart 8.3 Domestic and economic changes over the past three years, by age

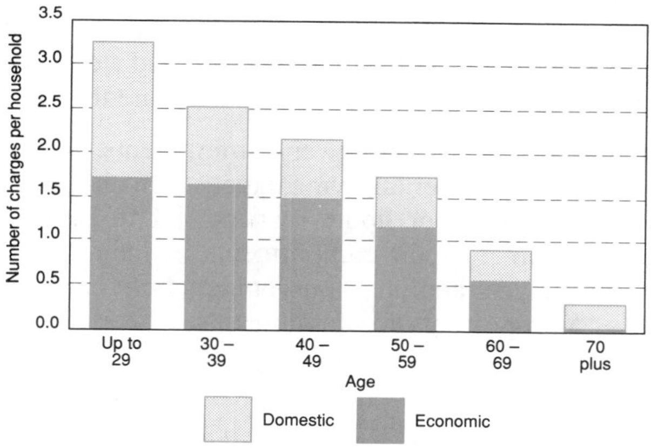

Source: PSI survey; analysis based on all householders

The survey confirms that young people led less stable lives than their elders. The average household in their twenties reported 1.5 domestic changes in the past three years: forming a household, marriage, a new baby, moving house and so on. The frequency of these domestic changes declined rapidly with increasing age: those at or after retirement age reported one fifth as many as those in their twenties (Chart 8.3, light). Economic changes – leaving jobs, finding them, changes in pay and so on – also tended to be more frequent among younger people than older people, although the rate of decline over the working phase of the life cycle was not so noticeable (Chart 8.3, dark).

In broad terms, this instability seems to explain the greater level of debt among the younger members of the sample. But we cannot pin this down specifically: for the most part, people who had experienced recent changes on either the domestic or the employment front were not much more likely to be in debt than people unaffected by change. There was some sign that households who had had a new baby or had experienced marital separation in the past few years had an above-average risk of debt. Similarly, losing or changing jobs was slightly associated with indebtedness. But only a small proportion of the overall problem could be attributed to these factors.

Another explanation might lie in the family life cycle. It will be remembered that the most important family influence on consumer credit was marriage; neither setting up one's own home nor having children had much effect on the number of credit sources in use. As before, we compare the main types of non-pensioner household in three steps, taking account of age whenever appropriate.

Non-householders vs young single householders Most non-householders were young people in their late teens or twenties, living with their parents. Compared with others of their generation who had set up their own homes they had a much lower risk of debt. One in twelve had a debt, compared with a quarter of young single householders. None had more than one debt.

Clearly non-householders had far fewer commitments, since they usually made just one payment to cover all living expenses, without the full range of household bills that tenants or home owners had to meet. They did, of course, take on consumer credit commitments in their own right. In fact young single householders and non-householders both had the same risk of debt expressed as a proportion of commitments – 5 per cent. The increased financial responsibilities of running a household therefore seemed to add to people's chances of being in debt.

Single householders vs couples without children Whereas couples used more consumer credit, single householders reported more debt – 0.32 problems per household, compared with 0.11. This was true across all non-pensioner age groups; indeed Chart 8.4 (left panel) suggests that marital status was more important than age among households without children. The risk of debt was nearly four times as high for single people (5.7 per 100 commitments) as for couples (1.5 per 100).

Couples with and without children Having children seemed to make some difference to young couples' use of consumer credit, but the effect had disappeared by the time they reached their thirties. Family responsibilities had a much stronger influence on the extent of debt. Chart 8.4 (right panel) shows that younger and larger families had many times more debts than older and smaller ones.

This is the first of several indications in this chapter that the influences on indebtedness interacted with each other. Neither age nor children was particularly important on its own. But in combination they provided a powerful explanation for the incidence of debt. It was young families who were most at risk.

Chart 8.4 Problem debts, by family type

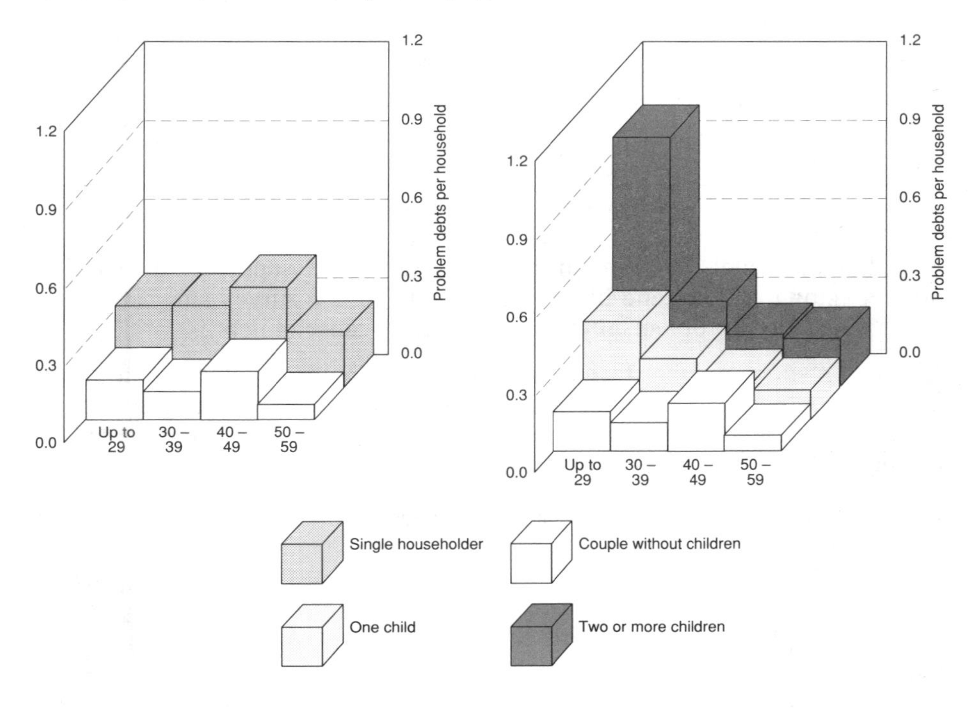

Source: PSI survey; analysis based on all householders

Lone parents also had a large number of problem debts: one each, on average – three times as many as single people without children. This provides partial confirmation of the effects of children, though the very low incomes of one parent families also need to be taken into account.

Economic influences

Income

Although the rich used most credit, it was the poor who had most debt. Table 8.5 shows that a few problem debts were reported right up the income scale. But the number of debts increased rapidly at the lower end. Householders with incomes below £100 per week accounted for only 12 per cent of non-pensioners' commitments, but reported 37 per cent of the debts. One tenth of the poorest group had three or more problem debts in the course of the year.

Table 8.5 Problem debts, by income

	Up to £100	£100 -£150	£150 -£200	£200 -£250	£250 -£300	£300 -£400	£400 plus
Total (=100%)	*255*	*176*	*255*	*201*	*177*	*284*	*206*
Proportion with							
any problem debts	33%	22%	13%	9%	10%	8%	2%
three or more debts	10%	4%	4%	2%	1%	1%	*
Average number of debts	0.69	0.40	0.29	0.19	0.18	0.13	0.04
Risk: debts per 100 commitments	12.8	6.5	4.2	2.6	2.3	1.7	0.5

Source: PSI survey, analysis based on non-pensioner householders

So, although much attention has been paid to the supposed increase in arrears among middle- and high-income families, the survey suggests that a much older set of problems remains the primary cause of debt.

Many of the extra debts faced by poorer households involved quite small amounts, which would have caused little difficulty to people with a substantial income. Five out of six debts of less than £100 were recorded by households with incomes below the national average.

Chart 8.6 Problem debts, by income within age and family type

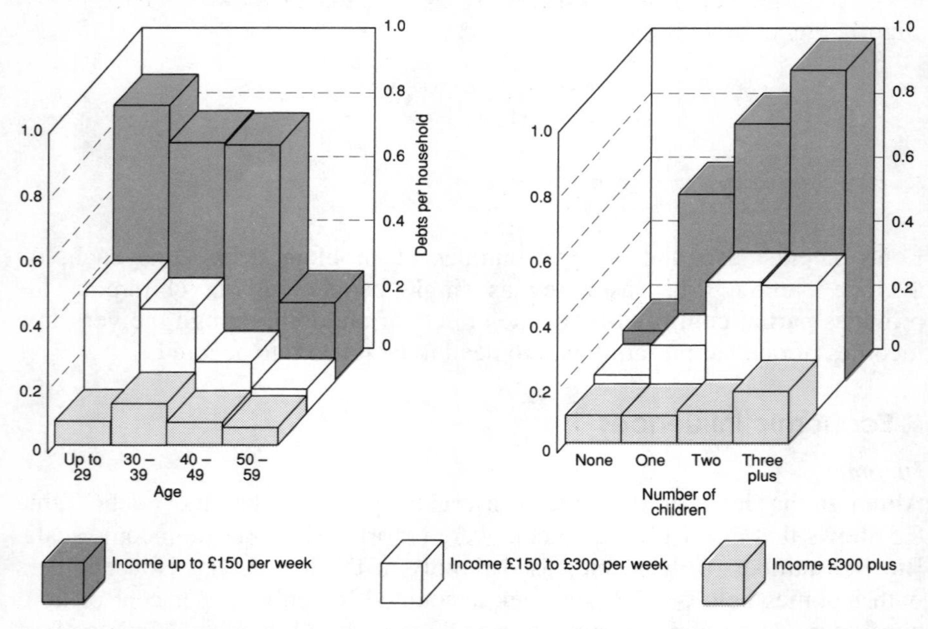

Source: PSI survey; analysis based on non-pensioner householders; the right hand panel is confined to married couples.

But low income was not nearly as simple an explanation for debt as one might have expected. Chart 8.6 shows that older people, and couples without children, had few debts, even if their income was low. Similarly young people, and couples with several children, rarely had debts if their income was high. The problems tended to arise when there were two risk factors both at the same time: younger householders with low incomes, or families with children on low incomes. A similar relationship has already been shown (Chart 8.4) between age and family type: debts were found in households which were both young and contained children. We can think, therefore, of a triangle of debt-inducing factors: age, children and income. Any combination of two from these three raised the risk of debt to a very high level.

Economic activity

Most people's income is determined largely by their earnings, or by the lack of them. Chart 8.7 shows how the extent of debt varied according to the economic activity of the chief earner in the household. For the most part, these variations were almost exactly in line with what would have been expected, given the ages and incomes of the people concerned. The large group of households headed by someone in full-time work, either as an employee or self-employed, had few debts. It was lone parents, unemployed people and students who were most at risk. Retired and disabled people had fewer debts than other non-workers, because they tended to be older, and had slightly higher incomes.

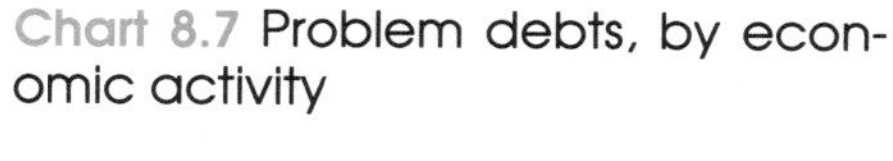

Chart 8.7 Problem debts, by economic activity

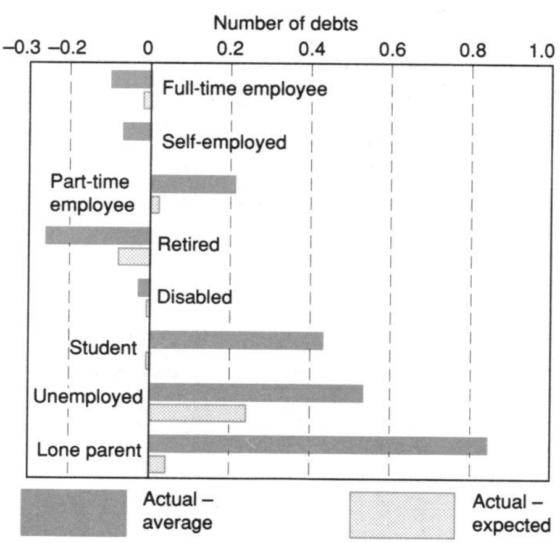

Source: PSI survey; analysis based on non-pensioner householders. See Box V

Although lone parents and students had high levels of debt, this was no more than would have been expected, given their ages and incomes. But unemployed people reported more debts than would have been expected. Table 8.8 examines unemployment in more detail. The most common problems were among those who had been in work and were now unemployed. This is exactly what would have been predicted, on the assumption that commitments built up during a period of prosperity were likely to cause difficulties during a period of reduced income. On the other hand, the long-term unemployed (who had not worked for at least three years) also recorded high levels of debt; and so did men and women who had returned to work after a previous period out of a job. In practice, most unemployed people have not been made redundant from a long-term well-paid job. They move in and out of a series of low-paid jobs. The real difference revealed by Table 8.8 is between those who were or had been on the dole, and those who had worked throughout the three-year reference period.

Box V Controlling for age and income

Several analyses in this chapter show the extent of debt among particular categories of household, after taking account of their age and income. This is done by calculating, for each member of the sample, the 'expected' number of debts, based on all households in the same age-group and income range. To the extent that the 'actual' number of debts is greater or less than expected, we can conclude that any difference (between, say, employed and unemployed people) is not simply explained by the ages and incomes of the two groups.

A related point is that non-pensioner claimants of income support – the means-tested minimum benefit for non-workers – had a very high level of debt: 0.90 per household. This was substantially higher than might have been predicted on the basis of age and income, so income support appeared to be significant in its own right. Claimants of the other two means-tested benefits – housing benefit and family credit – had more debts than average (0.45 per household), but no more than expected.

Table 8.8 Problem debts, by experience of unemployment in past three years

Number of debts

	Actual-average	Actual-expected
In work for three years	–0.13	–0.06
In work now, has been unemployed	+0.36	+0.34
Unemployed for three years	+0.46	+0.24
Unemployed now, has been in work	+0.61	+0.24

Source: PSI survey; analysis based on chief earners in work or unemployed. See Box V

Savings

It would not make sense to have debts at the same time as substantial savings, and very few people with more than £100 had any problems. The real risk faced people with no savings at all. The green area in Chart 8.9 shows that savings had an effect of their own, after allowing for the obvious association between savings and income.

Chart 8.9 Problem debts by savings

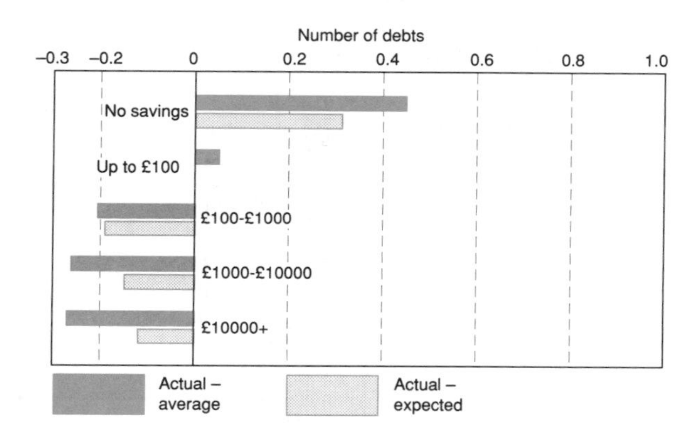

Source: PSI survey; analysis based on non-pensioner householders. See Box V

Consumerism and hardship

The analysis of credit use in Chapter 4 suggested that high-income households' use of credit was associated with an approach to purchasing which we labelled 'consumerism'. But low-income households used credit in circumstances of budgetary strain which we called 'hardship'. It is possible to argue that either of these might have contributed to indebtedness.

Households were defined as 'consumers' if they had bought durable goods such as cars, washing machines, or computers in the past year; or if they already owned them. Those who scored high on the consumerism index had relatively few debts; it was non-consumers who most often got into trouble (Chart 8.10, left). Actually, this was because the non-consumers tended to have lower incomes than the heavy consumers, rather than an effect of consumerism as such – the chart shows very little difference once age and income have been allowed for. Either way there is very little support for the view that 'consumerism' is primarily responsible for arrears and debt.

'Hardship' was defined in terms of being unable to afford things, running out of money before the end of the week, and difficulty in managing. The households shown to be in 'severe hardship' had many debts. 44 per cent of them had at least one problem over the course of the year; a quarter had three or more debts. The right hand side of Chart 8.10 shows that this was one of the strongest relationships identified in the course of the survey, and that it held up even after age and income were taken into account. In fact the minority of poor householders who were not in 'hardship' had far fewer debts than the minority of rich people who scored high on this index.

All this suggests that low income leads to indebtedness through the week-to-week budgeting problems it causes, rather than because poor people persist in buying consumer goods they cannot afford.

Chart 8.10 Problem debts, by consumerism and hardship

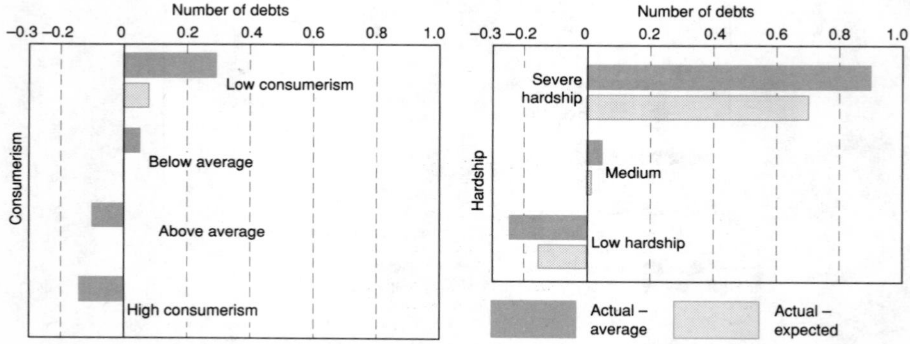

Number of debts
−0.3 −0.2 0 0.2 0.4 0.6 0.8 1.0
Consumerism
Low consumerism
Below average
Above average
High consumerism

Number of debts
−0.3 −0.2 0 0.2 0.4 0.6 0.8 1.0
Hardship
Severe hardship
Medium
Low hardship

Actual – average
Actual – expected

Source: PSI survey; analysis based on non-pensioner householders

Commitments

If income is one of the strongest influences on debt, we would expect families who had committed large amounts to housing, household services and consumer credit to be more at risk than those who had retained more freedom of action.

Logic suggests that it would be the amount of households' commitments which would be important, rather than the number: in principle a single bill of £100 should be neither more nor less difficult to pay than two of £50 or four of £25. But it turned out commitments measured in pounds were not consistently affected in the expected direction (Chart 8.11).

- Poor people (below £100 per week) had a high risk of debt, even if their commitments were relatively low. Remember (see Chapter 7) that virtually the whole of their income was committed anyway.
- But spending commitments did have an effect on households with moderate incomes – between £100 and £200 per week. Within this group, there were only 0.15 debts per household where basic commitments were limited to £30 per week; but this rose to 0.50 when basic commitments were as high as £100 per week.

Chart 8.11 Problem debts, by total amount of commitments

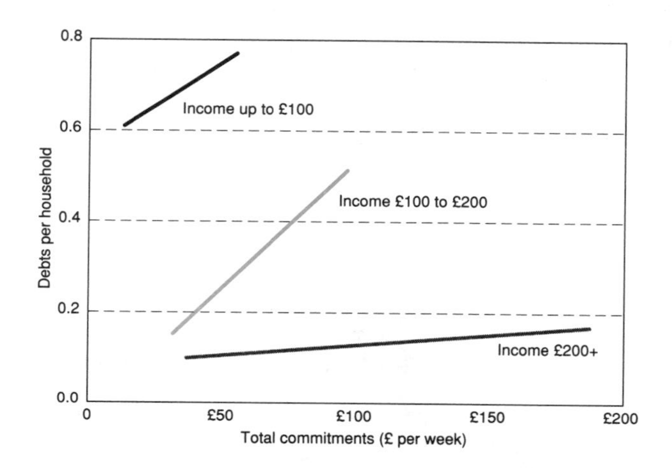

Source: PSI survey; analysis based on non-pensioner householders
Note: the chart is derived from a simple linear regression between the number of debts and the level of commitments, for each of the three income groups. For each income group it shows the estimated number of debts for a household with commitments one standard deviation below the mean, and for a household one standard deviation above the mean.

- Members of the middle and upper income groups (above £200 per week) had few debts, even if they had substantial commitments.

This is not the first study to have shown that levels of commitment are not the most important influence on indebtedness. Others enquiries have suggested that it is low income, not high costs, which causes the problem. [1]

The conclusion about the *amount* of people's commitments does not apply, though, to their *number*. Households which did not use any 'active' source of

Table 8.12 Problem debts, by number of active sources of consumer credit

	None	One	Two	Three	Four or more
Total (=100%)	*888*	*476*	*350*	*241*	*269*
Proportion with					
any problem debts	4%	13%	16%	21%	21%
three or more debts	1%	2%	3%	6%	8%
Average number of debts	0.05	0.21	0.28	0.45	0.55
Risk: debts per 100 commitments	1.2	3.6	3.9	5.6	5.2

Source: PSI survey; analysis based on all householders.

consumer credit in the course of the year had fewer problem debts than average (Table 8.12). Among credit users, the more sources they used, the more debts they had. The increase in debt was more than proportional to the increase in the number of commitments: non-credit users had a problem with 1.2 per 100 commitments; heavy users had a debt risk of more than 5 per 100.

Chart 8.13 Problem debts, by number of consumer credit commitments within income, age and family type

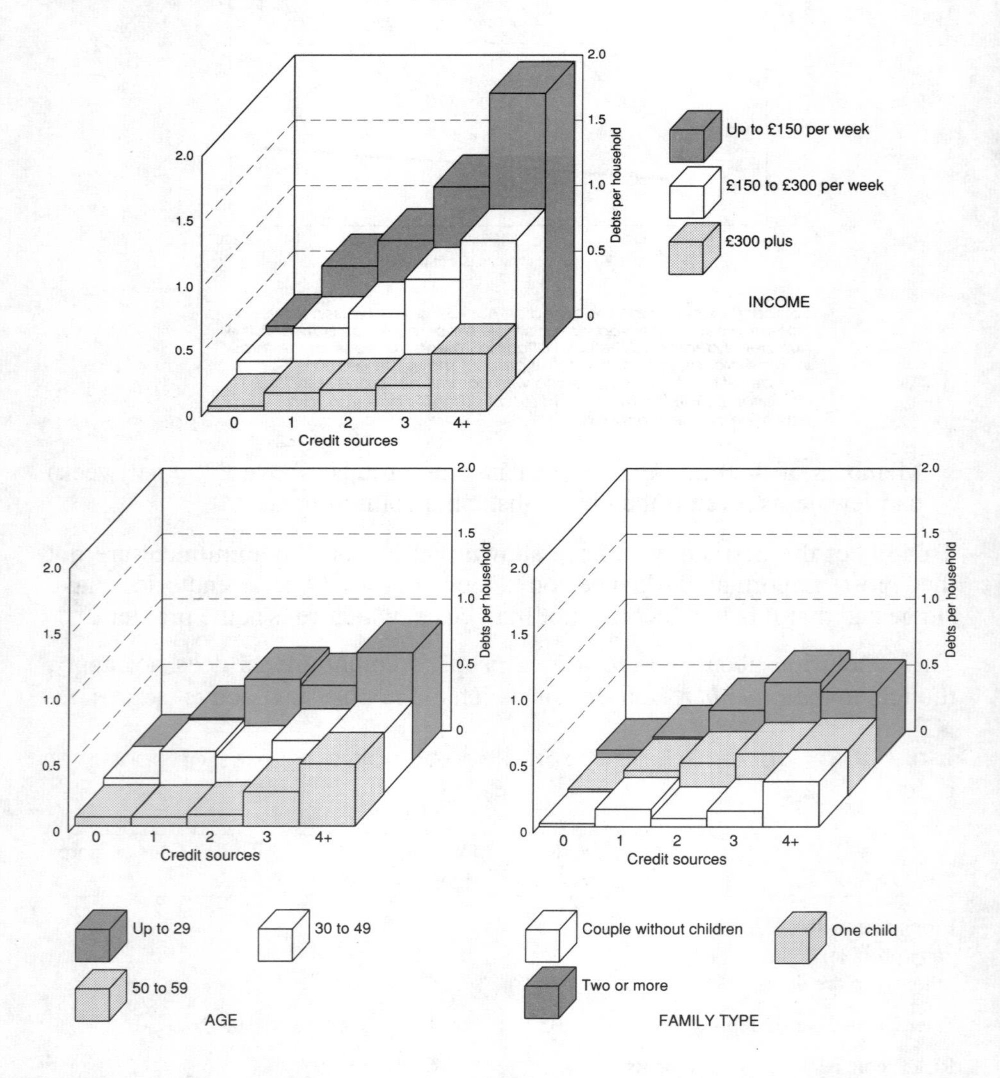

Source: PSI survey; analysis based on non-pensioner householders; the third panel is confined to married couples.

Non-credit users had few debts, even if their income was low (Chart 8.13, first panel). But the number of consumer credit commitments made much more difference to the poor than to the rich. Here is another example of debt being associated with a pair of factors in combination – in this case, low income and multiple credit use. The impact of credit use on low income families was very strong indeed – from 18 debts per 100 among non-users to 195 per 100 in the small group who had used four or more sources of credit.

The middle and third panels of Chart 8.13 show the relationship between credit commitments and debt, taking account of age and family type. The now-familiar pattern can be seen again, but it is less pronounced than it was in Charts 8.4, 8.6 or the first panel of 8.13. That means that the effect of consumer credit commitments interacted closely with low income, but was to a certain extent independent of age and number of children.

Budgeting and paying

It would be reasonable to expect arrears and debt to depend partly on the way in which households handle money, as well as on the size of their budget. The objective indicators of budgeting practices did make some difference. There was no variation in the extent of debt between couples who assigned different responsibilities to the husband or the wife. But people who budgeted by the week, and/or who had no current account, had rather more problems than those with a monthly cycle and an account with a bank or building society (Chart 8.14). These budgetary habits were much less important, though, than the impact of age, family, income and consumer credit.

Chart 8.14 Problem debts, by budgeting habits

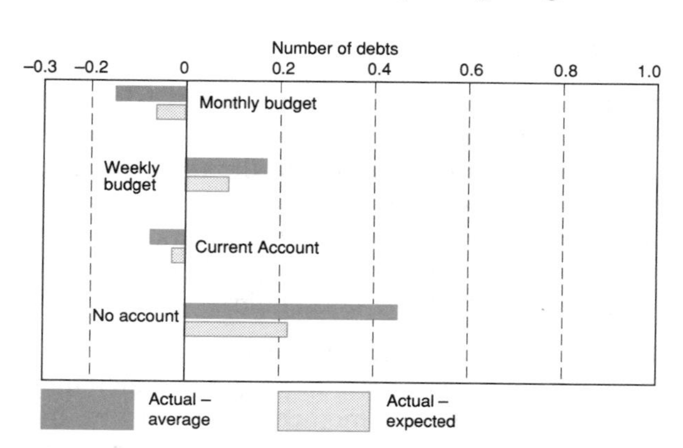

Source: PSI survey; analysis based on all householders

If the method of budgeting was not very important, the extent to which people kept a grip on their weekly income and expenditure seemed to have more of an influence. 'Grip' is not easily measured in a formal survey: the nearest we came to it was the question distinguishing those who felt that 'if the money is there, I find it just goes' from those (the majority) who said 'I always try to keep some money in hand for emergencies'. Those giving the 'easygoing' answer reported four times as many debts as the more cautious group – 0.60 per household, compared with 0.15. Chart 8.15 shows that a household's style of budgeting was important at all income levels, but the income itself was also important. Thus people who budgeted cautiously on a small income had more debts than those who adopted an easygoing approach with plenty of money.

Chart 8.15 Problem debts, by approach to budgeting, within income

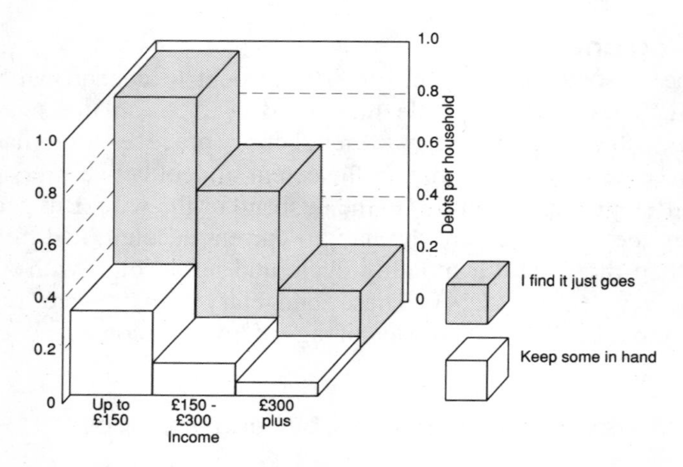

Source: PSI survey; analysis based on non-pensioner householders.

Another indicator of householders' control over their budgets could be derived from the series of money questions asked throughout the interview. Some respondents could put their hands on the relevant paperwork straight away; others gave precise estimates; and others an approximation. But some just did not know how much they were spending on particular commitments. The latter had higher levels of debt (0.42 per household) than those who could give precise answers (0.18 per household).

Among poor families, the difference between those who avoided debt and those who got into difficulty was often the extent to which they planned their expenditure. Compare two single mothers' accounts of their method of budgeting. The first had kept up with all her commitments during the previous two years.

I get my money weekly. I put so much away and don't touch it: put £10 away for certain bills; buy stamps – £5 for the telephone; put away for poll tax and electricity. . . Everything's budgeted for either weekly or monthly.

The other mother owed £63 on her rates, £60 for electricity, £20 for the telephone and £23 for her water rates. She had also run up an overdraft: the bank wrote it off, but withdrew the facility. She had just become a student, having previously received income support, and was finding it difficult to adapt to managing her grant.

I just don't know how to budget. It's a matter of practice. I'll just have to get used to it. I mean this first term's been a disaster, but next term I'll just have to spread. People will have to wait. I won't pay all the bills in one go, I'll just spread them out.

Asked if she worked out how much she spent on different things and then put the money aside, she replied:

I suppose I could if I sat down and worked it out. Not off the top of my head.

With a larger income she would probably have managed. But it was clear that the poor people who had everything planned to the last penny were the ones who had the best chance of avoiding debt.

Budget management is partly a matter of circumstances: the pattern of payments required from a given income. It may be partly a matter of skill. And it might be affected by how determined individuals were to keep up to date. One set of questions addressed the principles of repayment. Looking at the start of the process, almost everyone in the sample said that:

People shouldn't borrow money if they can't afford to repay it score 9.2

And how should people respond if they are in difficulties – where should their priorities lie? Most people felt that:

People should pay the money they owe straight away, even if that means going short on other things score 7.3

On the other hand, they also agreed that:

People should make sure their family has enough to live on before paying any money that they owe score 7.5

Effectively, the majority of respondents were agreeing with both of these contradictory statements. (They did not know when they were asked the first that the second was coming up. Another time we would want to put the quandary more directly.) While this hardly resolves the issue, it might be concluded that both points of view are legitimate – there *is* a quandary, and one might want to know more about the circumstances of a particular case before passing judgement.

What about people's own approach to arrears? Which of their bills and regular payments did they feel must be paid on time, come what may; and which could be delayed if money was short? This question was intended to help explain why some kinds of arrears were more common than others, but a clear pattern did not emerge. On average, 14 per cent of the householders reporting each type of commitment said that it could be delayed if necessary. The interesting point was that the majority said that *none* of their repayments could be delayed; they all had to be paid on time, come what may:

All must be paid on time	63%
More than half must be paid on time	24%
Half or less must be paid on time	12%

As before, these attitude questions, each with its own nuance, can be combined into a single summary indicator of the range of points of view about avoiding arrears. The calculation is explained in Box W. Some respondents took an absolutely rigid line: at every question they gave the answer most in favour of paying, and least in sympathy with not paying. The great majority were strongly in favour of paying, but tempered this with some moderation at one or two of the questions. But a third of the sample scored rather lower on this index, including a small group – under a tenth – who gave more answers in favour of non-payment than in support of payment (Chart 8.16)

Box W Priority on payments

The index was calculated from two sets of questions.

Each of the following was scored from 0 to 10:

People should pay the money they owe straight away, even if that means going short on other things (agree strongly = 10)

People shouldn't borrow money if they can't afford to repay it (agree strongly =10)

People should make sure their family has enough to live on before paying any money they owe (disagree strongly = 10)

The average of these scores (for husband and wife combined) contributed half the points to the overall index.

The other half of the points consisted of the proportion of bills and regular payments which must be paid on time.

Expressed as a percentage of the maximum possible score, the average was 75. We divided the sample into six grades, as follows:

Grade 1	91 to 100%	15 per cent
Grade 2	81 to 90%	33 per cent
Grade 3	71 to 80%	21 per cent
Grade 4	61 to 70%	15 per cent
Grade 5	51 to 60%	8 per cent
Grade 6	up to 50%	9 per cent

Chart 8.16 Priority on payment

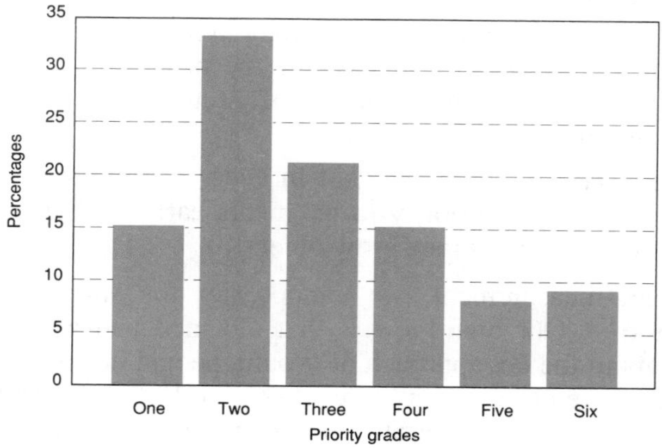

35
30
25
20
15
10
5
0
Percentages
One Two Three Four Five Six
Priority grades

Source: PSI survey; analysis based on all householders. See Box W for definition of categories.

Older people seemed to attach a very high priority to keeping up with their payments. Three-quarters of householders over the age of 70 were assigned to one of the top two priority grades. The proportion fell to one quarter for those in their twenties and thirties.

Chart 8.17 Priority on payment, by age

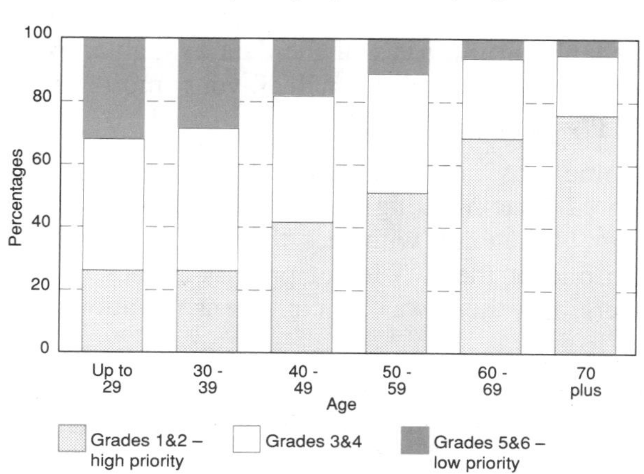

Source: PSI survey; analysis based on all householders. See Box W.

There are two types of reason why people in their twenties and thirties might have given answers so different from that of their elders:

- *a generation effect:* this assumes that the people who are now old would have given similarly high-priority answers if they had been interviewed forty years ago, while the current younger generation can be expected to maintain their 'low priority' stance for the next forty years. The lower priority answers are characteristic not of younger people as such, but of people brought up since the war.
- *a life-cycle effect:* this assumes that in every generation, people tend to attach a relatively low priority to payments early in their adult life, but develop a stricter view as they grow older.

With only one measurement, we cannot say for sure which of these hypotheses is true. Our own view is that old men and women have been complaining about the lax approach of 'young people nowadays' throughout history. If so, we are observing a life-cycle effect. But it is possible that there has also been some change in attitudes to debt over the years – a generation effect which could have intensified the difference observed between young and old at the end of the 1980s.

It is also unclear whether the differences should be ascribed to socio-moral or socio-economic influences. The moral explanations would lie in changing attitudes to financial obligation as interpreted in family, educational, religious or other networks. Such changes might occur over the decades (generation effect) or within the individual (life-cycle effect). The socio-economic explanations would lie in the extent of people's commitments, in their expectations of future income, in the arrangements made by creditors to collect their money and in families' experience of arrears. Both lines of argument are tenable on the basis of the data available. We can be sure of only one thing – that moralists will favour moral explanations, and economists will prefer economic ones.

As a rule, income was not nearly so effective as age in distinguishing between households placing a high and low priority on payment. One third of non-pensioner households with less than £100 per week gave answers placing them in one of the two lower priority grades, compared with one fifth of the others. But there was no consistent variation in attitudes above £100 per week.

Among the bulk of the population who attached average or above-average levels of priority to keeping up their payments, debts were very uncommon (Table 8.18). Those with a lower grading had more problems: the 17 per cent of the sample in grades 5 and 6 accounted for 62 per cent of all debts. The association between the attitude score and debt was as strong as any of the other factors identified in this chapter.

Chart 8.19 (left) shows that the strong relationship between the priority score and indebtedness was true in all age groups. So the relative frequency of

Table 8.18 Problem debts, by priority on payment

Grade	One (high)	Two	Three	Four	Five	Six (low)
Total (=100%)	*315*	*699*	*449*	*314*	*178*	*183*
Proportion with any debts	2%	3%	7%	15%	30%	41%
Average number	0.02	0.05	0.13	0.26	0.58	0.95

Source: PSI survey; analysis based on all householders. See Box W for definition of 'priority'

debt among younger householders may have been influenced by their more relaxed attitude to payment. It remains to be explained why they had adopted that view. One possibility is that it was their experience of arrears which had affected their attitudes.

The right hand panel of Chart 8.19 shows that attitudes made a difference to the risk of debt at every level of income, but it was among the poorest households that this factor was most important.

Chart 8.19 Problem debts, by priority on payment within age and income

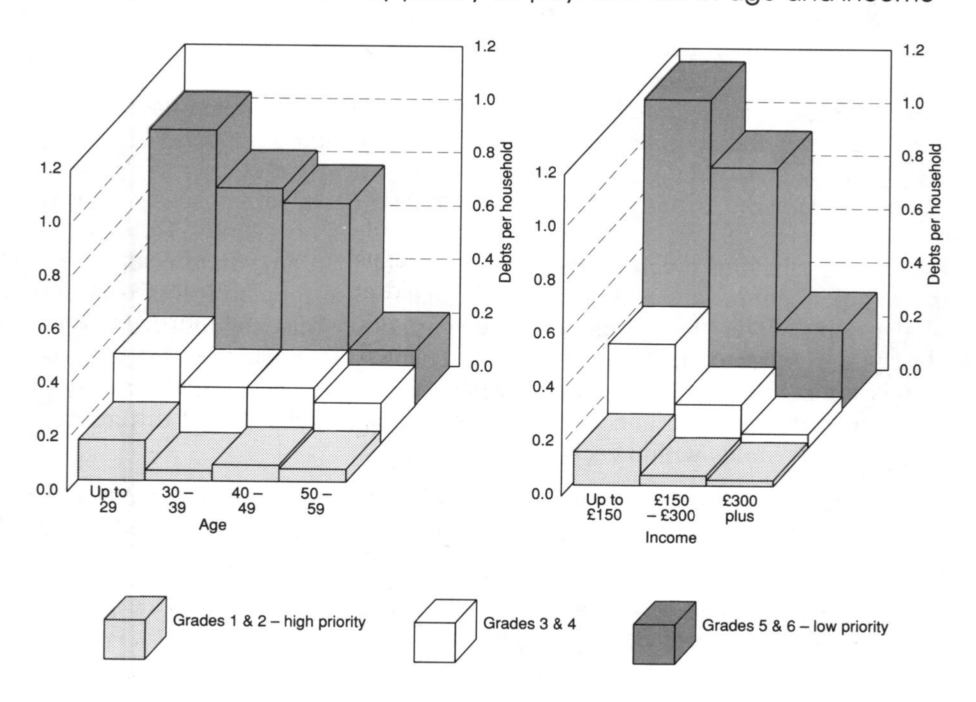

Source: PSI survey; analysis by age based on all householders; by income on non-pensioner householders.

Local influences

Although the survey collected data household by household, it is possible to reanalyse it to examine variations in the level of debt in different areas. This can be done by combining the information from all the households living near each other within a postal sector, as explained in Box X. Such a view of debt is of interest for two reasons. First, the social, economic or other characteristics of an area might have a direct effect on the arrears of the people living there. Second, it might be useful to identify the kinds of area where debtors can be found so that, for example, improved money advice services could be provided.

Box X Analysis by area

The samples of households in the general population (Samples A and B, as described in Appendix 1) were selected in clusters within 94 postcode sectors, which themselves formed a random sample of all postcode sectors in Great Britain. The analysis in this section is based on the respondents in 73 sectors for whom we had a minimum of 10 household interviews (in samples A and B).

In a post code, the sector is denoted by the first numeral in the second set of characters. PSI's postal sector is NW1 3.

The special sample of known debtors (Sample C) is excluded from the analysis. So are the Northern Ireland samples, except for the comparison between regions.

Debts were, of course, much more common in some areas than others. Chart 8.20 illustrates the complete range, where each column represents one local area in the sample. Many places, accounting for nearly a quarter of the total (22 per cent), were virtually debt-free (up to 0.05 debts per household). Then there is a range of rates up to about 0.50 debts per household. Three areas stood out as having much higher levels of debt than anywhere else. These three (4 per cent of the local areas in this analysis) accounted for 15 per cent of the debts. Over the complete range, variations between localities were clearly a significant factor, but it would wrong to conclude that debt is mainly a local phenomenon. Differences between areas accounted for only 7 per cent of the total variance; the other 93 per cent consisted of differences between households within each area.

We wondered whether local variations might have been caused specifically by rent arrears. But this was not the case: all types of debt contributed to the pattern.

One way in which an area could have affected the behaviour of the people living there might have been through social pressures. The hypothesis was that in some places everyone would agree that arrears should be avoided at all costs; elsewhere, debt might have been more familiar, and therefore less stigmatising. There was some evidence in support of this hypothesis, but the

Chart 8.20 Problem debts, by postcode sector

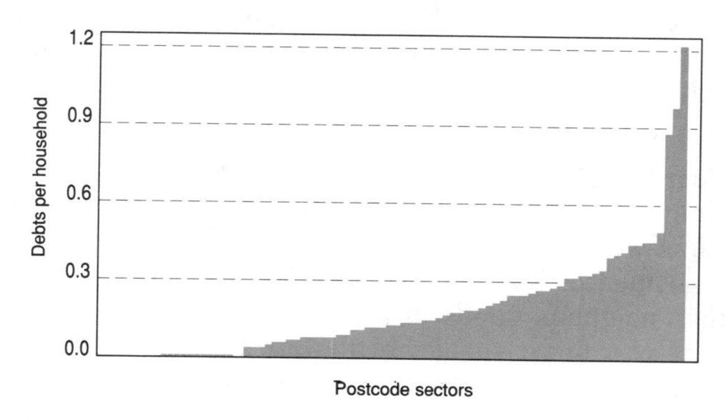

Source: PSI survey; analysis based on postcode sectors. See Box X.

effect was not particularly strong. The average score on the 'priority on payments' index was well below average in all three of the high-debt areas. The residents of several of the debt-free areas showed a high 'priority on payment' score. But over the sample as a whole, the ambient attitude in the area where people lived had very little effect on whether they themselves fell into debt: it explained about 1 per cent of the total variance.

To the extent that some local areas had higher levels of debt than others, what sort of places were they? Two of the three localities with very high debt rates were in the North West of England, out of a total of six sampling points in that region. This might indicate a special problem in that part of the country, or it might be a coincidence.

Chart 8.21 Problem debts, by region

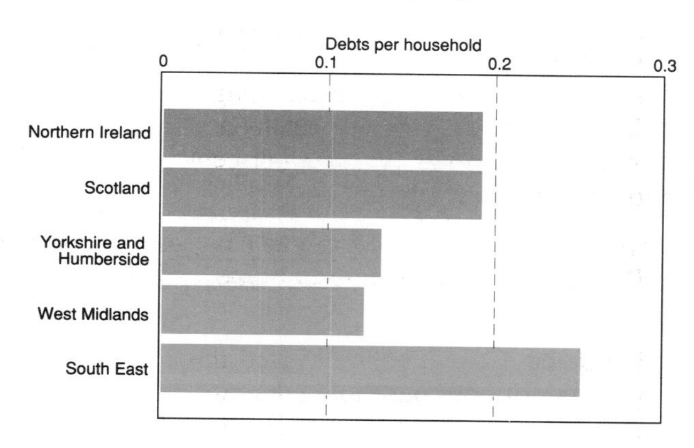

Source: PSI survey; analysis based on householders in selected regions, samples A and B

Looking more generally at regional differences, Chart 8.21 shows the number of debts recorded in each of the regions for which we have seven or more sampling points. The South East (including London) had more than any of the others. It is difficult to pick out a consistent pattern of variation elsewhere.

The three places which stood out from the rest seemed to have some other things in common. All three were in cities, while two-thirds of the debt-free sampling points were in non-urban areas. Two of the three were defined as areas of low affluence. So there are signs that debt is a special problem in deprived urban neighbourhoods. It is interesting to find, on the other hand, that this effect was more visible to the human observer than to objective statistical indicators. Table 8.22 compares the extent of debt between types of area, first as defined by formal measurements of such things as unemployment rates, density of population and so on; and second, as judged by the interviewers on the spot. The interviewers had two advantages. First, they could make distinctions between streets, and even along the same street, while the statistics summarise the situation in a wider area. Second, they knew whether the respondent had any debts when they recorded their opinion of the area, and may have been influenced by that information; this may be considered an unfair advantage. The interviewer assessment achieved a wider split between affluent/debt-free areas and run-down/debt-laden ones. Even so, the variation between types of area was less significant than the differences recorded earlier in this chapter between types of people. Area-stereotyping is not an effective explanation for debt: the problem depends more on who you are than where you live.

Table 8.22 Problem debts, by type of area

Average number of debts per household

Statistical definition	Debts per hh	*Total (=100%)*	Interviewer assessment	Debts per hh	*Total (=100%)*
Urban			Built-up		
Deprived	0.33	*202*	Run down	0.43	*194*
Average	0.28	*316*	Middling	0.18	*904*
Affluent	0.12	*102*	Prosperous	0.05	*206*
Mixed or rural	0.14	*811*	Country	0.11	*95*

Source: PSI survey; analysis based on all householders in Great Britain (samples A and B).

Influences on debt

The overwhelming majority of household commitments and consumer credit repayments are met in full and on time. The research has nevertheless shown that a substantial number of people face difficulties: over the course of a year 2 million households experienced a total of 5 million problem debts.

Most of this chapter has been devoted to an analysis of variations in the risk of debt. Five factors have stood out. In order of appearance, they were:

Age: the younger people were, the more debts they had.
Family: families with children had more debts than those without.
Income: the number of debts was substantially higher among poorer households.
Credit commitments: households who used several sources of credit had a high risk of debt.
Priority: those who consistently gave answers to suggest that it was all right to delay payments were relatively likely to have debt problems.

Other influences included:

unemployment;
savings;
hardship;
approach to budgeting;
area of residence.

Other factors which might have been expected to have a strong influence on the extent of debt turned out to be relatively unimportant. These included:

changes in household circumstances;
'young people' in the sense of teenagers living with their parents;
'consumerism';
amount of commitments (as opposed to number of sources of credit);
bank accounts and budgeting cycles.

The most striking finding is the number of contributory influences on the risk of debt, and the complexity of the interactions between them. For example, we found that neither age (on its own) nor income (on its own) was very strongly associated with debt. It was the interaction that mattered: the people at risk were younger-householders-with-low-incomes. Again and again we found that combinations of predisposing characteristics had a stonger effect than either of them taken on their own.

It was therefore useful to look at all five factors taken together. Some households were 'at risk' on four or even five of the criteria considered: they were young, had children, low incomes, many credit commitments and a below-average score for 'priority on payment' (see Box Y). These high-risk households had many debts. Among the small number who fulfilled all five criteria:

three-fifths had a problem debt;
a quarter had three or more debts;
they averaged 1½ debts per household;
problems were being caused by one fifth of all their commitments.

Box Y Interaction of factors

In order to identify households who were most and least at risk of debt, the sample was split in two on each of five questions. Households were considered 'at risk' if they were:

aged less than 40
had children
received an income of less than £150 per week
used three or more sources of active credit
scored 70 or less on the priority on payment index (see Box W).

Households were scored according to the number of these criteria they fulfilled. But all pensioners were assigned a score of nil. The distribution was as follows:

None of these factors	35%
One	19%
Two	19%
Three	16%
Four	9%
All five factors	3%

As Chart 8.22 shows, the rate of debt was directly related to the number of predisposing factors reported by each household. The two tall columns at the right of the graph represent only 12 per cent of all households, but account for 53 per cent of all debts. At the opposite end, debt was extremely rare among those who were not members of any of the at-risk categories. They represented 35 per cent of all households, but amassed only 6 per cent of all the debts between them.

Chart 8.22 Problem debts, by combination of factors

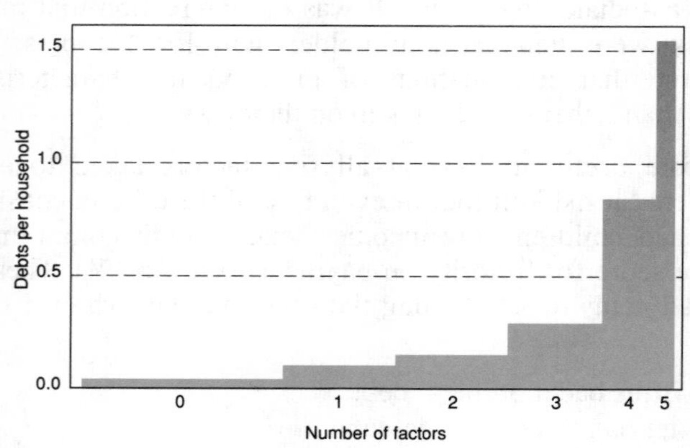

Source: PSI survey; analysis based on all householders.
Note: the width of each bar is proportional to the number of households

References

1. R. Berthoud, *Credit, Debt and Poverty,* HMSO, 1989

2. R. Berthoud, *Fuel Debts and Hardship,* PSI, 1981; S. Duncan and K. Kirby, *Preventing Rent Arrears,* HMSO, 1983

9 Debts to Different Creditors

The analysis so far has looked at debt as a single problem. But it has already been shown that some types of arrear were more common than others. Consideration of all debts tends to focus attention on the characteristics of the debtor, because that is the only thing that all types of debt have in common. Comparison of different types of creditor allows us to consider details of the commitment. There are two parties to every bargain, and arrears may be influenced by the actions or inactions of the creditor, either in accepting the commitment in the first place, or in the arrangements made for collecting payments

The first column of Table 9.1 shows how many people owed money to different types of organisation. The most common problems were rent arrears and debts on household services such as electricity and gas. But not everyone had the same commitments, and another way of expressing the same information is to work out what proportion of each type of payment had led to a problem debt (the second column of Table 9.1). The severity of the rent arrears crisis is revealed even more clearly by this treatment: one sixth of all tenants were in debt to their landlord. A high proportion of overdrafts on bank or building society current accounts were also in difficulty – note that the risk is expressed as a proportion of those with an overdraft, not as a proportion of all accounts. Other types of household and credit commitment recorded debt rates of between 1 and 5 per cent.

Box Z Samples of debtors

The number of households in the sample reporting some types of debt was rather small, and the findings in this chapter cannot be regarded as conclusive. The sample was adapted to boost the number of debtors, and the actual number of cases in each category is usually larger than the weighted total recorded in the tables. The actual and weighted numbers were as follows:

	Actual number	Weighted total
Rent	215	111
Mortgage	96	30
Local taxes	117	51
Household services	220	95
Overdrafts	74	51
Credit/store cards	46	31
Mail order catalogues	52	28
One-off advances	128	59

Table 9.1 Incidence and risk of problem debts

Percentages

	Incidence (Debts as percent of households)	Risk (Debts as percent of commitments)
Household bill debts		
Mortgage	1.3	3.3
Rent	5.0	17.7
Local taxes	2.3	3.1
Household services	4.3	1.6
Other household bills	1.9	2.3
Total	14.8	3.0
Consumer credit debts		
Overdrafts	2.3	16.2
Credit/store cards	1.4	4.5
Mail order catalogues	1.3	3.3
One-off advances	2.7	4.3
Total	7.7	5.2

Source: PSI survey; analysis based on all householders

Twice as many problems were reported with household commitments as with repayments of consumer credit. But there were three times as many household commitments in the first place. When this was taken into account the average risk of debt was rather higher for consumer credit than for basic household requirements.

Chart 9.2 Incidence and risk of household bill and consumer credit debts, by income

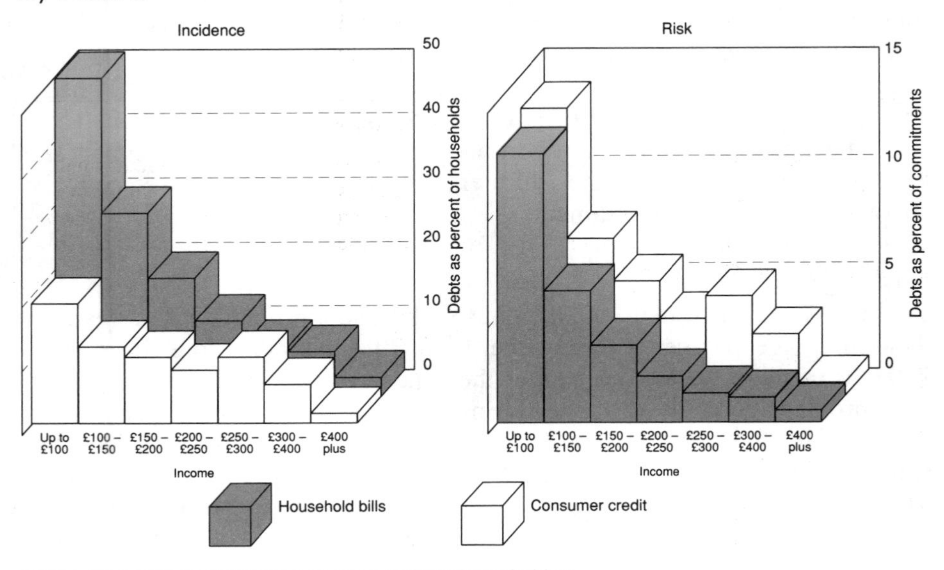

Source: PSI survey; analysis based on non-pensioner householders

The contrast is emphasised by a comparison between households with high and low incomes. The poorer a family was, the more debts they reported on household bills. The same was true of consumer credit debts, but the effect of income was much weaker (Chart 9.2, left). So for poorer families the number of household debts exceeded the number of consumer credit debts. This is because everyone has a similar number of bills to pay for their housing, fuel and so on, while, as we know, low-income households used fewer sources of credit. If we take account of the number of commitments, the *risk* of both types of debt was very similar at the lower end of the income scale; among the upper-income groups, there was a slightly higher risk of default on credit commitments than on household bills (Chart 9.2, right).

This distinction between the two types of problem has been discussed by Gillian Parker in terms of 'primary' versus 'secondary' debt.[1] According to this hypothesis primary debt consists of arrears on unavoidable household commitments, for which poverty is unequivocally to blame. Secondary debt occurs where people have taken on unnecessary credit; here voluntary overcommitment can be seen to play a role. Parker's analysis was based on a sample of multiple debtors, so risk rates could not be calculated. But the patterns in the two sides of Chart 9.2 lend some support to this way of looking at debt. On the other hand, it has been shown that a significant proportion of the 'consumer' credit taken out by poorer households was associated with hardship rather than with consumerism: it was required to make ends meet or to pay off household bills.

Five characteristics of a household helped to explain why some families fell into debt while others did not: age, family structure, income, credit commitments and the priority individuals attached to payments. Although Chapter 8 was concerned with debt in general, all these characteristics had a very similar effect on each of the different types of debt recorded in Table 9.1. There is little point in repeating this analysis time after time. The following discussion of the different types of debt focuses on the characteristics of the commitment.

■ Mortgage debts

The survey indicated that 300,000 households had a problem with arrears on their mortgage payments during the 12 months period before the survey. 170,000 of them were in arrears at the time they were interviewed. Those with problem debts at any time during the year represented 3 per cent of mortgage-holders. This is substantially lower than the rate of rent debt, but similar to the rate of debt on a wide range of other types of commitment. Mortgage repayments often accounted for a large proportion of a household's income, so that arrears mounted up rapidly – the median debt was £710.

The Council of Mortgage Lenders publishes the only reliable series of statistics on the extent of debt over the past decade (Chart 9.3). It shows that 80,000 households were at least six months behind with their payments at the end of 1989; the survey estimate for current arrears at that time – 170,000 – therefore includes a similar number who had missed between one and five instalments.

Chart 9.3 Number of mortgages six months or more in arrears, 1979 to 1991

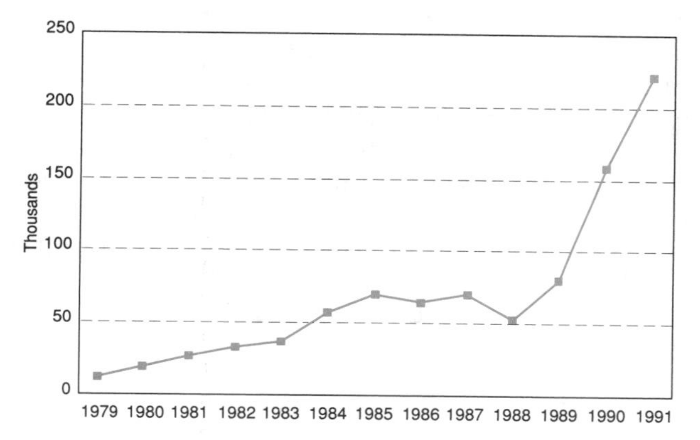

Source: Council of Mortgage Lenders;[2] the 1991 figures are based on the first half year; the 1979-1981 figures include some adjustments for missing data.

There has been a huge increase in mortgage arrears since 1979. The rise has occurred in two phases.

- The number of debtors owing half a year's payments rose from 12,000 in 1979 to 70,000 in 1985 – an average (compound) increase of one third every year. The reason for this trend remains a matter of controversy,[3] but it seems likely to have been associated with the relaxation in the constraints on lending as institutions competed with each other for low-to-middle-income customers.

- The level of arrears stabilised for two or three years towards the end of the decade. But an even steeper rate of increase in debt and repossessions is now in progress. It seems likely that the recent hike in the number of debtors has been caused by the rise in interest rates at the end of the 1980s, followed by the halt in the house price boom, described in Chapter 3 – see Charts 3.2 and 3.7. A family which was mortgaged to the hilt in 1988 would have seen their repayments increase more than one third over the first two years. Any attempt to retrieve the situation by selling up would have been blocked by the difficulty of finding a buyer and, in some parts of the country, the fall in the value of the property.

Over the period as a whole, the total number of mortgages has increased by just over half; the number six or more months in arrears by a factor of 18. A detailed analysis of lenders' statistics suggests that three-quarters of a million mortgage holders currently owe two months repayments or more.[4]

A few households had fallen behind with mortgages taken out many years ago; and some were already in trouble with commitments entered into within the past year or two. But the great majority of the debts affected households who had borrowed between three and ten years previously (Chart 9.4). The long-run impact of inflation on repayment commitments clearly leaves relatively recent purchasers most exposed to short-run fluctuations in prices and interest rates such as occurred at the end of the 1980s. We cannot project the survey figures forward to 1991 with any accuracy, but if it was assumed that the rate of debt has been multiplied by four (in line with the CML arrears statistics), then the risk among people who bought between three and nine years ago would now be as high as 18 per cent. Over this short high-risk period, the problem is as serious for owner-occupiers as for tenants.

Chart 9.4 Risk of mortgage debt, by years since purchase

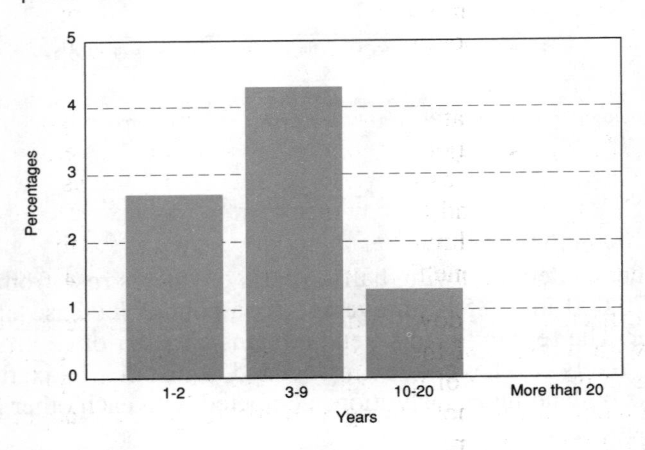

Source: PSI survey; analysis based on mortgage holders

On the whole, mortgages requiring higher monthly payments had a higher risk of debt than those involving small repayments. The average mortgage, not in arrears, was £224 per month, (equivalent to £52 per week); the average commitment where there was a problem debt was £314 per month (£73 per week). Although this accords with what one would have expected, the relationship was not particularly strong, nor consistent. Chart 9.5 indicates an upwards trend, but there is a sharp zigzag which we have not been able to iron out, even after taking account of the fact that higher earners

Chart 9.5 Risk of mortgage debt, by amount of mortgage payments

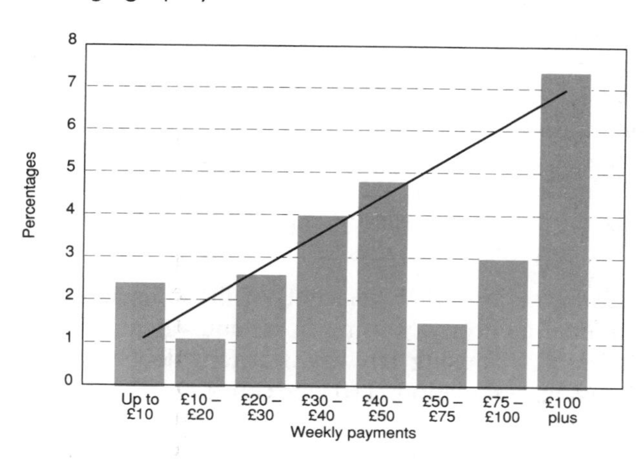

Source: PSI survey; analysis based on mortgage holders
Note: the solid line indicates the best fit between mortgage debt and income

tended to have larger commitments. With only a handful of debtors in each payment band, it is not possible to tell what the underlying relationship is with any confidence.

Mortgage-holders with relatively low incomes were also slightly more likely to fall behind than the majority with average or above-average resources – see below, Chart 9.7. But as on previous occasions, it was the interactions between high payments and low incomes which was most likely to cause a problem. Among the small number of people paying more than half their net income on the mortgage, one fifth (20 per cent) reported a problem debt.

It was also difficult to pin down consistent evidence that the risk of debt was associated with the size of the original loan, whether this was measured in pounds or as a proportion of the value of the property: the links were in the expected direction, but not strong enough to provide anything like an explanation for the problem.

Households who had negotiated an extension to their loan reported more problems (4.2 per cent) than those who had kept to the original amount (2.6 per cent). This may be associated with the fact that a number of the extensions had been taken out to help meet other commitments, though, again, the findings are indicative rather than conclusive.

First-time buyers on the open market had a higher risk of debt (4.2 per cent) than those who had already been owner occupiers (2.6 per cent). Those who had bought council houses or flats as sitting tenants did not share the higher risk of other first-time buyers (2.2 per cent).

The minority of mortgages borrowed from sources other than building societies had a slightly lower than average rate of problem debt (1.2 compared with 3.6 per cent).

Rent debts

More than one million tenants – 18 per cent of the total – faced a problem with rent arrears over the course of the year. Rent accounted for only 4 per cent of all commitments, but 22 per cent of all the debts reported by households taking part in the survey. Apart from bank overdrafts, no other commitment had anywhere near this level of risk.

The overwhelming majority (95 per cent) of the households with rent debts were living in local authority housing or its equivalent. Councils supply the lion's share of rented housing anyway, but rent debts were not so often a problem in housing associations (10 per cent in debt), and were relatively rare among private tenants (2 per cent).

Rents have been a matter of concern throughout the 1980s. Chart 9.6 traces arrears as a proportion of rent due, as recorded by local councils in England and Wales: the figure rose from 3.8 per cent in 1979/80 to 8.2 per cent in 1989/90. The accounting statistics cover technical arrears such as delayed transfers from the housing benefit office, as well as serious problem debts, but measurements based on tenants show the same picture. At the beginning of the decade, 6 per cent of council tenants in England were in 'serious' arrears of £50 or more; about 300,000 of them.[5] Our own survey suggests that 13 per cent of English council tenants owed £77 or more at the end of the decade – the equivalent at 1989 prices. Not only had serious arrears increased as a proportion of the (smaller) number of tenants; the actual number of cases had increased to nearly 600,000.

Chart 9.6 Rent arrears as a proportion of rent due, England and Wales, 1979/80 to 1989/90

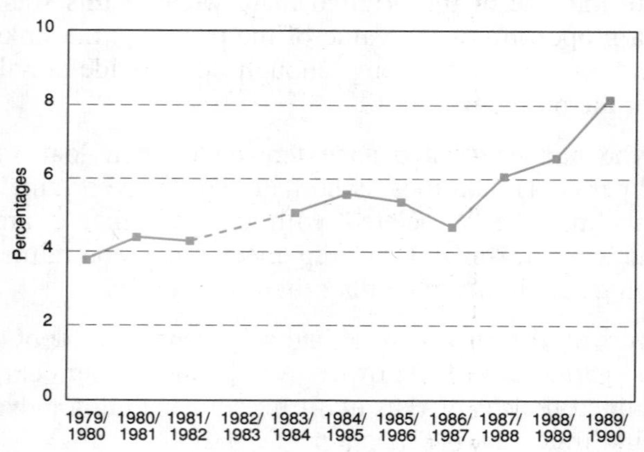

Source: Chartered Institute of Public Finance and Accountancy[6]

The comparison between the levels of debt on rents and mortgages is especially striking. Four types of reason are commonly advanced for the difference. The most obvious explanation, given what we know about the types of household most likely to fall into all kinds of debt, lies in the *incomes* of tenants and owner-occupiers. Public sector housing has always drawn its tenants from among the lower income bands, while most better-off families have taken out a mortgage. As middle-income council tenants bought their houses or flats during the 1980s, the remaining properties have been concentrated more and more among the poorer families, who might be expected to have greatest difficulty in keeping up with their commitments. It is true that problem debts were associated with income in both tenures. But, as Chart 9.7 shows, the risk of debt was far higher for tenants than for mortgagors, at all income levels. The gap between tenures was much wider than between income bands.

Chart 9.7 Risk of mortgage and rent debts, by income

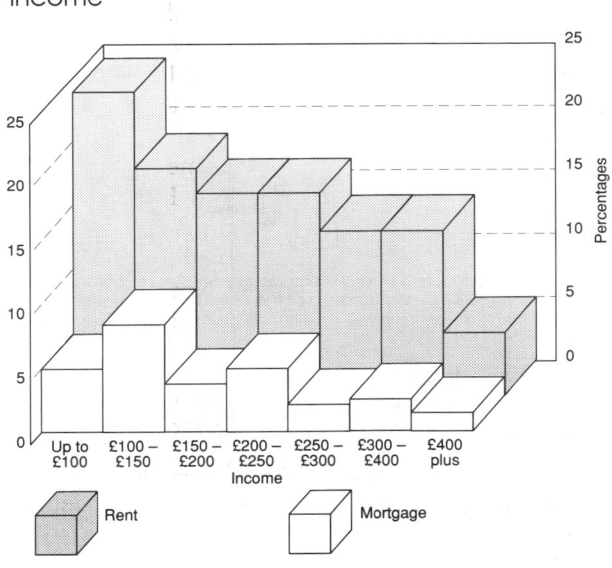

Source: PSI survey; analysis based on mortgage holders and tenants

A second hypothesis, more often advanced by inference than by direct accusation, is that council tenants have got into the habit of non-payment because they place a relatively *low priority* on meeting their financial obligations. The discussion is bound up with arguments about the culture of dependency. We expected to find that there would be at least some truth in this suggestion, on the grounds that if there was a minority of the population who were natural non-payers, they would tend to gravitate towards council accommodation as they were evicted from other tenures. Our index of 'priority on payment' did explain variations in the risk of debt *within* each tenure (Chart 9.8). But it turned out that the average 'priority' score was exactly the same for both groups, and this factor did not explain the difference *between* tenures.

Chart 9.8 Risk of mortgage and rent debts, by priority on payment

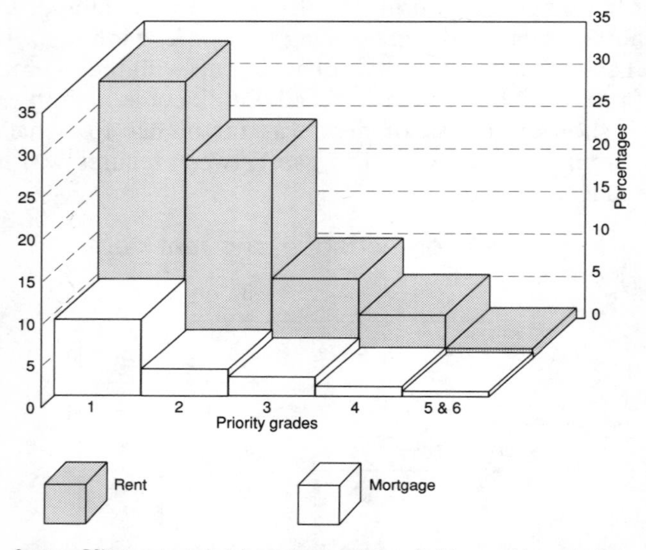

Source: PSI survey; analysis based on mortgage-holders and tenants. See Box W (Chapter 8) for an explanation of the priority on payment index.

Another line of analysis leads to the same conclusion. If the level of rent arrears was caused by some personal characteristic of the tenants, the same people should also have high levels of debt on other types of commitment. But if we leave out rent and mortgages and take account of income and other factors, council tenants had no more non-housing debts than owner occupiers.

A third potential explanation for rent arrears has been the level of rents, and especially the real increase in costs that has been imposed over the past decade. Our survey did suggest that the higher the rent, the greater the risk of arrears (Chart 9.9, and compare it with Chart 9.5), although such a relationship was not identified in the DoE's much larger study of rent arrears in 1981.[7] Rising rents may therefore help to explain increasing arrears; but they cannot possibly explain the difference between tenants and owners, because mortgage repayments have been rising even faster: the average weekly cost of a mortgage was more than twice the average rent; mortgage holders also paid a larger proportion of their income.

Chart 9.9 Risk of rent debt, by amount of net rent

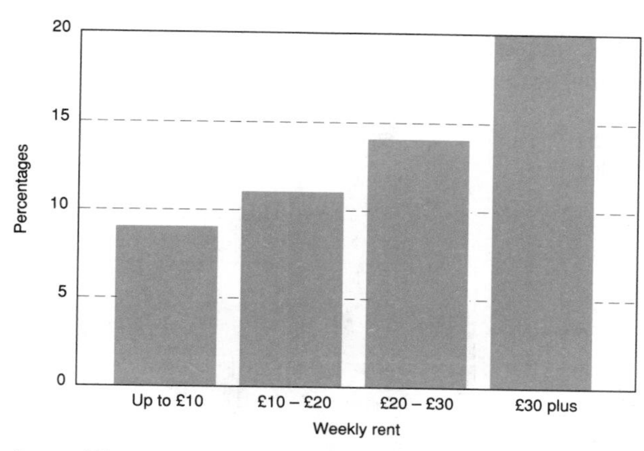

Source: PSI survey; analysis based on council tenants not receiving a 100% rebate

Chart 9.9 does not include the tenants who received 100 per cent rebates and therefore had no rent to pay. Until 1982, unemployed and other recipients of supplementary benefit claimed the amount of their rent as part of their weekly income, and were responsible for paying it to their landlord. Since housing benefit was introduced, claimants in public housing have had the rent paid at source. The change was intended, among other things, to cut down on arrears. It is therefore surprising to find that one fifth (20 per cent) of council tenants with full rebates had a problem rent debt – the same proportion as those, at the opposite end of the scale, paying more than £30 per week. These illogical arrears accounted for one sixth of council tenants' rent debts. The tenants may have had arrears before they claimed benefit, but our survey does not allow us to investigate them in any more detail.

The fourth potential explanation for the increasing number of tenants in arrears lies in the *rent collection* and arrears recovery procedures of the landlord authorities. The DoE's 1981 survey showed that the clearest influence on rent arrears was the method of payment. [8] The same was true in 1989 (Chart 9.10). Landlords have increasingly been asking tenants to pay their rent through the post office, and this is now the most common method (see Chapter 3). But it is also the method most associated with debt: nearly a quarter of the families expected to pay at the post office had a problem with missed rent payments during the year. Only a small proportion of tenants still had their rent collected, yet this was the method associated with the lowest level of arrears. Only 4 per cent of tenants who had their rent collected were in debt – a rate comparable with mortgage debt.

Payment by standing order or direct debit was also associated with below-average rent arrears. It is, therefore, interesting how few tenants paid their rent in this way, while it would be the most common method of paying a mortgage. In fact a half of tenants had no current accounts and so could not take advantage of standing order payments; but among the half who did have an account, only a small proportion paid in this way.

Chart 9.10 Risk of rent debt, by method of rent collection

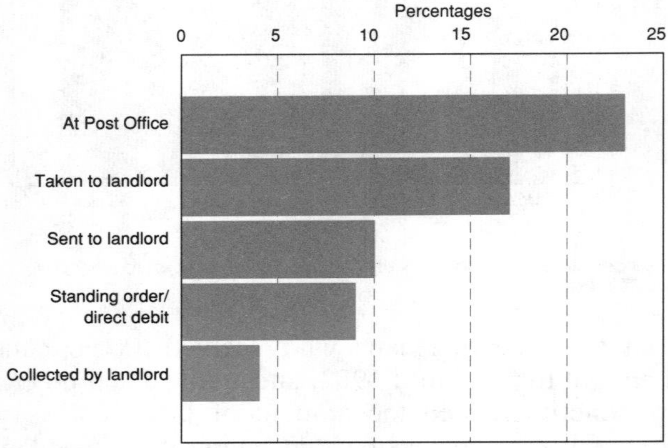

Percentages
0 5 10 15 20 25
At Post Office
Taken to landlord
Sent to landlord
Standing order/ direct debit
Collected by landlord

Sources: 1989, PSI survey; analysis based on tenants with rent to pay.

Local taxes

An assessment of local tax debts is complicated by the fact that there have been five different regimes over the past five years: rates with full rebates were the standard system in 1987-88; a minimum contribution was introduced in 1988; the community charge was introduced in Scotland in 1989; and in England and Wales in 1990; both sets of poll tax were reduced by £140 in 1991. The rates have continued in Northern Ireland throughout the period. Our own survey took place in 1989, and allows a comparison between the rates (in England, Wales and Northern Ireland) and the poll tax (in Scotland).

Almost every householder in Scotland was liable to pay the community charge directly. Elsewhere, most council tenants paid their rates together with their rent; they were liable to the tax, but they would not have been conscious of it as a separate item. Only people with 100 per cent rent rebates paid their minimum contribution to the rates as a separate payment. Among other tenants, half said that they paid rates separately; the others paid the tax at the same time as, or as part of, their rent.

There are, therefore, two measures of rates arrears. Among those paying it as a separate commitment – mostly owner occupiers – 3.5 per cent had a problem debt over the course of the year. But those who paid their rates with their rent automatically fell behind with their rates when they missed the rent. If the people with combined rent and rates arrears are added to the calculation, the risk of rates debt rose to 6.3 per cent. The risk was higher than for most other types of commitment, not because of a specific problem with rates payment, but because of the rent connection.

The survey's definition of debt was based on a pair of questions (see Box U, Chapter 8). If people had missed one or more payments in the past year, that was called 'arrears'; if they were worried about the arrears, or said that it was a problem, then it was referred to as a 'problem debt'. For most types of commitment, about one third of 'arrears' turned out not to be a 'problem'. In Scotland, a few months after the community charge had been introduced, one fifth (20 per cent) of those liable had missed one or more of their poll tax payments. This was one of the highest arrears rates identified. But more than two-thirds of the people concerned said that it was neither a worry nor a problem; only 6.1 per cent reported a problem debt. This is higher than the level of pure rates debt in the rest of the United Kingdom. But it is very similar to rates debt if combined rates and rent debts are included in the comparison.

Should the level of non-problem community charge arrears be a cause for concern? It is not clear from the survey whether the shortfall was a temporary feature of the start of any new tax, or whether there would be long-term administrative difficulties. Nor is it clear how many of the non-payers were acting on a genuine political principle; how many were taking advantage of the unpopularity of the tax to avoid meeting their obligations; and how many were just confused. The arrears were a problem for local authorities and for the government, whatever their cause. And in the long run they were likely to become a problem for those whose debt was allowed to build up over this period. It can be imagined that many of those who started as *won't pays* eventually became *can't pays* by the time they owed hundreds or thousands of pounds.

Household services debts

Fuel and telephone bills were less likely than many other types of commitment to fall into arrears. 2 per cent of electricity customers and of gas customers reported a problem debt over the past year. No-one had a debt for other types of fuel, except in Northern Ireland where solid fuel remains the usual source of heating, and 1 per cent of its users were in debt to their supplier. The risk of debt on phone bills was only 0.7 per cent.

On the other hand, virtually everyone had to pay for electricity, and the majority of households also had gas and phone bills. So, although the risk of debt on these commitments was low, the incidence was relatively high: there were getting on for one million household service debts, nearly as many as for rent.

The current survey concurs with the findings of more detailed studies,[9] that fuel debts are related to the same factors as other forms of problem – income, age, family type, credit commitments and priority on payment. Indeed the electricity and gas debts were more strongly associated with poverty than any other commitment: the mean income of those owing money to their fuel board was only £120 per week, lower even than for rent debt.

Electricity showed a fairly consistent link between the risk of debt and the size of bills (Chart 9.11). But gas customers were about equally likely (or unlikely) to report a problem, whatever the scale of their commitment.

Chart 9.11 Risk of fuel debts, by size of bills

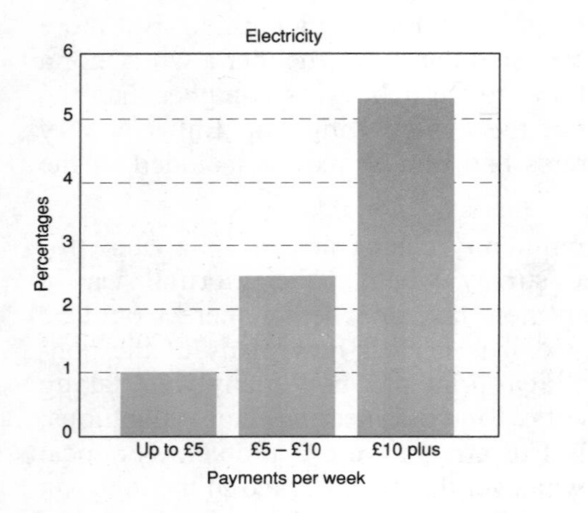

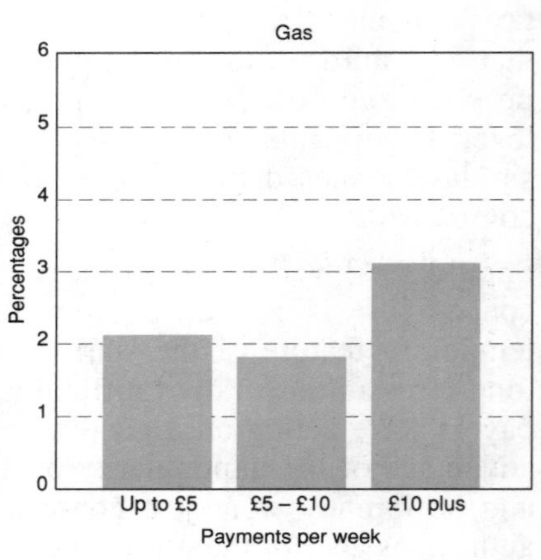

Source: PSI survey; analysis based on the customers of each fuel

It would be valuable to show which method of billing and payment was least likely to lead to fuel debts. In practice many households change their payment schedule after they have fallen into debt. As a result it was those currently using the pay-as-you-go methods who were most likely to have owed money.

Consumer debts

The survey provides the first detailed evidence about the extent and nature of arrears and debt on consumer credit. Since there have been no previous surveys, and no statistics are published, it is impossible to say with any certainty whether consumer debt is increasing at the same rate as the housing debts discussed earlier. Since the volume of credit has doubled in real terms over the past decade, a first assumption would be that the volume of debt has also doubled. But it would be possible to argue in principle against that assumption, in either direction.

- Lenders might have expanded their market by being less selective in their choice of customers. If so, the new lending could be riskier than the old, and debt would increase more rapidly than credit. This is the argument of those who oppose the growth in consumer credit.
- Lenders might have become more skilful in their selection of customers, and this would have enabled them to reduce the risk on new business. If so, debt would rise more slowly than credit; it might not rise at all. This is the argument of the credit industry.

Either of these arguments is legitimate in principle. Only factual evidence would tell us which has been true in practice. The following facts provide an indication of the answer.

- A 1981 survey of council tenants indicated 2.2 per cent had consumer credit arrears.[10] Applying as far as possible the same definitions to the current- and ex-council tenants in our own survey suggests an increase to 8.2 per cent.
- The Finance Houses Association reported that the proportion of accounts two months or more in arrears increased from 5 to 7 per cent between 1979 and 1984.[11] More recent figures are not available. Remember that the big increase in consumer credit occurred between 1982 and 1989 (Chart 4.3).
- Official statistics show that the number of court cases involving consumer credit increased from 175,000 in 1979 to 414,000 in 1987[12] (see Chapter 10, Table 10.7).

Any one of these sources of information would be very weak evidence on its own. But they all point in the same direction, and in the absence of evidence to the contrary, the balance of probabilities appears to support the view that there has been a substantial increase in consumer debt.

Overdrafts

The majority of households had at least one current account with a bank or building society. But (see Chapter 5) only a quarter of accounts had an overdraft facility, and a tenth of customers used their account as an active source of credit. The risk of problem debt can therefore be expressed in three ways:

1.9 per cent of all current accounts
8.1 per cent of overdraft facilities
16.2 per cent of accounts actively used as a source of credit.

The third version is the closest to the definition applied to other credit commitments. Looked at in this way, overdrafts were almost as likely to cause difficulty as rents. There were about half a million problem debts on current accounts over the course of the year.

The risk of debt was the same, whether the overdraft was agreed in advance or unauthorised. Accounts which were overdrawn by more then £500 at the time of the survey were nearly twice as likely to be in difficulty as those which were less than £500 in the red.

Current account overdrafts were a form of credit commonly used by households with above-average incomes. Among those who made use of these facilities, the chance of getting into difficulties was associated with low income, in the usual way, but the variation between income bands was weaker here than with other forms of commitment. As a result, overdraft difficulties were a relatively up-market type of debt. The mean income of the debtors was £220 – just above the national average. Overdrafts accounted for only 5 per cent of the debts faced by households with less than £150 per week; but for more than a quarter (27 per cent) of the small number of debts of those above £250 per week.

Most overdraft debts were the sole financial problem experienced by that household. There were some signs that customers with overdraft facilities used their current account to pay off other commitments, so that difficulties in paying any of a number of items would tend to show up as an overdraft problem.

Credit and store cards

To many people credit and store cards are almost synonymous with debt. But they have default rates that are no higher than other forms of credit. 'Arrears' were identified in two ways: 6 per cent of those using a card as an active source of credit had missed even the minimum payment at least once during the year; 6 per cent had gone over the credit limit for more than just a short time. Some customers reported both difficulties; 9.4 per cent had defaulted in one way or the other. But just under half of them were worried or felt that it was a problem, so the risk of problem debt was 4.5 per cent. The number of card problem debts is estimated to be about 300,000 over the course of a year.

These figures express arrears and debt as a proportion of the accounts which were used as an active source of credit. If cards which were paid off every month are included in the total, the risk of arrears was 4.0 per cent; and of problem debt, 1.9 per cent.

There was no significant difference in the risk of debt between credit cards and store cards. But customers who had an agreement to pay a set amount each month were substantially more likely to report debt problems (9.3 per cent) than customers with the more flexible arrangement of choosing how much to pay off each month (1.4 per cent). Chart 9.12 (green bars) suggests an association between the risk of debt and the scale of the customer's repayment commitment.

Chart 9.12 Risk of card and mail-order debts, by repayment commitments

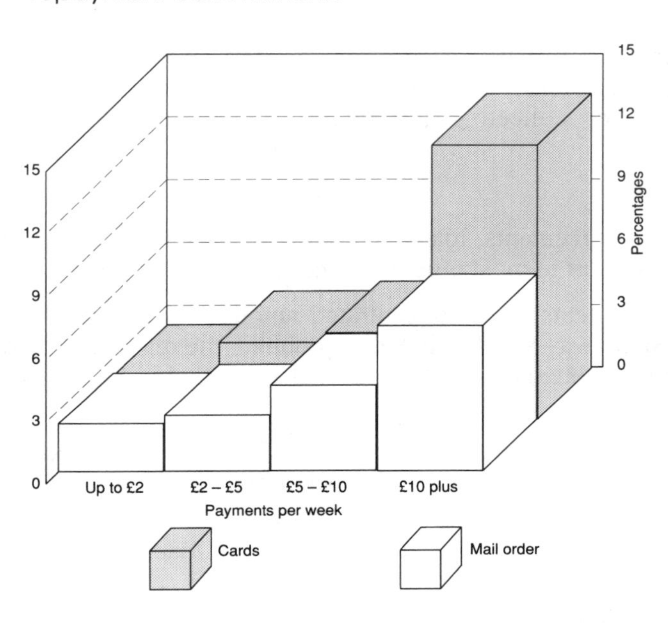

Source: PSI survey; analysis based on credit/store cards used for credit and on mail-order commitments. See Chapter 4, Box J for definition of repayment commitments.

People with high credit limits on their cards seemed to have no greater risk of getting into repayment difficulties than those with more restricted accounts – if anything, their risk of debt was lower. Almost all of the very small number of cards which had their credit limit decreased during the year had been in arrears. This suggests that card companies acted to restrict the facility where the card holder had got into difficulties.

Mail-order catalogues

Mail-order catalogues were commonly used by poor families. In spite of this, catalogues had one of the lowest level of default of all types of credit: 3.3 per cent. One reason was the age profile of catalogue customers: a relatively high proportion of them were pensioners, hardly any of whom had a problem with their payments. Three-quarters of the catalogue debtors were below the age of 40.

Chart 9.12 (white) showed that mail-order debt was related to the size of people's commitments, in much the same way as credit and store cards.

People who acted as agents for the mail-order companies were more likely to be in debt than their customers. 5.4 per cent of agents had a problem because they had failed to make some payments to the mail-order company during the year. Only 1.5 per cent of people who bought through an agent had missed an instalment. People who sent off from catalogues on their own account were in between (2.6 per cent). Sample sizes are too small to draw any clear conclusions, but the indications are that local and personal arrangements for collecting instalments provide a valuable control on arrears.

One-off advances

HP instalment agreements, loans and borrowings, taken together, had a risk of debt very similar to most other types of commitment: 4.3 per cent.

Although these debts were concentrated among low-income households in exactly the same way as other types of problem, the real distinction appeared to be between different classes of lender, as identified in Chapter 4.

- Banks, specialist dealers and building societies tended to lend to customers with above-average incomes. The debt risk among these *up-market commercial* lenders was 3.0 per cent.
- *Middle-market* transactions with a broader customer base included HP from high-street stores and fuel boards, and loans direct from finance houses. The risk of debt in this sector was 4.7 per cent.
- Money lenders and check companies specialised in small advances to poorer customers. The risk of debt among these *down-market commercial* lenders was 23 per cent.
- Poorer people could, however borrow from *down-market interest-free* sources: relatives, friends and the social fund. Only 0.8 per cent of these borrowings had become a problem debt.

Thus a large proportion of debts were concentrated among the specialist down-market commercial lenders. They accounted for 4 per cent of all one-off credit advances, but a quarter of the one-off problem debts. The concentration is even stronger among households whose income was below £100 per week: 15 per cent of their advances came from money lenders or check companies, but no less than 43 per cent of their one-off debts. (But look at this from another perspective as well. The majority of poor people's debts were not loans at all, but rent arrears and unpaid fuel bills. The specialist down-market lenders accounted for only 4 per cent of all problem debts reported by households below £100.)

The opportunity to borrow from local lenders appears to be of value to many poor people – otherwise they would not do it, and continue to do it. One of the advantages put forward for this type of loan is that the repayment commitments need not be seen as too rigid an obligation: the door-to-door collector accepts that a payment may be missed one week and made up the next. The Consumer Credit Association suggests that most loans extend beyond the original contracted period, typically lasting 30 rather than 26 weeks, at no additional cost to the customer.[13]

In the context of our survey, the down-market lenders argue that the irregularity of repayments should be seen as 'arrears' rather than as 'problem debts': neither party worries about them too much. This was certainly borne out by the comments people made about owing moneylenders repayments. Typical remarks included:

> *They aren't pressing me. They aren't pleased but they know I'll pay when I can.*

> *They know I'll pay when I can. If I'm skint they can't have it.*

Even so, almost all the members of our sample who reported arrears on such loans said that they were worried about them. In that sense, at least, they were genuine 'problem debts'.

A possible explanation for the high level of risk faced by money lenders and check companies might have been the very low incomes of so many of their customers. Among all other commercial lenders combined, the risk of arrears rose as high as 12 per cent if the borrower had an income below £100 per week. But for the downmarket lenders, the risk of arrears was 32 per cent. So low income on its own provides no more than a partial explanation for the high risk in that sector. It is likely that lenders' expectation that payments will be missed become self-fulfilling. Customers believe that the lender knows 'I'll pay when I can' and so miss payments on their loans rather than on other commitments. An alternative explanation might be that the moneylenders and check traders service the needs other loans do not reach, by accepting applications from high-risk candidates who have been or would be rejected by the mainstream creditors. The survey offers no direct evidence on that point.

In order to look in more detail at the characteristics of advances which may be associated with debt, the following analyses are confined to what we refer to as the mainstream creditors: interest-charging companies, *excluding* moneylenders and check companies.

Debt risks were very similar for both large and small loans, with long and short repayment periods and high and low instalments.

Even in the mainstream market, loans taken out to help repay existing debts, or to make ends meet, had a higher risk (11 per cent) than other advances (3.4 per cent).

There were some signs that debt might be associated with high levels of interest. Virtually none of the advances offered at zero interest had become a debt (0.1%). 2 per cent of the advances with charges below 100 per cent APR had led to a problem. The risk rose to 10 per cent among the small number of mainstream loans with a calculated charge in excess of 100 per cent.

In Chapter 6 we discussed a series of specific concerns about 'responsible' lending and borrowing. All but one of the questions listed in Table 9.13 turned out to be associated with an above-average risk of debt.

In fact, the more of these factors identified with a particular advance, the more likely it was to become a debt (Chart 9.14): the risk rose from 0.4 per cent of advances with none of the characteristics listed in Table 9.13, to

Table 9.13 Risk of debt on one-off advances, by aspects of 'responsible' lending and and borrowing

Percentages

	Debt risk among advances with this characteristic	Debt risk among all other advances	*Number with this characteristic (=100%)*
No deposit (instalment agreements)	6.1	3.0	*203*
Attracted by advertisement (loans)	3.5	3.0	*54*
Spur of the moment or emergency	5.8	3.0	*252*
Creditor did not check	7.3	2.4	*270*
Interest rate not known	5.4	1.9	*523*
Borrower expected difficulty	8.6	2.8	*161*

Source: PSI survey; analysis based on one-off advances from mainstream creditors

Chart 9.14 Risk of debt on one-off advances, by index of responsible lending

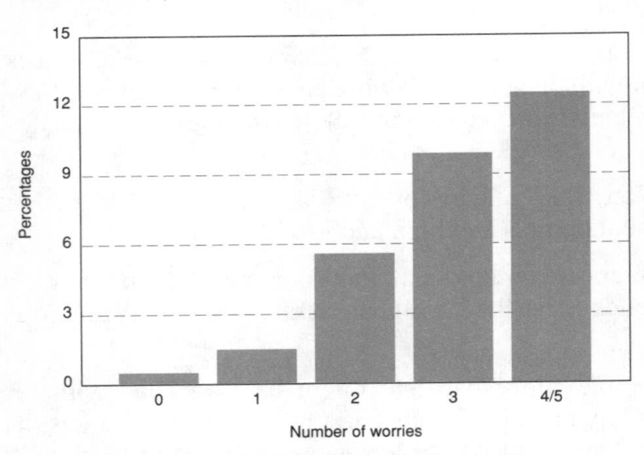

Source: PSI survey; analysis based on one-off advances from mainstream creditors. The index of responsible lending is based on the questions in Table 9.13, as explained in Chapter 6, Box R.

12 per cent of those exhibiting four or five of the problems. 'Irresponsible' lending/borrowing did, therefore, seem to be implicated in the level of debt. On the other hand, they were far from providing anything like a complete explanation. The problem cannot be 'blamed' on irresponsible lending or borrowing behaviour, any more than any other single cause.

References

1. Gillian Parker, *Getting and Spending: credit and debt in Britain*, Avebury, 1990

2. Council of Mortgage Lenders, *Housing Finance*, No.11, August 1991

3. See M.Boleat, *Mortgage Repayment Difficulties*, Building Societies Association, 1985; J.Doling, V. Karn and B.Stafford, *Behind with the Mortgage*, National Consumer Council, 1985; J.Doling, J.Ford and B.Stafford (eds), *The Property Owing Democracy*, Avebury, 1988; J.Ford, *The Indebted Society*, Routledge, 1988

4. See J. Ford, *Mortgage Arrears*, Institute for Employment Research, 1991, for more detailed analysis of building society arrears statistics.

5. S. Duncan and K. Kirby, *Preventing Rent Arrears*, HMSO, 1983

6. CIPFA, *Housing Revenue Actual Statistics*, 1979/80-1989/90

7. See note 5

8. See note 5

9. R. Berthoud, *Fuel Debts and Hardship*, Policy Studies Institute, 1981; Julia Field, *Electricity Council and Electricity Consumers' Council Survey of Code of Practice Payment Arrangements*, Social and Community Planning Research, 1989

10. PSI reanalysis of the data from the survey cited in note 5

11. Finance Houses Association, *Consumers and Debt*, FHA, 1985

12. Lord Chancellor's Department, *Judicial Statistics*, HMSO, 1979-1989

13. 'Memorandum submitted on behalf of the Consumer Credit Association of the United Kingdom in relation to Consumer Credit Act 1974; Extortionate Credit', May 1991

10 The Experience of Debt

The primary objective of the research was to find out how many households got into debt to different creditors, and what sort of people they were. But we were also concerned about what happened to them once they had fallen behind. Some families had had a purely temporary difficulty – no worry at all. Others had faced serious problems in repaying the money, while many still did not know what the solution could be. A small number of multiple debtors were in a permanent state of insolvency, and it was they who were likely to have had dealings with creditors, the courts and advice services.

Feelings about debt

People did not always worry if they missed one of their payments. More than a third of the 'arrears' recorded in the course of the survey were 'not at all' worrying, and had caused no problem. It was the remaining two-thirds, referred to as 'problem debts', that have been the focus of attention.

Not surprisingly, rich and poor households had different experiences at every stage of the process. Chart 10.1 shows that households with less than £100 per week had six times as many arrears as those earning more than £400. Nearly three-quarters of the poorer households' arrears were a 'problem'; just over a quarter of those of the richer group. Half of the well-off households' problem debts had been paid off by the time of the survey; a quarter of those in the lowest income band.

Chart 10.1 Arrears and debts, by income

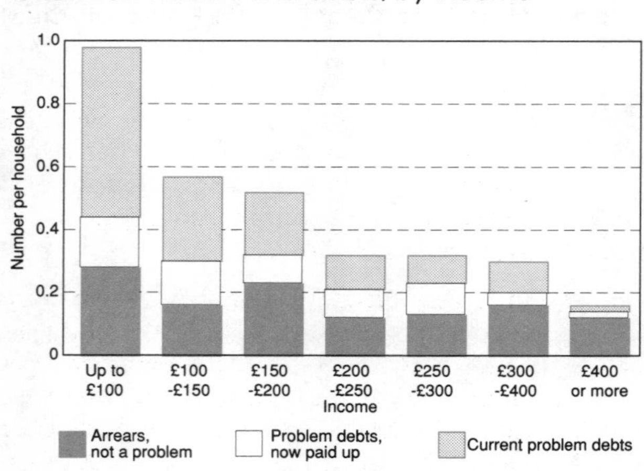

Source: PSI survey, analysis based on non-pensioner householders

The majority of debtors were very (45 per cent) or rather (25 per cent) worried about their problem debts. The most worrying were housing commitments or fuel bills – 56 per cent of these problems were 'very' worrying, no doubt because of the risk of eviction or disconnection. The least worrying, according to this measure, were problem debts on plastic cards or mail-order catalogues; only 25 per cent of them were very worrying, perhaps because customers felt that a few missed payments on revolving credit facilities could fairly easily be made up.

There was some sign that those debtors who had fallen into arrears in spite of a placing a high or very high priority on maintaining their payments were more concerned about their problems (64 per cent very worried) than others whose 'priority' score was low or below average (42 per cent). (See Chapter 8, Box W for the definition of 'priority on payment'.) There were, on the other hand, no signs that anyone took a care-free attitude. If some people had come to accept that they could not keep up to date with all their commitments, that seemed an adaptation to the strain of living on a low income over a long period. As one lone mother said:

> *I don't like being in debt. I know it sounds like I do, but I really don't... being on income support for five years I was never able to catch up with myself.*

Paying back

That last phrase – never able to catch up – is an important one. The analysis in Chapter 8 showed that debt was a rare problem for most people, but for particular groups of household – young, poor and families with children – it was a common experience. If half or more of the members of those groups experienced debt in the course of a year, it stands to reason that many must experience it from year to year. For some of them, it must be a frequent, perhaps even a continuous problem.

The debts identified by the survey – all those experienced in the course of a year – do not provide a particularly appropriate sample for studying the course of events once payments had been missed. For that purpose, we should have picked up a sample of cases at the beginning, and followed them through until they had been resolved. But we can gain some impression of the outcome from the available information.

Not that the impression is very clear. We know that there were 5.1 million problem debts over the course of a year, and 3.4 million outstanding at the end of the year. On the assumption that the total number of debts was stable, that suggests that 1.7 million debts started and 1.7 million were cleared up over the 12 month period – 140,000 per month. These calculations imply a mean duration of 24 months (3.4 million divided by 140,000); or a median of 16 months (at a constant clear-up rate of 4 per cent per month).

Direct questions suggested a broadly similar conclusion. For current debts, the average length of time since the arrears started was 13 months (mean) and 7½ months (median). Since (on average) it can be assumed that each current debt was in the middle of its trajectory, the overall duration would have averaged 26 or 15 months (mean and median respectively).

Both of these estimates are concerned with the 'stock' of debts – all of those outstanding at a particular time. Another perspective is the 'flow' – all the debts starting over a period. Long-lasting problems have a greater chance of appearing in the stock than in the flow. We estimate that if we had had a sample of debts starting in the course of a month, the average durations would have been about 6 months (mean) or 3 months (median). This is reflected by respondents' reports of the length of time they had had a problem with the debts that they had experienced earlier in the year, but which had now been resolved. These resemble a 'flow' sample. Three-quarters of the closed episodes had been completed within six months. Chart 10.2 compares the reported duration of current debts and of those which had already been repaid.

Chart 10.2 Duration of problem debts

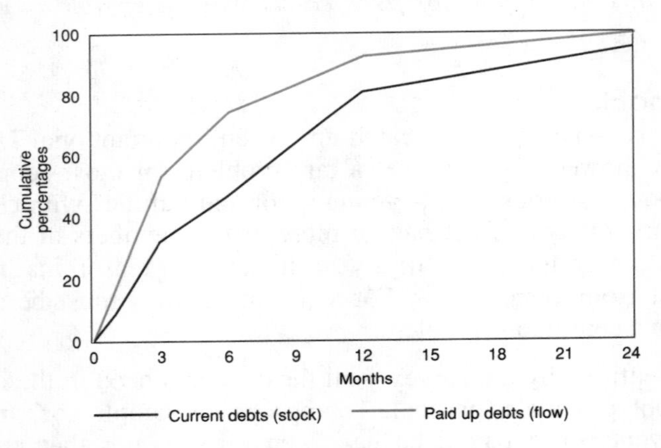

Source: PSI survey; analysis based on problem debts

Among current debts, the smaller amounts tended to have been owing for shorter periods: if the arrears were £100 or less, two-thirds (65 per cent) had been a problem for less than six months; if £500 or more, only 3 out of 10 (29 per cent) were as recent as that. This makes sense, but it is not clear which is the more important reason: large arrears might take a long time to pay off; and the longer the period, the more arrears might build up.

The small number of people above the age of 60 who had any debts tended to take a long time to resolve the problem: only one sixth of them had cleared it up within six months.

One of the difficulties of measuring the duration of debts was that the end was not always a clearly identifiable event. Nearly half (46 per cent) of the commitments which were reported to be back on an even keel had been repaid by instalments. 'Paid up to date' might mean that the arrears had all been paid off; or it might mean that the instalment plan had been adhered to. Another 10 per cent of debts had been paid off by taking out another loan or by borrowing from relatives or friends; this was another way of spreading the repayments over a period. There was some sign that poorer families used instalment arrangements more often than the small number of debtors with higher incomes did. But the sample of repaid debts is now so small that it is impossible to analyse the alternative payment methods in any more detail.

While most individual debts were repaid within a few months of the first missed payment, a number of clues suggest that the problem was often far from temporary. While some were cleared up quickly, others went on for many months, even years. Many of the debts which had been settled involved a prolonged repayment plan, or could only be repaid out of borrowed money. Once low-income families got into difficulties, it was almost impossible to get straight again unless there was a dramatic improvement in their circumstances. Of all the households who had been in debt at any time over the course of the year, three-quarters (73 per cent) were still, or again, in debt at the end of that year.

Among twelve low-income debtor families reinterviewed a year later, only two were no longer behind. One of those had been in arrears with their mortgage. The husband's income had increased considerably and the extra money was used to repay the debt. The other was a recently-widowed mother whose brother had taken out a bank loan to clear her rent and gas bill debts.

Many of those still in debt said it was a struggle to make ends meet, let alone pay back the money they owed. Most had paid off some of their creditors only to get into debt to others. It was apparent, though, that the creditors who had been repaid were the ones who had either threatened or taken further action. Eight of the ten families still in debt had repaid some of their creditors. Of these two were about to be disconnected by utilities, one was taken to court by a mail-order firm, one had a court order for repossession of their council house and a fifth, living in Northern Ireland, had had the Payments for Debt Act used to recover the money.

> *[They said] pay up or we'll cut your water off. I haven't said anything. I'll just try and get the money or borrow it somehow to pay for it. Off my mother most probably.*

Most were 'robbing Peter to pay Paul'. More worrying was the fact that three of the five families who remained in multiple debt during the year had used further loans to pay off earlier commitments. One had run up a large overdraft within days of being granted the facility. She spent up to her limit of £350 only to receive a letter from the bank to say they had made an error and the limit was only £250. She was still waiting to hear the outcome.

Another two families already had large loans from a check company but had increased the amount borrowed. One, with a weekly income of around £100, owed £500 which they had borrowed at various times to pay bills. Their loan was constantly being added to as new bills came in that they could not pay, with the result that they owed £200 more than when we had interviewed them a year earlier. There were signs that they were reaching their credit limit with the company.

> *I couldn't have it off the Provvy; we've got too much on. It's just continually the same isn't it. It never gets any better. It's got worse. If you have a look at what I did last year I'm more up to my eyes in debt than then.*

Negotiations between creditor and debtor

Debt recovery practices vary between different creditors and, sometimes, between different offices of the same company. Even so, many organisations adopt a broadly similar approach. Typically the early stages of debt recovery begin with a series of letters, at first reminding the customer that the money is overdue and gradually adopting a firmer line until they include explicit threats of court action or other sanctions. Some creditors also try to make personal contact with customers who are in arrears, either speaking to them on the telephone or visiting them at their home.

We were not able to study debt recovery procedures in detail, looking at them from the creditors' perspective as well as the debtors' point of view. We have only the debtors' accounts of what happened when they fell behind with their payments.

Four out of five debtors said that their creditor had made contact with them: in almost all instances by letter. Personal contact occurred much less frequently. Only one in ten (11 per cent) of debts had been followed up by a visit from the creditor and an even smaller number (3 per cent) had been pursued by a telephone call.

Many creditors claim to attempt to establish personal contact with customers who are in arrears, but they clearly vary in the effort they put into this. Some try hard, while others appear to make no serious attempt. Almost half of consumer credit loans that were in arrears had been followed up by either a telephone call or a home visit. It must be remembered, though, that a significant proportion of these were loans taken out from companies who collected weekly payments from their customers anyway. Landlords too stood out as being likely to have made personal contact; they had visited nearly a quarter of tenants with rent debts. Of course tenants often live relatively close to one another, unlike the customers of most creditors, and would be much more easily visited. Very few mortgage debtors had been visited in person. Mail order firms very rarely did more than write to their customers who had got into arrears and three out of ten catalogue debts appeared not to have been followed up at all.

Whatever the method of communication, an important question facing every debt collection procedure is what message to convey. Creditors generally feel it is important to make it clear that the money must be repaid, that the sooner this happens the easier it will be and that failure to do so will lead to court or other action. At the same time responsible lenders recognise that customers who are genuinely unable to pay should be given time to do so and the opportunity to negotiate a way of repaying that is within their means. In other words creditors need to be firm but fair.

According to the people we interviewed, the most common message they received from creditors who contacted them was a reminder to repay the money they owed. Half of all debts were followed up in this way. In general, creditors were more likely to take a firm line, demanding payment or threatening further action, than they were either to try to identify the cause of the problem or to arrange a way of repaying the arrears in instalments.

Table 10.3 Messages received from creditors

Percentages

	Reminder to pay	Asked for immediate payment	Threatened action	Suggested way of paying	Asked if had problems	*Total (=100%)*
Rent	36	18	47	32	9	*97*
Mortgage	66	15	7	17	27	*21*
Electricity	41	32	57	20	6	*39*
Gas	45	31	35	34	15	*31*
Cards	70	53	30	16	19	*25*
Catalogues	79	51	55	2	9	*20*
Instalments	69	24	30	5	4	*20*
Loans	59	18	22	20	24	*22*
Overdraft	55	39	11	31	20	*36*
All	52	32	34	21	13	*399*

Source: PSI survey; analysis based on all debts where the creditor made contact, Percentages read ***across*** *the table.*

Some creditors took a much firmer line than others and there were some interesting contrasts between similar creditors (Table 10.3). Local authorities are frequently held to blame for the mounting levels of rent arrears. Yet rent debts were frequently pursued with a 'firm but fair' approach while the most common response of mortgage lenders was simply to send a reminder that payments were overdue. We have already seen that landlords were more likely than mortgage lenders to make personal contact with their debtors.

They were also more inclined to take active steps to ensure that the debt was repaid, including both firm and fair approaches. Tenants with rent debts were threatened with further action far more often than mortgage defaulters. But, at the same time, landlords suggested ways of repaying the arrears in instalments almost twice as often as mortgage lenders did.

Fuel boards also behaved rather differently from one another. There was almost no difference between the proportions of gas and electricity debts being followed up by reminder letters or requests for immediate repayment. But there the similarity ends. Gas boards were much more likely to ask if there were problems or to suggest a means of repayment, while the electricity boards tended to threaten further action.

Comparison of the two forms of revolving credit – plastic cards and mail order catalogues – also shows some interesting differences. Mail-order firms generally took a 'firm' line to recover their debts if they made contact at all. Half of their follow-up letters were said to contain threats of further action. And they were less likely than any other creditor to have tried to find out if the people owing them money faced problems or to have suggested a way of repaying the arrears. In contrast, credit and store card companies were much less inclined to threaten further action, while being more prepared to suggest a means of repayment or to ask if there were special problems.

Similarly, the recovery practices differed for the two main types of one-off credit. Credit given as a loan seemed to be treated more sympathetically if it became a problem debt than was credit arranged as an instalment agreement, such as HP or credit sale, made with the supplier. Loan companies were far more likely to suggest repayment arrangements and to try to discover whether there was a particular problem.

There was, however, little evidence that creditors took account of the circumstances of the people who owed money to them during these early negotiations. Young and old, rich and poor seemed to be treated in much the same way.

Overall, seven out of ten debts were resolved without the need for further action: two out of ten had been repaid in full and five out of ten were being recovered through arrangements to repay over time. Repayment agreements were twice as common where the creditor had contacted the customer than they were when no contact had been made. Three-quarters of the debts that had been followed up by the creditor had been settled.

Interestingly, it seemed to be the creditors who took a more understanding line who were most successful at settling the debts owed to them. Those who had suggested a means of repaying the money owed resolved nine out of ten of their debts. Threats of further action led to three-quarters of debts being resolved, and letters demanding immediate repayment only two-thirds.

At the same time, there seemed to be a trade-off. Creditors taking firm action on their debts persuaded a greater number (between a quarter and a third) of their customers to pay up in full but did so at the risk of an equal number reaching no repayment agreement at all. Creditors suggesting repayment over time reached agreements with nine out of ten of the people owing them money, but most of these were in the form of instalments and far fewer (one out of ten) of their customers paid up in full.

The debts most likely to have been resolved were for rent, mortgage repayments and fuel bills; mail-order catalogues had the highest proportion of unresolved debts. In part this can be attributed to the level of contact made by the creditor – as we have seen mail-order companies followed up the smallest proportion of their debts. It also seems as if the approach taken by the creditor was important. This does not, however, explain why landlords and mortgage lenders resolved similar numbers of debts, despite employing rather different approaches to debt recovery. In the same way, the two fuel utilities also used different approaches but had similar end results, as did the two forms of revolving credit and the two types of one-off credit. A plausible explanation is that creditors' success in resolving their debts depended as much on the sanctions they had available to them as on the debt recovery methods they employed. The knowledge that the debt could lead to eviction or fuel disconnection may have been a greater incentive for people to reach an agreement with the creditors they owed money to, than the possibility of being taken to court.

Both creditors and money advisers complain that people who find themselves getting into difficulties with payments do not, themselves, make contact with their creditor. In fact, two-thirds of debtors said that they had made contact. While creditors most often made contact in writing, debtors more commonly used the telephone or visited the creditor's office (one quarter each). Only one debtor in five wrote to the creditor.

People contacted their creditor with several objects in mind. The three most common reasons were:

- to explain why the payments had not been made (57 per cent);
- to ask for arrangements to repay the money owed (51 per cent);
- to tell the creditor that they expected to have difficulty in making the payments (41 per cent).

Creditors claim that, if the customer contacts them with a repayment offer, they are usually willing to negotiate. Our findings support this view. This was especially true where the contact had been by 'phone or in person. Nine out of ten personal visits to the creditor had resulted in a repayment agreement. Fewer than half of debtors who had not contacted the creditor had agreed repayment arrangements.

In general, more people had contacted their creditor about rent, mortgage and electricity debts and fewer had initiated any contact with commercial credit companies or banks. Again it seems plausible that concern about the sanction available may have been as important in encouraging contact as the approach the creditor took to debt recovery.

We have seen that five out of ten debts involved some form of arrangement to repay the money owed over time. Most of these were being repaid in instalments; the average agreement involving payments of £9 a week over a period of 12 months.

Money advisers express concern that, in an attempt to appear reasonable, many people offer unrealistic debt repayments to their creditors; repayments they subsequently find they cannot meet. There was some evidence that this was so. Three out of ten agreements had been broken. In most cases this involved late payment or the occasional missed payment but, in a small number of cases, no payments were made at all. Although there was no link between the rate of default and the size of the instalment, there was a relationship with the household income of the debtor. Only a half of the poorer households, with incomes of less than £150 a week, had made all their payments on time, compared with seven out of ten of households with incomes above this level.

Looking back over the negotiations as a whole, only half of the people with debts felt their creditor had been either very or fairly helpful. Most commonly this was because they had been understanding or had worked out a way of repaying the debt. A single mother, in multiple debt, had successfully negotiated a way of repaying her store card debt:

> *Well they did ask if I had any problems and were willing to listen to them. And they were willing for me to pay them back by instalments directly through the bank.*

Three out of ten people said their creditor was either not very or not at all helpful, chiefly because they had been unpleasant or uncooperative.

> *They were not very helpful. It was just their attitude. They just wanted the money and they don't care about the state you're in.*

Only a minority of creditors were criticised for administrative inefficiency or for refusing to accept an offer of repayment. A small number, one in twenty, were criticised, perhaps unreasonably, for not writing off the debt.

It was clear that different creditors could react quite differently to the same set of circumstances. A young couple had got badly into debt when the husband lost his job shortly after the wife had given up work to have a baby. They had got into arrears on their mortgage, rates and electricity and had put their house up for sale to clear their debts and start again. When they explained their situation to the local electricity board they received a sympathetic ear:

> *Well they were going to cut us off. That's when I phoned them up. I explained to them that we were moving and the man was very nice. When we move they will come and read the meter and we will pay it off.*

In this instance the local authority was far less accommodating about the rates debt:

> *I asked if I paid half of it, would it do until October. And they said no, we must pay it in full.*

At the time we interviewed them, they were waiting for a court summons for the rates.

It was also apparent that responses from the same creditor and even the same branch office could differ widely. A young man, who became unemployed for 13 months shortly after buying a flat, contacted his mortgage lender.

> *When the problem first occurred, the manager at the time wasn't very helpful. He didn't suggest anything constructive. However the new manageress has been extremely helpful. She offered me the facility to increase the mortgage to clear the arrears.*

It has been shown that one in three debts were not resolved through negotiation. In the nature of things, some of these would have only recently gone into arrears and creditors would not have started trying to recover the debt. But others had passed into the later stages of debt recovery. One in ten debts had been passed to either a solicitor or a debt collector for recovery; with solicitors being used twice as often as debt collectors. Again there were some interesting differences between creditors, reflecting the ease with which they could enforce payment of the debt. Debt collectors were mainly used by the consumer credit industry; one in eight debts on mail-order catalogues were put into the hands of debt collection agencies as were one in ten loans and instalment agreements. Creditors with more punitive debt enforcement procedures at their disposal seldom used a debt collector but were more inclined to pass the case on to their solicitor. These included landlords and mortgage lenders, who could threaten legal proceedings to repossess the house, and fuel boards, who could disconnect supply without the need for court proceedings.

Debt enforcement

Different creditors have different courses of action that they can follow to enforce repayment of the money owed to them. Electricity, gas and telephone companies may disconnect supply without recourse to a court; water companies may also disconnect, but only after getting a court order.

Rent and mortgage debts are usually enforced by eviction following a county court repossession hearing. Local authority housing departments may use bailiffs to seize goods without a court order. Consumer credit debts are generally enforced through the county courts, although hire purchase companies may repossess goods without a court order if less than a third of the price has been repaid.

Rents and mortgages

The most common way of enforcing housing debt is by getting a county court Possession Order. Local authorities have the right to send in the bailiffs without a court order; a process known as 'distraint'. In practice most local authorities use possession action rather than distraint. Consequently, although rent debts were extremely common and landlords frequently threatened further action, the survey identified only one instance where bailiffs had been sent in, without a court summons.

Court records on possession orders granted to private landlords include a variety of disputes apart from unpaid rent. But it is known that the great majority of court cases brought by social landlords are concerned with arrears. Chart 10.4 shows that the number of orders awarded to councils and housing associations rose to a peak in 1982 and fell in the mid-1980s. They have risen sharply over the past few years to reach 92,000 in 1990. Surprisingly, there seems to be no information about the number of tenants actually evicted – a court order is a stage in the process which does not necessarily lead to repossession.

Chart 10.4 Repossession actions, 1979 to 1991

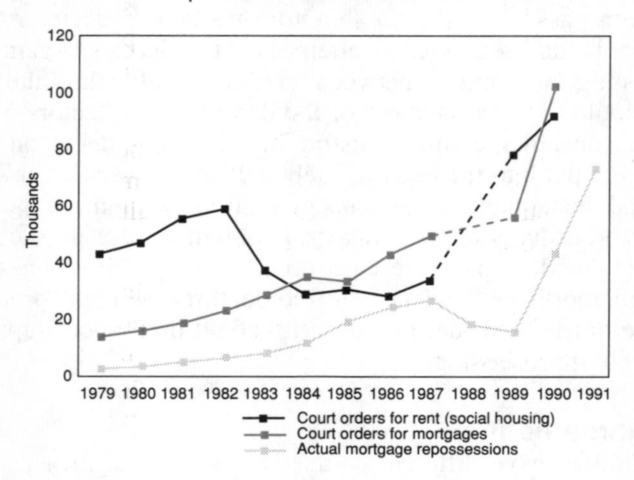

Sources: Court orders, DoE;[1] *Actual repossessions, Council of Mortgage Lenders*[2]
Note: the statistics for court orders cover England and Wales; the actual mortgage repossessions cover Great Britain. The 1991 repossession figure is based on the first half year.

Chart 10.4 also shows that the number of repossession orders granted for mortgage debt was substantially lower than for rent arrears at the beginning of the 1980s. But the rate of increase has been steadier and more rapid in the owner-occupied sector, and the number of mortgage repossession orders passed 100,000 in 1990. The Council of Mortgage Lenders' statistics on actual evictions suggest that less than half of the orders lead to the ultimate sanction. The most recent figures show a huge rise in the number of repossessions caused by the combination of high interest rates and falling house prices. The rate of repossession was 25 times higher in the first half of 1991 than it had been in 1979.

Utility debts

The most common sanction for non-payment of fuel and other utility debts is the disconnection of supply. The electricity and gas supply industries have the right to disconnect customers in arrears without needing to use a court. For many years they operated a voluntary code of practice designed to 'help where there is real hardship'. In spite of this, the majority of those disconnected showed some evidence of hardship such as low incomes, or they were families with children.[3] These findings are confirmed by the credit and debt survey: considering all utilities together, we found that almost all the people who had been disconnected had incomes that were below average. Four out of ten of them were families with children.

Since 1989 in the case of British Gas, 1990 for the electricity supply companies, the fuel industries have had to comply with more stringent licence provisions for dealing with customers who owe them money. These conditions require them to take into account their customers circumstances and identify those who are unable to pay, making payment arrangements which take this into account. Where these arrangements break down a pre-payment meter should be supplied.

The Water Act 1989 limits the circumstances under which the water companies can disconnect customers owing them money and effectively requires them to obtain a court order first. As a result the water companies have become major users of the county courts.

The debtors in our sample said that electricity boards threatened disconnection more often than British Gas. This difference in approach is borne out by official statistics on disconnection. In 1989, 20,379 customers had their gas supply disconnected; 69,975 had their electricity supply cut off; and 7,181 lost their water supply. Official statistics show that the rate of disconnections has always been lower for gas than for electricity. In both cases, though, the level of disconnection has fallen in recent years (Chart 10.5).

This has been particularly noticeable for British Gas. At least part of the explanation for the trend lies in the availability of prepayment meters.

Chart 10.5 Electricity, gas and water disconnections, 1980-1990

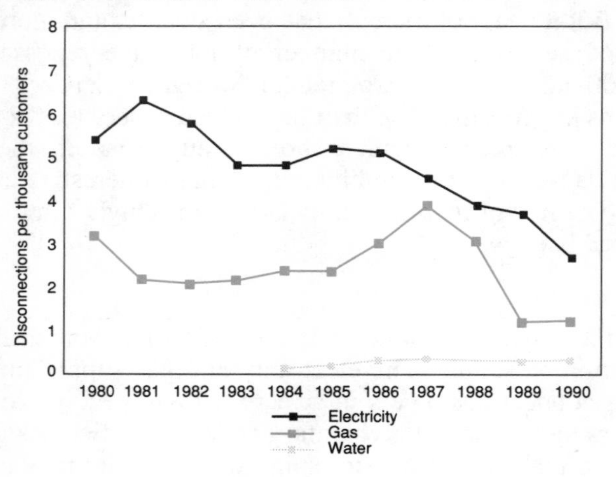

Source:Industry statistics [4]

Chart 10.6 compares the rate of disconnection with the rate of supply of prepayment meters for the period from 1980 to 1990 and shows an inverse relationship between the two. From 1981 to 1985 the rate of installation of meters exceeded the disconnection rate. Concerns about the security of cash meters led fewer of them to be installed and this was accompanied by a rapid increase in disconnection until 1987. Since then there has been a rise in the number of meters installed, and a rapid fall in the level of disconnections.

Chart 10.6 Gas prepayment meters and disconnections, 1980-1990

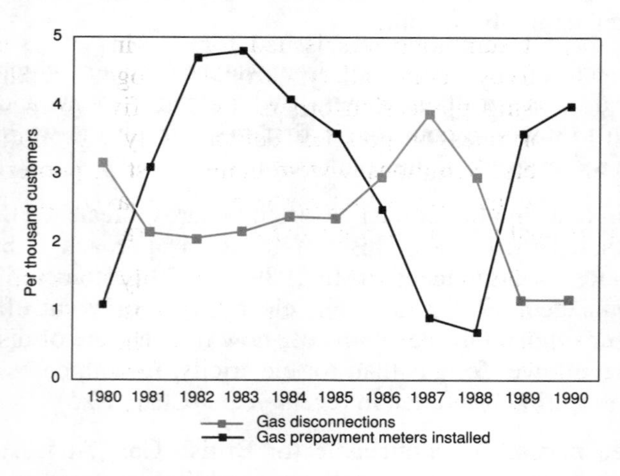

Source:British Gas and OFGAS [4]

Consumer credit

Recent statistics on County Court 'money plaints' are difficult to interpret in terms of consumer credit debt. But a consistent run of figures is available covering the period up to 1987. In that year there were about 300,000 court cases initiated for 'money lenders' claims and loans'; and a further 100,000 for 'HP and credit sale' debts. There had been some decline in the number of HP cases, but this was more than offset by a large increase in the number of loan cases.

Chart 10.7 County court actions to recover consumer credit debts

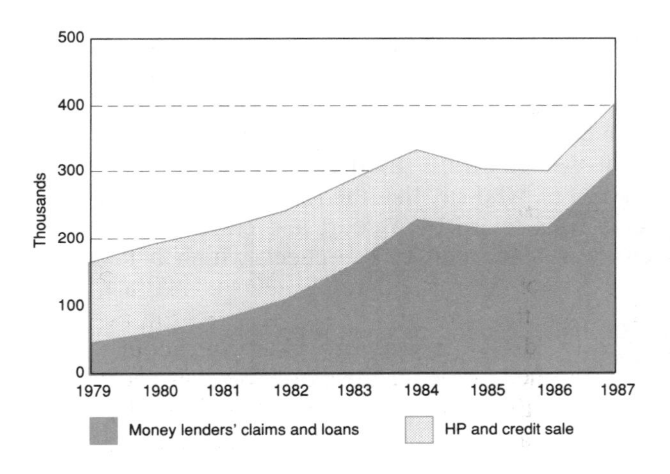

Source: Lord Chancellors Department[5]

Court summonses

Some kind of court summons was issued for one in ten of all the debts identified in our survey, taking all types of debt together. Almost half of these were for housing possession orders. One in five were taken out by local authorities for rates or poll tax default; only a minority were for consumer credit debts. Summonses were commonest in poorer households. Debtors with below average incomes were twice as likely to receive a summons as those with incomes that were above average.

Unexpectedly, households with multiple debt ran only a slightly greater risk of being summonsed for any particular debt than those who owed money to only one creditor. This suggests that households who had been in debt to more than one creditor were rotating their repayments, managing to pay off many commitments before receiving a court summons.

Only half of the households receiving a summons replied to it, usually by filling in and returning the form that the court had sent to them. Nearly four out of ten proceedings were avoided by the debtor reaching an agreement with the court about paying the money owed. A further third of people with a summons said they had either not received a date for the hearing or they were waiting for their case to come to court.

A court hearing was, therefore, known to have occurred for about a quarter of debts where a summons had been issued. Surprisingly, two-thirds of people who knew that there had been a court hearing said that they had attended in person (or, more rarely, had been represented). Court records indicate that just over a half of cases are heard with no-one present. There are several possible explanations for this discrepancy. Some of the people we interviewed may not have been aware that they had received a court summons, or they were not admitting to having received one. An alternative explanation is that many of the people who said their case had not come to court were not aware that a hearing had taken place. Certainly we would have expected a court hearing to have resulted from more than the quarter of summonses that we identified. Further support for this explanation comes from money advisers, who say that their clients are frequently not aware that their cases have been heard by a court and consequently do not attend the hearing. There is no way that we can check which of these explanations is right.

The people who had attended or been represented at the hearing had almost all done so to make arrangements to repay the money they owed. Repayment arrangements were, therefore, reached for two-thirds of all the debts which had been enforced by a court summons. A third of these were set up by the court following a hearing and two-thirds were agreed without the need for a hearing.

As things turned out, a third of people had failed to make all the agreed repayments on time and the court took further action on one in ten of debts for which they had issued a summons. The most common action was to issue a possession order, but there were also a very small number of instances of prison sentences, distraint orders and fines.

Payments for Debt Act

From 1971 public bodies in Northern Ireland were able to use the Payments for Debt (Emergency Provisions) Act (Northern Ireland) 1971 to recover money owing to them. This enabled them to have debt repayments deducted at source from both social security benefits and wages. In 1986-87, for example, £37 million was taken from benefits, but only £1.8 million from earnings. Always a highly controversial power, it was repealed in January 1991. Its use had been declining in real terms as a greater use was made of ordinary powers to deduct from benefit. In contrast to Britain, where deductions can only be made from income support, in Northern Ireland deductions can be made from any social security benefit.

Chart 10.8 Social security deductions under the Payments for Debt Act (Northern Ireland), 1979-80 to 1988-89

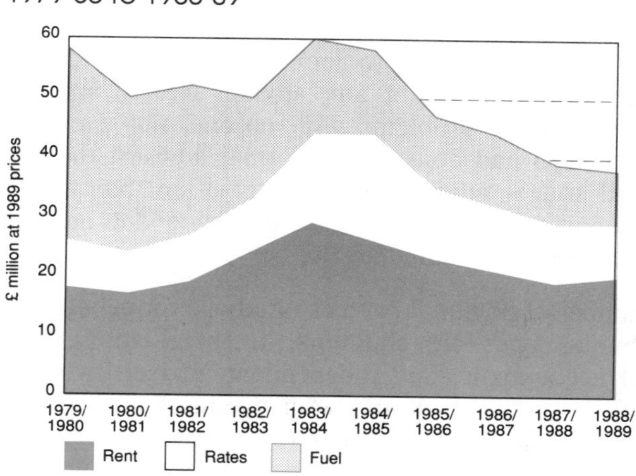

Source: Hansard[6]

Money Advice

Debt recovery procedures are a relatively straightforward routine for creditors and they each have a clear set of debt recovery sanctions that are used regularly. They employ a range of specialist staff, including financial and legal experts who are experienced in the legal processes open to them to recover the money owed.

The procedures are a great deal more confusing for debtors, putting them at a distinct disadvantage. They have far less experience of debt recovery than the staff of the creditors who pursue arrears, and are often facing the situation for the first time. They have little knowledge of the process of negotiation and will almost certainly have not been involved in court proceedings before. If they owe money to several creditors they will be faced with more than one set of procedures and legal sanctions. Few are likely to be aware of their rights or of the best course of action in trying to sort out the situation.

Studies of money advice clients[7] suggest that they were confused by the sequence of demands from their various creditors. Often they did not realise they were in a process of negotiation – creditors seemed to be saying 'pay up or else' and they assumed the courts would automatically take the creditor's point of view. The sanctions open to some creditors are drastic ones, involving eviction, disconnection or even, in a small number of cases, imprisonment. The need for expert advice is acute.

These same studies suggest that creditors' staff generally act in ignorance of the circumstances of the debtor, and especially of the other commitments and debts the household may face. So creditors, too, benefit from the intervention of an adviser able to determine a debtor's exact financial problem.

In the survey, everyone with a problem debt during the previous year was asked whether they had sought any advice. Nearly six out of ten had discussed their financial problems with no-one, not even their family or friends. Only a third had consulted a formal adviser; those with three or more debts had sought advice only slightly often than others with fewer debts. The proportion of people seeking advice did not, however, vary between different ages or income levels.

There are a number of potential sources of advice for people who are in debt. The most obvious ones are solicitors, financial advisers such as bank managers and accountants, and independent advisers working in citizens advice bureaux or specialist money advice centres. Together three-quarters of the people who had sought help from a formal adviser had turned to one of these three groups of people. They were also the advisers who were found most helpful by those who consulted them.

These groups of advisers were used by different people for different purposes. Financial advisers such as accountants and bank managers were most often consulted by people who had above average incomes and who owed money to only one creditor, while those who had been to independent money advice centres and citizens advice bureaux had below average incomes and were in multiple debt.

There was also an interesting comparison between people with different types of debt. Half of those seeking advice specifically about a debt on a consumer credit commitment had consulted an independent advice agency such as a citizens advice bureau or money advice service; half had been to see their bank manager or financial adviser. But bank managers were mainly consulted about difficulties with overdrafts and although respondents referred to them as advisers, strictly they had contacted their creditor. When this was taken into account, three-quarters of all other consumer credit debt enquiries were taken to an advice centre. This finding is particularly relevant to the current debate about the responsibility of the consumer credit industry to finance independent money advice services. It is clear that if people with consumer credit debts go anywhere for advice it is to an independent advice agency.

In contrast, people with debts on household commitments had sought advice from a much wider range of organisations, including solicitors, social services and the Department of Social Security. Even so about four in ten enquiries about household commitment debts had been made at an independent advice agency.

About half of those people consulting an official adviser were given advice and information only; about another half were helped to negotiate with their creditors, but very few were represented by advisers at court hearings. Again there were clear differences between the different groups of advisers. People who consulted a financial adviser most commonly received advice and information, while those who had visited an advice agency were frequently helped to negotiate with their creditors. Just about everyone who had been represented in court had been to a solicitor.

Chart 10.9 Assistance given by advisers

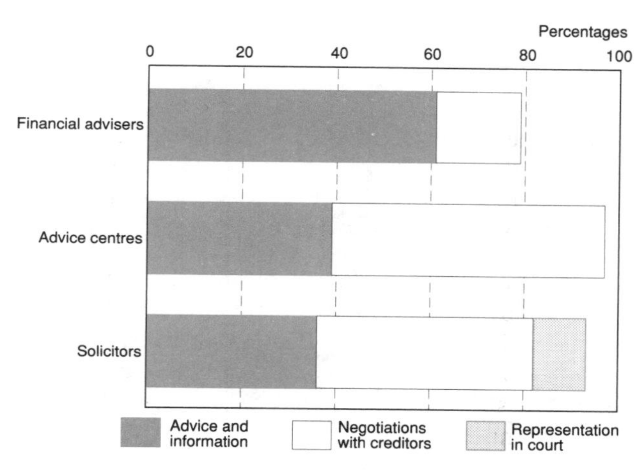

Source: PSI survey, analysis based on householders who had sought advice about debts

Altogether six out of ten people with problem debts had sought no advice at all, not even from their friends or relatives. Only one in 20 of them said that they had managed to sort things out with their creditor. The most common reason for not seeking advice was a preference for sorting things out themselves and not letting others know their business. Frequently this was because people were ashamed or thought they had only themselves to blame. A married woman with three children and living on a low wage, supplemented by family credit, was in debt on their rent, television rental and four loans to money lenders:

> *Because I was planning to save up and pay off the bills I thought I didn't need any help. I feel I must sort it out myself.*

A newly married couple, with a new baby, had got into debt on their mortgage, electricity and rates when the husband lost his job as a shop fittings designer:

I think we were ashamed really. That stopped us going for advice. That's the only reason.

The only other common reasons were that people did not know where to go for advice about debt, or they were either not worried or were deliberately withholding the money they owed.

Chart 10.10 Main reasons for not seeking advice, by number of debts

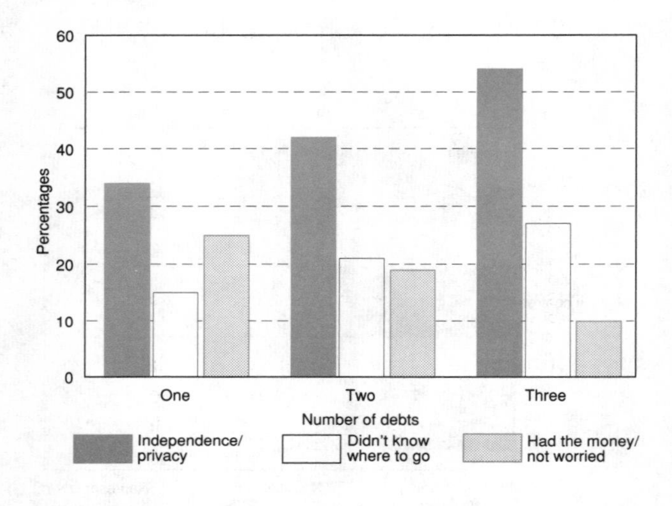

Source: PSI survey, analysis based on householders who had not sought advice about debts

Unsurprisingly people who said they were not worried or had the money to pay were more likely to have had only one debt and to have debts they had paid off. But the proportions of people who wanted to sort things out themselves or said they did not know where to get help were greatest among those with multiple debt and who had current debts.

Setting aside those who said they had the money to repay their debts or were not worried about the situation, there were still about one million households who had current debts at the time of our survey but had sought no advice. About 200,000 of these owed money to three or more creditors. Almost by definition they would be unable to afford to pay for advice, and since a high proportion of people in debt did not have a bank account they could not consult a bank manager.

Help from solicitors is likely to be rather limited for two main reasons. The means test for legal aid excludes many who need help: even two-child families living on two-thirds the average male earnings are expected to pay

Chart 10.11 Main reasons for not seeking advice, by status of debts

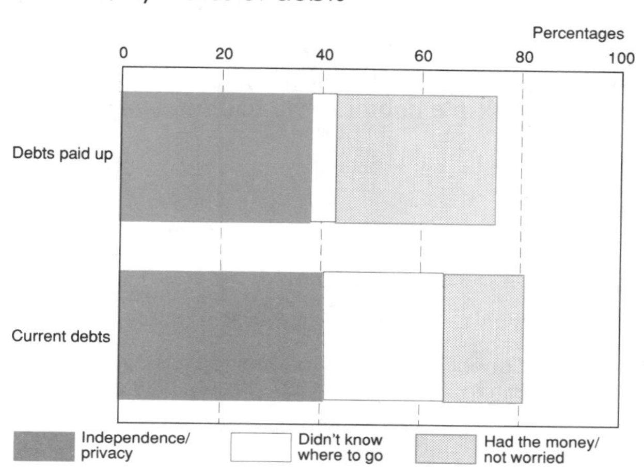

Source: PSI survey, analysis based on households who had not sought advice about debts

substantial contributions. Full legal aid is not available for defendants in county court proceedings, even for those meeting the means test. The only help available is advice and assistance under the legal aid 'green form' scheme which does not cover the lengthy negotiations with creditors needed for people in multiple debt. In fact, national figures show that only 55,000 people received help with debt problems under the green form scheme in the year we carried out our survey.[8]

This leaves the independent money advice services. The number of money advisers has grown rapidly in recent years but even so the most recent survey has shown that there is only the equivalent of about 270 full-time money advisers in the United Kingdom, about 60 of whom are volunteers.[9] In addition there is the equivalent of about 50 people working full-time in units that provide support and training services for money advisers.

Most of these specialist workers assist people in multiple debt. This is a lengthy process involving a number of different stages. The adviser's first action is to inform all creditors about all debts, so that they can stop asking for money which is not there. They then see if they can increase the client's income, especially from social security benefits. The next stage is to calculate the client's income and expenditure and, from this, to calculate how much is available for the repayment of debts. It then becomes possible to make offers to the priority creditors – those with serious sanctions at their disposal. Finally, the adviser negotiates with the remaining creditors asking each to accept a regular payment from what remains of the client's income.

This is generally a time-consuming process and it has been estimated that each adviser can assist only 100-150 clients during the course of a year.[10]

In other words, each year the current number of specialist money advisers can be expected to assist up to 40,000 people in serious debt – a long way short of the 200,000 multiple debtors who had not sought help at the time of our survey.

References

1. Department of the Environment, *Housing and Construction Statistics*, HMSO

2. Council of Mortgage Lenders, *Housing Finance*, October 1991

3. R. Berthoud, *Fuel Debts and Hardship*, Policy Studies Institute, 1987

4. Electricity Consumer Council and OFFER annual reports (England and Wales); British Gas and OFGAS (Great Britain); Hansard col.527, 19 July 1988 and OFWAT (England)

5. Lord Chancellors Department, *Judicial Statistics*, HMSO

6. Hansard written answers, 12 February 1988 cols 395-6 and 22 June 1989, col 223

7. T. Hinton and R. Berthoud, *Money Advice Services*, Policy Studies Institute, 1987

8. *Legal Aid*: 40th Annual reports of the Law Society and the Lord Chancellor's Advisory Committee (1989-90)

9. National Consumer Council, *A Report on Debt Advice Provision in the UK*, NCC, 1989

10. See note 7

Part IV
CONCLUSIONS

11 Policy on Credit and Debt: whose responsibility?

Stereotypes of debtors abound. In some commentators' minds debt is entirely due to low incomes and poverty. Others focus on young people over-spending on credit cards to maintain a consumer lifestyle they cannot afford. More recently concern has turned to middle-income families hit by high mortgage interest rates. In reality the situation is a good deal more complex than any of these stereotypes implies.

Our survey has shown that age, numbers of children and income all related to a household's risk of debt and any combination of two from these three debt-inducing factors raised the risk of debt to a very high level.

We found little evidence to support the view that 'consumerism' was primarily responsible for debt. It seemed that low income led to indebtedness through the week-to-week budgeting problems it caused, rather than because poor people persisted in buying consumer goods they could not afford. People who were heavy credit users had an increased risk of debt, but the number of credit commitments made much more difference to the poor than to the rich.

Similarly the style of budgeting was important at all income levels, but had its greatest effect among low-income families. Even so, people who budgeted cautiously on a small income had more debts than those with plenty of money who adopted an easygoing approach.

Finally we have found a link between debt and the priority people assign to keeping up with their payments. In this case there was a strong inter-relationship with age, but it was not clear whether this was a generation or a life-cycle effect. Attitudes made a difference to the risk of debt at every income level but, again, it was among the poorest households that this factor was most important.

In other words, people get into debt for any number of reasons: poverty, changes in circumstances, poor money management, over-commitment and even deliberate non-payment all have a part to play and also interact with one another. Money management clearly has a far greater effect in poor families than in those with more money to spend. Some commitments which now seem impossible to maintain might have appeared perfectly rational at the time they were taken out; the problem might have been caused by a rise in interest rates, breakdown of a marriage, or redundancy.

If we are to begin to tackle the problem of debt then we must look beyond stereotypes. Many people get into financial difficulties through no fault of their own. They may be struggling to make ends meet on a weekly income that many would not think twice about spending on a meal in a restaurant. They may have budgeted carefully and taken on modest commitments and then experienced an unexpected drop in income.

More than 10 per cent of households experience debt in the course of a year. But there is still a great deal of stigma attached to debt. Stereotypes which stress individual inadequacy reinforce the stigma and cause unnecessary hardship. Many people struggle with impossible financial situations rather than contact their creditor to arrange a way of tackling the problem, or seek advice from one of the few independent money advice services. Most people who have their homes repossessed neither contact the court nor appear at the hearing. District Judges have powers to avoid repossession which they are unable to use if the defendant does not attend the court.

Household incomes

Much of the analysis in this report has been concerned with the relationship between credit, debt and household incomes. We found that poorer people spent rather less on their household commitments than richer households, but they used up a far higher proportion of their resources in meeting these basic needs. Indeed, households with an income below £100 per week appeared to have nothing left at all after paying for their housing, household services, minimum personal needs and credit repayment commitments. Not surprisingly, a very high proportion of all household debts were reported by respondents at the bottom of the income scale.

Taking one year with another, the 1980s was a period of rising incomes for many people, and of rapid increase for some. One would expect such a trend in incomes to be associated with increased use of credit, especially after the relaxation of so many controls on lending. As long as the incomes went on rising, there would be no fear that the credit could not be repaid, and for many people this has been true. But incomes have not been rising for everyone: the number of families depending on social security has increased, and their benefits have been held at the same real value throughout the 1980s; the transfer from direct to indirect taxation has also affected their spending power.

People with low incomes used significantly less credit than those with more money to spend, though their repayment commitments represent a larger proportion of their available income. Poorer households using commercial credit facilities had a high risk of falling into debt. But at the bottom of the income distribution, household debts were much more common than consumer debt, because the use of consumer credit was relatively low.

It is clear that low incomes are one of the most important factors contributing to the extent of debt. Features of the market for housing, fuel and consumer credit are also important factors, which will be discussed later in this chapter. But it is also relevant to look more closely at the policies affecting the resources with which households enter those markets.

This survey was not needed to show that households with very low incomes faced money problems and hardship – that was already clear. The evidence in this report will encourage those who have argued that social security rates are too low, and that claimants are in poverty; and it should persuade those who have argued that benefits are already adequate to think again. To a certain extent the argument is about scale rather than absolutes. It can be argued in principle that if the risk of debt is directly related to levels of income, raising the income of the poorest would reduce the extent of debt. The kind of increase in benefit rates which might possibly be considered – £5 or £10 per week – would help, but it would not eliminate the problem.

Pensioners

Lack of income is evidently not a complete explanation, on its own, for the extent of debt. Pensioners were very rarely in arrears, even though the great majority of them have a standard of living below the national average. It is true that pensions and other social security benefits for retired people are a little higher than those available to other types of claimant, but the difference is not large enough to explain their low level of debt. An alternative explanation lies in the stability of pensioners' incomes. They have known for many years that they could expect a reduction in their income around their 60th or 65th birthday; they know for certain that their income will not increase in the future. A related explanation lies in their lifestyle. Pensioners are at a time in their life when they may be moving to a smaller home and discarding rather than replacing possessions. As a consequence the strains on their budget will be reduced. We have also seen that older people adopt attitudes against borrowing and place a high priority on payments. All of these factors would reduce retired people's propensity to borrow, or to fall behind with their household commitments.

Unemployment

The number of people without work was in the millions throughout the 1980s, compared with hundreds of thousands in the previous decade. The trend was downwards at the time of our survey, but has turned up again since then. Unemployed people have been affected more severely than any other group by changes in social security benefits in recent years: many may be worse off now than they were in 1979.[1]

This is not the place for a discussion of the cause of unemployment, or of possible solutions.[2] But it is clear that it has serious consequences in terms of debt in three main ways. Sudden loss of earnings, through redundancy, creates immediate pressures on the commitments that had been entered into during a time of prosperity. Second, a substantial proportion of unemployed people have irregular job histories with frequent moves between low paid jobs and unemployment. Others suffer a sustained period of unemployment and low incomes. It is difficult to work out whether sudden, intermittent or long-term unemployment would be more likely to cause indebtedness – and in practice the survey showed that all three groups suffered to a similar extent.

Lone parents

Another group of people on low incomes has expanded rapidly. In 1980 there were about 800,000 one-parent families; the latest estimate is 1.2 million. Many lone parents have always had to rely on the social security system for a minimum income, but the proportion on benefit has been growing too. New measures to increase absent fathers' maintenance contributions, to be introduced in 1992, will help a small proportion of them to increase their incomes above the income support line, but the great majority, remaining on benefit, will be no better off.

The combination of low income with family responsibilities makes lone parents the population group at greatest risk of debt, alongside unemployed families with children.

Families with children

People with children are not especially likely to use consumer credit, compared with others in their twenties, thirties and forties; but those are the decades when people are most likely to borrow, and families with children are as heavily committed as anyone else. They were, however, much more likely to be in debt than others of the same age.

One of the most important conclusions of the analysis is that neither low income (on its own), nor children (on their own), nor heavy credit commitments (on their own) was strongly associated with indebtedness. Households in debt tended to have two or three of these characteristics at the same time. It was low-income families with children who were most at risk; and this risk was higher if they used consumer credit as well as the usual household commitments.

Earlier evidence about the extent of debt among benefit claimants with children was one of the reasons why the government has adopted low income families as a priority group since 1985. There has been some argument about how effective this priority has proved in practice. On the one hand, the family premium was introduced in 1988, and benefit rates for families with children were increased in 1989 and 1990. On the other hand, this group were the main losers from the abolition of single payments.[3] And local taxes and water rates have increased more rapidly than the benefit system had allowed for. But at least families with children have been protected from the cuts in benefit which have affected unemployed people without children.

Although the very poorest families have the highest rate of debt, it is clear that income and family size are also implicated in arrears across a wide range of households with moderate incomes. This is partly because many mothers either give up paid work, or go part time, during the period when they are also responsible for children. While mothers' participation in the labour market has been increasing for many years, it remains true that family responsibilities often lead to an absolute fall in income. The children themselves add to household costs, at every level of income. The results of the survey clearly show the impact of these two factors on the extent of debt among families with children.

Part of the government's priority for low-income families has taken the form of family credit, a means-tested benefit for low-paid workers with children set at a higher rate than the previous family income supplement. This has benefited a number of families, especially lone parents, who would otherwise have found themselves little better off in work than on benefit. But its effects have been counteracted by the stagnation of wage levels in semi- and unskilled occupations. Families with incomes just above the family credit level have been hit by the attrition of the real value of child benefit between 1985 and 1990. Both of these trends have whittled away at the resources available to the majority of families with below-average incomes.

Household bills

Successive governments have pursued a policy of encouraging greater home ownership, while reducing the role of local authorities in the direct provision of housing. At the same time, there has been a move towards charging 'economic rents' by both local authorities and housing associations. Low-income households are protected from rent increases by the housing benefit system, but a tightening of eligibility criteria has reduced the number who now qualify for help. There was always a risk that these policies might lead to an increase in housing debt, as people with moderate incomes took on mortgages and poor tenants faced rising rents.

Unanticipated expenditure, bills that are larger than expected, can disrupt even the most well-planned family budget. Their effects in low-income families can be sufficient to cause real hardship and debt. Few poor families can afford to put money by for such expenses; they either borrow or let other bills mount up when the need arises. 'Robbing Peter to pay Paul' is, for many, a way of life.

Borrowing can never be a long-term solution for making ends meet, whether it be from family, the social fund or commercial lenders. We look later at other solutions to spreading the expense of bills.

Mortgages

Over the ten years from 1979 to 1989 the proportion of households owning their home grew from a half to two-thirds, while the proportion of council tenants fell from a third to a quarter. In part this has been a result of incentive schemes such as the Right to Buy, which has allowed more than a million council tenants to buy their home at a substantial discount.

Critics of government housing policy argue that young people now have little choice but to buy, given the decline in council house building and the sale of a fifth of the housing stock to sitting council tenants. As a consequence, many people may have been encouraged to buy who could not really afford to do so. Their risk of mortgage arrears is increased because, unlike tenants, home owners with low-paid jobs do not qualify for help with housing costs. Only those who are unemployed and receive income support can get the interest paid on their mortgage. This anomaly could be overcome if home owners were entitled to housing benefit on the same basis as tenants. The Joseph Rowntree Foundation has estimated the cost of doing this at £275 million.[4]

The Right to Buy policy itself does not seem to have encouraged families to take on a commitment that they could not afford. If anything, households who had bought their council homes had a lower rate of mortgage arrears than other home buyers and a good deal lower than first time buyers who bought in the open market. This is hardly surprising given the discounts that they received and the characteristics of the households that exercised the right to buy their home. In the main they were couples whose families were grown up and leaving home. Their incomes were a good deal higher and more secure than other tenants. In other words, they tended to be people who had a lower than average risk of debt.

Our findings also suggested that, before the rapid increase in interest rates, mortgage arrears were much less of a problem than rent arrears. Even when income, type of family and other characteristics are allowed for, home buyers were much less likely to default on their housing costs than were tenants.

When we carried out our survey mortgage interest rates had only just begun to rise and house prices had yet to fall. Since then, the number of families with mortgage arrears has risen to about one in twelve of borrowers.

There can be little doubt that the level of mortgage repayments plays a large part in determining mortgage arrears. This relationship is not entirely straightforward since there have been other periods of high interest rates when arrears were nothing like as high as they are at present. What is different now is the stagnation in the housing market coupled with declining house prices and rising unemployment. In earlier periods of high interest rates home owners could trade down to a cheaper home and either avoid getting into debt or use some of the equity released to repay any arrears they had built up. At the present time many home owners are finding it difficult if not impossible to sell. A mortgage rescue scheme would help tackle the problem. Typically such schemes involve part purchase of homes by a council or housing association, which would then charge a low rent. The owner would retain the share of the property not mortgaged. At the time of writing (December 1991) the government is discussing mortgage rescue schemes with the Council of Mortgage Lenders.

It has been suggested by some commentators that we should return to some form of control on mortgage lending: a ceiling on the percentage of house price that can be borrowed or a ceiling on the earnings to loan ratio. Our findings suggest that, while either of these suggestions would help to contain mortgage arrears, the calculation needs to be similar to that used to assess housing benefit entitlement and take into account both level of income and family composition.

Unlike consumer credit institutions, mortgage lenders have not, traditionally, used either credit referencing or credit scoring techniques to screen their customers. There are signs that this is now changing. A register of mortgage default is being established and most mortgage lenders are now developing credit scoring systems to assess the risk associated with lending to a particular household. Both are welcome developments. Credit scoring for mortgages could well include not only a risk assessment of mortgage applicants but a calculation of the amount that they could afford to borrow. Given these developments and the costly lesson lenders have already learnt, it seems likely that they will inevitably be more cautious in future even without controls on mortgage lending.

Even with careful screening of borrowers, there will always be some who experience an unexpected drop in income at a later date. Nearly a half of the people we interviewed who had a problem mortgage debt gave a drop in income as the reason for their arrears. This was far higher than for any other type of debt. Mortgage protection plans are increasingly being offered to borrowers which will cover their mortgage repayments for many of the events that can cause an unexpected drop in income: redundancy, sickness and disability. As we experience the second recession in a decade, there is a strong case for these to be even more widely available.

Rents

The factors associated with rent arrears were far from straightforward. Our analysis suggests that there are three groups of factors that play a part: characteristics of tenants; central government housing policy; and the policies and practices of landlords.

As better-off council tenants have taken the opportunity to buy their homes, the remaining tenants include a much higher proportion of low-income households, families with three or more children, lone parents and households headed by an unemployed person, all of whom have a high risk of debt. This makes it especially important that local authorities and housing associations should take steps both to prevent arrears occurring in the first place and to ensure that swift action is taken once a tenant has defaulted.

As in the 1981 survey of rent arrears, carried out by the Department of the Environment,[5] we found that different methods of rent collection had widely different levels of arrears. More worrying is the fact that fewer tenants now have their rent collected, the method least associated with rent arrears; while many more use the Giro system which is related to very high levels of arrears. For security reasons, it is unlikely that landlords will return to the use of rent collectors. There are, however, other options open to them that have rent arrears levels that are significantly lower than the Giro system. Standing orders and direct debit had an arrears level about a third of that of the Giro system and only marginally higher than rent collectors. About a half of tenants had a current account, yet only one in ten paid their rent by standing order or direct debit. More could be done to encourage tenants to set up such arrangements where they are in a position to do so. Local authorities might also help credit unions to develop bill-paying services for those tenants without current accounts.

It was also clear that swift action by landlords helps to stop arrears mounting further. It is commonly said that local authorities encourage rent arrears by being too easy-going. In fact, compared with other creditors, including mortgage lenders, landlords were more inclined to take a firm line when people got into arrears. They were also especially likely to suggest ways that the arrears might be repaid. Local differences in arrears levels suggest that some landlords are more lenient than others, so there may be further scope for tightening things up. On the whole, though, they are doing rather better than some commentators would have us believe. Landlords are always likely to have a higher level of default than mortgage lenders because so many tenants have low incomes and because they cannot sell up to pay off debts.

The survey suggested that, among tenants with rent to pay, higher levels of rent were associated with a greater risk of arrears. The increase in net rents over the past decade may, therefore, be implicated in the growth of debt.

Housing benefit is designed to ensure that low-income families can afford their rent. The high levels of rent arrears suggest that the taper by which housing benefit is withdrawn may be too steep.

One of the difficulties in the way of a more generous level of rent rebates and allowances is that the present mechanism for calculating benefit (the 'fixed taper') could have a potentially damaging effect on the housing market. But alternative mechanisms have been proposed (a 'dual taper', a 'proportional taper' or a variable earnings disregard) which would limit that effect.[6]

Since the introduction of housing benefit, council tenants claiming supplementary benefit/income support have had their rents rebated at source instead of receiving their rent money as part of their cash income. This might have been expected to reduce the number of tenants with rent arrears. In fact we found tenants on income support who nevertheless had rent debts. Some will have started claiming benefit after they had got into arrears; others found administrative problems with benefit payments which had caused their arrears.

A significant number of tenants attributed their rent arrears to problems arising from the housing benefit system. We carried out our survey about eighteen months after there had been substantial changes to housing benefit administration and many local authorities faced problems setting up systems to handle the changes within the timescale required. As a consequence there were delays in processing claims and incorrect assessments leading to the over-payment of benefit to some claimants. We may have been picking up the longer-term effects of this transition period, but local authorities should be aware of the extent to which benefit administration may be precipitating families into rent arrears.

Local taxes

Council tenants on income support are now expected to make separate payments for their water rates and 20 per cent of local taxes; previously most of them had been paying for these with their rent. A completely new budgeting problem was therefore introduced.

The domestic rates were replaced by the community charge in 1989 in Scotland, followed a year later in England and Wales. There is whole sequence of reasons why the poll tax bore more heavily on poor households than its predecessor: because of the flat rate, coupled with the 20 per cent minimum payment; because the level of poll tax turned out to be higher than had been assumed when basic benefit rates were calculated; and because councils levying the highest charges tended to have lower income populations. Even the poll tax reduction of £140 introduced in the 1991 budget and paid for by increased VAT, may hit the poorest families. Those paying 20 per cent of their poll tax will gain only £28; but they would expect to spend about £60 per year in additional VAT.[7]

The survey was able to compare arrears of the poll tax in Scotland with the domestic rates still in force, at that time, in England and Wales. A very high proportion of Scots were in arrears with their community charge. A large number of them had either not paid for administrative reasons or were deliberately withholding payment. The political unpopularity of the tax led many people to withhold payment on grounds of principle, and this must have affected the determination to pay of those whose difficulty was financial. There was a similar increase in the number of debtors when the community charge was introduced in England and Wales a year later.

Fuel bills

Although only 3 per cent of fuel commitments had caused a problem, electricity and gas bills represented a high proportion of all debts, especially among low-income families. Half of the poorest households are billed for their gas and electricity quarterly. In the past the fuel boards were reluctant to instal prepayment meters because of the security risks. Meters were often broken into and staff who emptied the meters were judged to be at risk. As a consequence, the proportion of customers with prepayment meters fell considerably over the 1980s. The electricity companies now have an electronic token meter. British Gas are in the process of developing one and, meantime, are using a mechanical token meter. Problems over the supply of these new meters have restricted their availability. We found only a quarter of the poorest families paying for their fuel in this way. Meters are frequently offered only after a family has got into arrears and as an alternative to disconnection. Fuel boards should clearly be offering low-income families pay-as-you-go facilities as a matter of course.

Using social security to aid budgeting

While the total income available to low-paid workers and unemployed people is clearly the most important influence on their ability to budget, it is worth considering how far the design and administrative arrangements of the social security system might be adapted to assist people to pay lump sum bills out of a small weekly income.

Remember that most of the debts faced by low-income households were for household commitments; and that a significant proportion of their consumer credit arrangements were to pay bills, repay debts, to make ends meet or to buy something in an emergency. It is sometimes argued that help with budgeting would merely enable people to cope with their poverty, rather than solve it. An alternative argument is that people would prefer to cope with their poverty than get into debt. One suggestion is that the social security system might perform some of the services for the poor that banks provide for middle- and upper-income people.

Most budgetary assistance is associated with income support, the means-tested benefit which aims to provide the safety net of the social security system.

- *Direct deductions* Claimants who have fallen behind with their rent, electricity or gas can have payments of arrears and/or current commitments deducted from their benefit at source and paid direct to their creditor. Although this reduces available weekly income even lower than basic benefit rates, the signs are that those affected are glad to be relieved of anxiety about these debts.
- *Voluntary savings* Until 1988 claimants who were having difficulty budgeting were allowed to ask for part of their benefit to be withheld each week, to be drawn upon when a bill arrived or a need arose. The scheme was little used, possibly because claimants had to plead their inability to budget before joining, but it was popular among those who did use it.
- *Grants for one-off needs* Until 1988 weekly benefit was intended to meet regular needs, while lump-sum grants were available to meet 'special' expenses. Many claimants, especially families with children, found these grants a useful method of supplementing their basic benefit when difficulties arose. The difficulty lay in drawing a line between the regular needs covered by weekly benefit and the special expenses eligible for grants, when millions of claimants faced the 'routine' problems of poverty. Grants were offered, and later withdrawn, first for fuel bills, then for children's clothing, then for furniture and furnishings. Widely available grants were abolished in 1988; 'community care grants' are offered in a much more narrowly-defined set of circumstances.
- *Budgeting loans* Since 1988 loans have been available to help some claimants with ordinary but irregular expenses. The policy has been extremely controversial, largely because the scheme was introduced as a way of reducing expenditure on grants. The objection is that loan repayments push claimants' available income below the 'poverty line' implicit in the basic benefit rates. The argument in favour is that poor people need credit, and would prefer an interest-free advance. The issues are examined in the section on social loans, later in this chapter.
- *'Bonuses'* A suggestion which has found some favour both with commentators and with claimants themselves is that people should be paid additional benefit once every six months. Knowing that such a lump sum was on its way could make all the difference when an irregular expense arose. It has been estimated that an extra week's benefit paid every six months would cost about £500 million per year.

Current accounts

Families with current accounts can set up direct debit or standing order arrangements which enable them to spread the costs of household bills evenly across the year. Those with an overdraft facility can meet their bills when they are due even if they have insufficient money at the time. One in five families, however, had no current account. Most of these were on low incomes, so that half of non-pensioner households with weekly incomes below £100 had no account. Only one in ten of them had a current account with an overdraft facility. Two-thirds of them received their income weekly and managed their family budget by the week. For these families bill-paying is especially difficult. They can, of course, use the Giro system to make payments. But without a bank account the charges are high. Girobank, through post offices, charges the least (70p per transaction); most banks charge about £2 a transaction.

In some countries, all benefits have to be paid into bank or post office accounts. The requirement to open and operate such an account might make a difference to poor people's budgeting arrangements. The privatisation of the Girobank means that such a system would be less easy to set up in Britain than it has been elsewhere. On the other hand, banks and building societies are developing sophisticated computer systems that will enable them to monitor their customers' accounts much more closely. This should have the effect of widening the availability of both current accounts and overdraft facilities.

Bill-paying services

Even so, it is unlikely that there would be universal access to a current account. Another possible solution is to develop bill-paying services. To a limited extent these exist already. There are a small number of commercial services licensed as deposit takers under the Banking Act 1979. One of the largest home budgeting companies operates primarily in the Midlands, but has some outlets in the North as well. Customers usually make regular weekly payments direct to a collector, and in turn most of their major commitments are met from the account. Charges tend to be on a sliding scale according to the size of the payments made, but are normally in the region of 1.5 to 2.5 per cent.

Problems can, however, arise when the account is in arrears, since the company may suspend payment on any liability without reference to the customer. Indeed we interviewed people who had got into debt on their commitments whilst believing them to be covered by a bill-paying company.

Bill-paying companies also offer loans, at APRs ranging from 45 to 350 per cent, and payments on these are taken directly from the customers' account, assuming priority over other liabilities. Linking loans to a bill-paying service in this way is also unlikely to discourage borrowing to pay bills. On the contrary, there are financial advantages to companies to *encourage* people to borrow.

In both Northern Ireland and the Irish Republic, bill-paying services are commonly offered by credit unions. Where such services exist in the Britain they tend to be through workplace unions and, therefore, to serve the needs of middle- rather than low-income families. Birmingham Settlement, which pioneered money advice services, hopes to offer a similar service to poor families in the Midlands. This innovatory scheme deserves careful monitoring to discover how low-cost bill-paying facilities can be offered to poor families throughout the country.

Consumer credit

The volume of credit outstanding more than doubled over the past decade and more than three-quarters of households have one or more credit facilities. Many argue that things have gone too far and that we are living well beyond our means; they call for a curb on lending. Others put a moral case, arguing that all credit is usury, causes misery and should be severely curtailed if not banned outright.

There may be a case to be made for credit controls on macroeconomic grounds, but as far as individual households are concerned the great majority use credit without getting into repayment difficulties. Credit enables young families to spread the cost of setting up a home over a number of years and, in effect, to smooth out their lifetime earnings. It is an irony of life that our earning capacity is at its highest when we may least need the income; in the middle years when we have established our home and brought up our family. When we first set up home and start a family earnings are a good deal lower.

At the same time, it has to be acknowledged that heavy credit use is associated with higher risks of debt. While it may not be necessary to implement draconian curbs on lending, it is clearly important that we address ways of encouraging both responsible lending by the credit industry on the one hand and responsible borrowing by consumers on the other.

Credit marketing

There is a prevailing belief that credit marketing has become too aggressive. It is felt that direct mail advertising encourages people to take on more credit than they need; that advertisements fail to give sufficient information so that consumers borrow more than they can afford to repay and that 'instant credit' encourages both impulse buying and ill-advised use of credit.

Only a minority of the people we interviewed had selected a source of credit as a result of direct mail advertising and those who had done so had only an average risk of default. At the same time, we discovered that attitudes towards credit had become more negative since 1979. The government will be making regulations requiring credit circulars to advise consumers that they can register their wish not to receive further direct mail.[8] This seems an appropriate response to the situation. Those who do not want to receive details of consumer credit products are unlikely to become customers and there seems to be little commercial advantage in mailing to them.

There is clear evidence that consumers need more information both to assess the level of credit commitments they can afford and to judge value for money. Earlier studies have shown that, although APR is a good way of enabling different forms of credit to be compared, few consumers understood how it was calculated. Most judged affordability in terms of the size of the repayments. In fact half the people we interviewed did not know the level of interest that they were paying, and these had an above average risk of default. People who had taken out one-off credit agreements in response to a newspaper advertisement also had a very high risk of default. We would, therefore, support the government's proposal to issue regulations requiring all credit advertisements which include any information about price to give not only the APR but also the frequency, number and amount of repayments as well as the total amount payable under the agreement. This could be further strengthened by requiring creditors to give similar information to all applicants.

We also found that just over a third of people who had defaulted on their one-off credit commitments had anticipated that it would be difficult to make the repayments when they had signed the agreement. This lends weight to the government's planned regulation requiring both credit advertisements and credit agreements to carry a health warning advising potential borrowers not to enter a credit agreement unless they are sure that they can afford the repayments.

The area of greatest public concern is, however, the marketing of 'instant credit'. In practice most people are screened in some way for the credit they obtain. There remains, however, a concern that consumer goods and credit are marketed alongside one another. Not only can retailers increase their sales by offering credit, but because they derive further profit by selling credit they will be tempted to encourage customers to borrow rather than pay cash. The situation is made worse when retail sales staff receive commission for both the goods *and* the credit they have sold. In fact we found that most people used credit for planned rather than impulse purchases. Only a minority bought on the spur of the moment, but these people had double the average risk of default. One solution to this problem, and the one being pursued by government, is to amend the Consumer Credit Act 1974 to give consumers a 'cooling-off period' during which they can cancel credit agreements that have been signed on impulse. On the face of it this is an attractive proposition, but it may be more difficult to put into practice. A more radical approach would be to find out if there are financial incentives for retail sales staff to encourage customers to take out credit and to see if they need to be controlled.

Secured lending

There is also a continuing concern about the need to protect consumers who take out secured loans, without understanding that they risk losing their home should they default on their payments. Such commitments are a relatively small part of the overall credit market. During 1989, 4 per cent of households had extended their mortgages and 2 per cent had taken out other loans secured against their home. Of particular interest are secured loans to consolidate existing commitments, since the risk of default on these loans was considerably above average. Our research suggests that about 200,000 households were risking their home in this way.

Provided that borrowers understand the risk that they are taking, such loans offer borrowers who have heavy credit commitments a way of reducing their level of repayment. They are, however, a very vulnerable group who often have no other way of coping with their situation. They often ignore or fail to understand the danger they run of having their home repossessed. Most were attracted to a secured loan by newspaper advertisements, which are now required to carry a plain English warning of this risk. The government intends to introduce regulations requiring a similar warning to be included in the signature box of secured lending agreements.

Much of the sales pressure to take out secured consolidation loans comes from brokers who receive commission for each loan sold. In 1987 the National Consumer Council drew attention to the dangers of this practice and called for careful monitoring to identify irresponsible behaviour by brokers. This is an area that still requires further investigation.

Secured loans under £15,000 made for purposes other than house purchase are generally covered by the Consumer Credit Act 1974 and the regulations made under the Act. Our evidence suggests that about one eighth of secured loans were for more than £15,000, putting them outside the terms of the Act. The upper limit under the Consumer Credit Act needs to be high enough to cover problem loans.

Credit granting

The nub of responsible lending, however, lies not with marketing but with the credit-granting process. The ease with which checks of credit-worthiness can be made lead many consumers to believe that they have not been checked at all. In some instances this may be true, but for the most part checks *are* made.

Most lenders now refer to the registers maintained by one or more of the credit reference agencies, in some cases by direct electronic link to the agency's files. These contain details of credit commitments taken out both by the applicant and anyone who has lived at the applicant's address in the last six years, including whether all repayments were made on time and details of any default. They also include details of any county court judgments in the last six years that have been recorded against the address. The main credit reference agencies also provide an optional service, which monitors current consumer credit accounts. Use of this is restricted to subscribing companies who submit regular updates of their customer accounts, including the date, period and amount of the loan, the balance outstanding and the payment history for the past twelve months.

As they stand at present, then, the registers rely heavily on information about the past behaviour of applicants. More weight should be given to their capacity to repay, including the total amount already owed in relation to their income. To do this, however, would require three things. First, all lenders would need to provide current credit account information to the credit reference agencies, rather than for the scheme to be optional as at present. Secondly, registers would need to include income details. Finally, borrowers should be given the option of not allowing the information to go forward, but with the understanding that this may affect the outcome of their application.

Although lenders need accurate and detailed information about potential borrowers, there is understandable concern about privacy of personal financial information. The Data Protection Registrar, in particular, has taken a firm line on the use of third-party information in assessing credit-worthiness. The Registrar's concern is not whether third-party information helps responsible lending, but that it contravenes the legislation on data protection because the information is used unfairly. Our analysis largely supports this view. It suggests that there is a fairly clear association between the repayment records of husbands and wives, but there was no evidence of a link between members of households other than husbands and wives.[9] In 1990, the Registrar initiated legal action against the main credit reference agencies and the resulting tribunals have partly upheld his case. From January 1993 credit reference agencies will not be permitted to use information about a third party with a different surname in assessing an applicant's application for credit unless they know that they are part of the same household. The tribunals have ruled that it should be permissible to use information about other people with the same surname.

The heavy reliance on credit references has been diminished by the development of more sophisticated methods of risk assessment. They now form one part of a more complex system including techniques of application scoring, which look at the characteristics of an applicant and assess whether, on the basis of past experience of other borrowers like them, they are likely to be a good or a bad risk. There can be little doubt such credit scoring has allowed lenders to lend to a wider range of people while keeping risks under control.

Interesting developments are also taking place in the area of behavioural scoring. Banks and building societies, in particular, are able to take advantage of developments in this area. Through the constant monitoring of both current and credit accounts they are able to adjust the amount of credit that they offer each individual. So creditors are able to lend small amounts of money to people who score as a bad risk, many of whom will not default.

The amount lent can either be increased or cut off immediately depending on the borrower's repayment record. This should have the effect of extending mainstream lending to a larger number of high risk families who have previously been denied access. At the same time they will have access to cheaper sources of credit. The facility to monitor accounts means that high-risk borrowers can be given low initial credit limits that can be increased gradually.

Costs of credit

The final area of concern centres on the costs of credit and, in particular, the high rates of interest charged to low-income and high-risk borrowers. We found many poor families borrowing to pay their bills. The lucky ones had families they could turn to; those less fortunate had to resort to borrowing from commercial lenders. As we have seen, these loans can be expensive even from reputable lenders: small advances to be repaid by weekly collection normally cost the equivalent of more than 100 per cent per annum. We identified a handful of loans in access of 1,000 per cent APR. The loan may well help with the immediate financial problem, but often at the risk of creating a worse situation in the long term. We interviewed families who had borrowed so often to make ends meet that repaying the loans ensured that they could not pay the next bill without borrowing further.

In parts of the United States and Europe interest rates are regulated, with a ceiling set for the interest that can be charged for various types of lending. This approach has never found favour with either regulators or consumer organisations in this country. Deciding on a limit that is practicable poses many problems. The other arguments against interest-rate ceilings are that they would encourage lenders to set rates at or near the limit when they could be lower and they would result in a reduction in lending to the most disadvantaged borrowers, pushing them out of the legitimate credit market. Equally it is clear that the current protection, which allows agreements that are 'extortionate' to be reopened by the courts is not tackling the problem. As we have seen, many borrowers are unaware of the interest rate they are paying and do not understand APR. Court staff, similarly, have little knowledge of prevailing interest rates for different types of credit. Borrowers are also understandably reluctant to take legal action against lenders. People generally end up paying high interest rates not through choice but because they have no other option open to them. They are unlikely to jeopardise the only source of lending they have at their disposal.

The debate about interest-rate ceilings was reopened by a consultative document produced by the Office of Fair Trading.[10] In their report the OFT conclude that 'the extortionate credit bargain provisions of the Act have not dealt effectively with the problems to which they were addressed'. Their proposals are designed to improve the working of the Act rather than set specific ceilings for interest rates. If ceilings are not to be adopted then we at least need guidance on the levels of interest that are unacceptable. These will clearly vary for different types of credit and will need to take into account the costs that have to be recovered through interest rates as well as the level of risk faced by the lender.

Part of the problem lies in the fact that poor people have a limited range of credit options open to them. Those who are least able to afford high interest rates are the ones who are forced to pay them. Lending to poor and high risk people is expensive and even reputable companies have high costs. To avoid a high level of default they use door-to-door collection methods. They also adopt a flexible approach to repayments so that most credit commitments take longer to be repaid than was originally agreed. It is hard to see how a commercial company could make a profit lending to poor people without taking steps such as these. The solution to cheaper lending for low income families must, therefore, lie outside the commercial credit market.

Social loans

One possibility is the development of credit unions, which have proved an effective means of providing affordable credit in Ireland and elsewhere. Credit unions have, however, been extremely slow to get off the ground in Britain. Those that are most successful tend to be used by middle income families who have a range of other sources of credit open to them.[11] Some local authorities have invested a good deal in trying to get credit unions established in their area, but a more innovative approach seems to be needed to make them more attractive to low-income families. The bill-paying service that is being explored in Birmingham is one such approach and should be monitored in detail.

If innovation is one of the strengths of the voluntary sector then patchy development is its chief drawback. In the longer term the solution almost certainly lies in the development of public institutions which provide credit at costs that could not be offered by commercial organisations. Such institutions exist in other countries; the municipal banks in the Netherlands, for example.[12] To some extent the social fund fulfils this role for families claiming income support. Criticism of the social fund focuses on the fact that interest-free loans are now given where previously claimants would have received a grant; and cash limits mean that, in practice, there are restrictions on the items that loans will be granted for. High repayment levels have also been criticised. In theory, though, it offers a possibility for developing a source of low-interest credit for low-income people. A more serious criticism is the administrative cost of the social fund. Unlike commercial lenders the social fund does not have high costs associated with collecting repayments, but with making the loans in the first place. Because discretion is a labour-intensive process it costs nearly £50 to administer each grant or loan.[13]

To be fair the social fund was, of course, never designed as a credit-granting organisation, but as a way of assisting claimants faced with exceptional needs. If one were designing a source of credit for low-income families then one might design a very different type of organisation. Certainly it would be available not just to people claiming income support but to all households dependent on social security, other than child benefit, for at least part of their income. It would also operate with more generous cash controls, giving loans without staff needing to exercise discretion but charging interest at just above the basic bank rate. Repayment through attachment of benefits would keep costs of collection and default to a minimum. The question remains whether such a scheme could be self-financing or would require subsidy. Also, at the end of the day, credit, even social loans, is no substitute for lack of income.

These and other ideas are currently being followed up by a separate study of the ways that low-income families make ends meet. The Joseph Rowntree Foundation has provided funds for PSI to investigate the needs for a low-cost credit-granting organisation and to identify ways that the need might be met.

Responsible borrowing

Lenders cannot be expected to bear the total responsibility for the way that credit is used. Borrowers, themselves, must share the responsibility.

In the United States, most people have a clear idea of their credit-worthiness and regulate their use of credit accordingly. The concept is poorly developed in this country, perhaps because wide-spread credit use has developed here more recently.

The Office of Fair Trading has a commendable track record in the area of consumer information and education on the use of credit. Through its publications and cooperation with the media it has played an important role in encouraging responsible borrowing. Through their work it is possible to identify areas where efforts need to be concentrated.

Consumers need to be encouraged to shop around for the cheapest source of credit, yet, as we have seen, many are unaware of the costs of using credit. People are more interested in whether they can afford the regular repayments than with the total cost of borrowing or whether they could borrow more cheaply from a different lender. Indeed, it is probably fair to say that many people do not think of borrowing as buying money. The proposed regulation requiring credit advertisements to include the total amount repayable on agreements will help potential borrowers to compare the total costs of using different sources of credit.

The National Consumer Council has suggested that the Office of Fair Trading might collect and publicise the range of APRs for different types of credit – short-term, long-term and secured loans – and publicise these through newspapers. This is an attractive suggestion which would not cost much.[14]

Consumers also need to be educated on how to avoid the high pressure sales techniques used by some creditors. If we can recognise *how* pressure is being applied we will be better placed to resist it.

Responsible borrowing is, however, best seen in the wider context of money management. Managing a household budget for the first time is one of the most challenging things that most of us have to face. We receive little or no guidance in advance and most of us learn on the job. What is more we learn at a time in our life when our budget is under the greatest strain. There can be little doubt from our survey that careful money-managers who plan their expenditure have less need to borrow and have a far lower risk of getting into debt than those who spend as they go.

There has been a number of initiatives related to money management over the past ten years involving the expenditure of large sums of money, yet there are still calls for more to be done in this area. Perhaps the time has come for a review of the successes and failures of the schemes that have been tried.

■ Arrears and debt

There is no single solution to the problem of debt. We have seen that people fall into arrears with their household and credit commitments for many different reasons; some are circumstances that are outside their control while others they have created for themselves. Tackling the problem involves preventing debts occurring in the first place, swift and responsible debt collection and providing practical help and support for people who have got into debt.

Preventing debt

The old adage that 'prevention is better than cure' applies as much to credit as it does to health. Many of the ways of avoiding debt have already been discussed but are worth restating.

First, it is clear that different methods of payment have widely varying levels of default associated with them. In general the commercial sector has been quicker to recognise this than the public sector. Credit companies lending to low-income people tend to retain control of the payment system; check traders and money lenders use door-to-door collection methods; mail-order companies recruit local people to act as their agents.

In contrast, local authorities have tended to change to rent payment systems that give them less control. Door-to-door rent collection is now rare, and has largely been replaced by Giro payment. Only a half of non-pensioner households with incomes of less than £100 a week pay-as-they-go for their fuel. About half of these low-income households have current accounts but few of them pay their rent on standing order or direct debit or have budget accounts for their fuel bills. Bill-paying services could provide an alternative for those without current accounts.

Secondly there needs to be careful screening of people applying for mortgages or consumer credit. In part the responsibility for this lies with the lender; in part with the borrower. We have seen that lenders are developing improved techniques for screening applicants and have commented that they should take more account of people's existing commitments in relation to their income. At the same time consumers need to be made aware of the costs of credit and the problems of overcommitting themselves.

Even with both responsible borrowing and careful screening there will be people who get into debt because of an unexpected event which leads to a drop in income. This applies particularly to mortgages but also affects other large or long-term credit commitments. Insurance policies are available which will cover credit and mortgage repayments, but not all of them are comprehensive. There is a strong case for borrowers to be offered credit insurance against the main causes of repayment problems – illness and unemployment – at the time they take on a new commitment. The cost of such insurance should be included in the advertised cost of the credit.

The unresolved question is whether insurance cover should be arranged automatically by the lender unless the borrower asks to opt out, or whether it should only be arranged where the borrower has requested it. There are serious objections to any form of inertia selling and it seems unlikely that opt-out schemes will be accepted by the government. On the other hand, an optional scheme is most likely to be used by people who are at greatest risk. If this were so, it would increase the cost of the insurance. Current schemes add about 10 per cent to the costs of credit. Lenders' associations might explore the possibilities of a joint non-profit fund to underwrite credit insurance on an industry-wide basis as one way to keep costs low.

Finally, consumers need to be encouraged to contact their creditors when their financial problems first begin, rather than wait until they have got into arrears. This can be achieved in a number of ways. Many creditors already inform their customers that they are willing to be understanding if financial problems make repayment difficult. This practice should be a matter of routine so that people are told when they first become customers and are reminded periodically afterwards whenever they are billed. At the same time creditors should follow up arrears promptly and not allow them to build up. These steps need to be supported by more general consumer education with the mass media having a large part to play. All too often press stories and radio and television programmes focus on reckless borrowing. Stressing individual inadequacy in this way only reinforces the stigma of debt. There needs to be much greater recognition that many people get into debt for no fault of their own and should feel no shame about their circumstances.

Debt collection

It is in no-one's interest for arrears to be allowed to build up. Both the speed and the nature of the response by creditors are critical in containing arrears. The sooner people in arrears are contacted the more easily the problem can be resolved, since at each stage in the debt recovery process the majority of people contacted repay, or arrange to repay, the money owed. Letters asking about the causes of the difficulty and suggesting ways of repaying are particularly successful. In general we found that creditors who threatened to take further action if they were not repaid were more likely to have the debts cleared immediately than those who suggested repayment arrangements, but this was achieved at the expense of losing contact with a much higher proportion of customers.

It was also noticeable that, while creditors usually chose to communicate in writing, the people who owed money to them preferred more personal forms of contact. As we have seen, most people get into debt for a complex set of reasons which may be easier to explain in person or on the telephone than in writing.

Taken together, these findings suggest that debt recovery is best pursued by a swift response as soon as the problem arises, encouraging customers to telephone or visit the office to discuss their financial difficulties.

Enforcement procedures

The legal system allows creditors to use different ways of recovering their money depending on the type of debt. Some of these require a court order, others do not.

Disconnections The utilities – electricity, gas, water and telephone – may disconnect customers who have not paid, although water companies must get a court order first. Their codes of practice do, however, require them to identify households who are in hardship and to find alternatives to disconnecting them. All the utilities are undergoing substantial changes following their transfer from public into private ownership.

The licences of both British Gas and the electricity supply companies require them to make prepayment meters available to customers who get into arrears. There have been times when the demand for meters has exceeded availability, but that problem seems largely to have been solved. The development of token meters has been accompanied by a fairly dramatic drop in fuel disconnection. In the case of gas, the level of disconnection has now stabilised while electricity disconnections continue to fall. But two concerns remain. Consumer groups expected to see disconnections disappear altogether, yet experience with gas is that they have levelled out chiefly because no contact is made with a proportion of households in arrears. It is not known whether these are people who deliberately withhold payment or whether they include households who should not be disconnected under the terms of the licence. The other concern is the level at which arrears are recovered through prepayment meters. Most households which have meters installed have very low incomes and if rates of arrears recovery are set too high then either they will default on other commitments or else they will voluntarily disconnect themselves.

While meters are a clear solution to fuel disconnection, they are more problematic for water. Until recently this was an academic consideration, partly because the level of disconnection was very low and partly because appropriate meters had not been developed. Until the 1988 social security changes, supplementary benefit claimants had their water rates met in full. They now have to meet the costs out of weekly benefits and charges are projected to rise steeply. In addition, council and housing association tenants usually paid their water charges together with their rent and so were often protected against disconnection. In our survey 70 per cent of council tenants and 55 per cent of housing association tenants did not make separate water payments. These included a high proportion of low-income households, lone parents and people not in work, all of whom had a high risk of debt in general and on water charges in particular. Following privatisation many local authorities and housing associations have discontinued the collection of water charges and more are likely to follow suit. This can only mean that the level of water charge debt will rise. At the same time prepayment water meters are being tested by at least one water authority. There is concern that the installation of meters with high levels of arrears recovery could lead to self-disconnection by poor families and create a public health hazard.

British Telecom has tackled its debt problem somewhat differently. Like credit lenders it now screens potential customers through the use of credit reference agencies. It has also introduced deposits for customers it believes to be a high risk. In general this seems to be an appropriate solution, if public call boxes are generally available for those unable to obtain a phone of their own. A telephone, unlike fuel or water, is not an essential service. It is not, however, entirely without problems. Social services departments are finding that they face problems supplying telephones to people, such as those who are disabled or chronically sick, that they are required to help.

Possession actions Rent and mortgage debts are usually pursued through county court possession actions. With the rapid increase in mortgage debt, the number of mortgage repossessions has risen steeply and attracted a good deal of attention in the media. There are signs, though, that mortgage lenders are increasingly reluctant to repossess during a period of slump in house sales.

Possession cases are heard by district judges, who have a range of discretionary powers they can exercise. They may postpone or suspend a mortgage possession to give the borrower time to pay provided they are satisfied that the arrears will be paid off in a reasonable time. Possession of council homes, in theory at least, should involve a review of the reasons for the arrears and the tenants' financial circumstances. A possession can be suspended if it would cause 'exceptional hardship'. The chief problem is that the majority of defendants fail either to communicate with the court, or to attend the hearing. Yet, on the evidence of our survey, they could well have avoided repossession if they had done so. Clearly this is unsatisfactory and more needs to be done by both creditors and court staff to make defendants aware of the advantages of contacting the court and arranging a way of repaying the money owed. Press coverage of mortgage arrears should also stress that repossession might be avoided by responding to a court summons.

County court default summonses Consumer credit debts, including the repossession of goods bought on hire purchase, are largely enforced through county court summonses. Judgement is usually entered by default; court records show that two-thirds of defendants fail to reply to their summons. Again we found that, of those people who did reply, most made offers of repayment that were acceptable.

The Courts and Legal Services Act 1990 includes some important changes to the present procedure that will be brought into force over the period to 1995. Some of these act to reduce the pressure on courts, others reflect the fact that many people get into debt because they are unable rather than unwilling to pay.

Fewer cases will involve a full court hearing in front of a district judge and there will be more 'paper disposal hearings'. Defendants will send their reply to a summons direct to the creditor with the court getting involved only if agreement cannot be reached. Where there is no agreement about repayment, court staff will make a decision based on written submissions from both defendant and creditor. These decisions will be devolved to senior court officials and money advisers are concerned that the quality of the decision making will be lower than that of district judges. A more positive aspect is that the admission form will now collect much more information about the defendant's financial situation. It has always been a matter for concern that courts set repayment levels without considering the defendant's ability to pay.

The courts will no longer offer a 'banking service' for payments made either before judgement or between judgement and enforcement. Such payments are now made direct to the creditor who is responsible for keeping records of the money paid. Payments after enforcement are still mostly made to the court.

It remains to be seen how these arrangements will work in the long term, but there has been a good deal of initial confusion about payments among both creditors and debtors. Creditors are also complaining about the extra work that they now have to undertake. One possible consequence of the changes is that creditors will avoid using the courts wherever possible and rely instead on debt collectors. This could be a mixed blessing. On the one hand, fewer people will face the trauma of a court summons. On the other, debt collectors could well be a trauma in themselves, and are more likely to want the arrears repaid in full. If this proves so, and fewer debtors are be offered the chance of repaying their arrears in instalments, it will be a retrograde step.

The Act also places further restrictions on the goods that can be seized by bailiffs, effectively limiting them to luxury goods. Bailiffs cannot seize vehicles or tools that are necessary for the defendant's work, nor can they take normal household goods. This should avoid situations where poor people have basic items seized and sold for very little money, leaving them still owing most of the debt they were sued for.

Administration orders The Courts and Legal Services Act will introduce important changes to administration orders, reflecting the fact that most people who get into debt genuinely do not have the means to repay. At present someone who has at least one judgement debt and owes less than £5,000 in total to their creditors can apply to the court for an administration order to cover all their debts. In practice this means the court sets the level of repayment, the debtor makes one regular payment to the court and the court arranges for this to be distributed pro rata to the different creditors.

In future administration orders will be available to many more people as a result of several significant changes.

- The upper limit of indebtedness will be removed so that people owing more than £5,000 can apply. It is not, however, clear whether they will now include mortgages and secured loans.
- There will be no need for someone to have a judgement debt before they can apply for an administration order.
- Applications for administration orders will no longer be limited to debtors or their representatives. Despite the fact that an administration order is the best means of people in multiple debt resolving their situation, few apply for them, chiefly because they are unaware of the procedure. In future creditors or court officials will also be able to apply. This opens up the possibility that court staff will be able to identify people who have serious debt problems from the financial statements included in their admissions and arrange for them to repay all that they owe through an administration order.

Possibly even more significant is that administration orders will last only three years and it is likely that at the end of that time the debt would be wiped off. At present they must usually pay until the debts are cleared. This will offer people who have got into serious difficulties the prospect of being able to start again.

Advice

Clearly, the management of financial affairs is a very complex process for many of the people who get into debt. Not only does it involve negotiation with large bureaucracies but also frequently involves recourse to the law. Few of us have the skills and experience required to handle this alone and we need specialist advice and help.

It is, however, widely accepted that the need for money advice far outstrips the current level of provision. As we have seen, two and a half million households had problem debts in 1989, about half a million of them in arrears to three or more creditors. One in 10 of all debts resulted in a court summons.

Legal aid In theory at least, help can be sought from solicitors through the legal-aid scheme. Advice and assistance can be given under the 'green form' scheme to anyone meeting the financial means test. The Legal Aid Reports show that only 60,000 people with debts were advised in this way in 1990/91. There are a number of reasons for this.

First, few people even know that the 'green form' scheme exists and repeated studies have shown that many are reluctant to consult a lawyer because they are concerned about the likely costs. To a large extent they are right to worry since the means test sets a very low income level for free assistance. For example families with two children and living on two-thirds the average wage would be required to make substantial contributions towards their legal aid costs. For families who are in debt this is clearly out of the question.

There are also restrictions on the help a solicitor can give. Initial advice and assistance is covered by the 'green form' scheme, but most debt cases are excluded from full civil legal aid. So in cases involving court proceedings solicitors can advise their clients but cannot represent them unless they are prepared to do so without payment.

It seems unlikely, given the current government concern to curb legal aid spending, that we shall see solicitors providing the level of service needed to help all those needing advice and help with debt problems.

Money advice services Most people, in both creditor organisations and consumer groups, look instead to independent money advice services to meet the need.

Recent research, for the National Consumer Council, identified 286 organisations offering specialist money advice and assistance for people with debt problems.[15] Together they employed the equivalent of around 270 full-time staff, about a fifth of whom were unpaid volunteers. Most of these worked within generalist advice centres, such as citizens advice bureaux, that provide assistance with a wide range of problems other than debt. There were just six organisations that specialised in money advice.

In our earlier study of money advice services we found that a full-time money adviser can handle only 100-150 multiple debt cases a year.[16] The work is complex and time consuming, involving unravelling some very complicated finances, a great deal of negotiation and letter writing and frequent preparation of cases for court hearings.

If all the 500,000 households we identified as having three or more debts had sought advice this would have required 3,000 full-time money advisers, or more than ten times the number at present. Even a more conservative estimate of 200,000, based on those with current debts they could not repay and who had not sought advice, suggests a shortfall of more than 1,000 advisers.

This extensive shortfall was addressed by a working party that was set up by the Finance Houses Association under the chairmanship of Lord Ezra.[17] One of the main recommendations of their report was that the finance industry had a responsibility to provide funds to extend the money advice network. The Money Advice Trust has been established to take this recommendation into practice. To date the emphasis has been on a voluntary scheme, with creditor organisations being asked to make contributions based on the size of their turnover. The response has been disappointingly slow and the 1991 Consumer Congress called for a statutory levy on the finance industry to meet the costs of money advice.

There can be little doubt that commercial creditors, including the building societies and utilities, should meet part of the costs of advising those who get into debt. Consumer credit problems were most common in households with multiple debts. It was also clear that if people with consumer credit debts go anywhere for help it is to an independent money advice centre. But the credit industry cannot be expected to take on the whole responsibility for money advice. Both local and central government will need to share that responsibility.

As we have seen, the most common debt was for rent, with local authority landlords having the highest level of arrears. It is also clear that the central government policy of high interest rates has caused many households to get into arrears with mortgage and other payments. It is true that many local authorities already fund advice services but it is far from the rule. The restrictions placed on local council spending by the government have led to many of those who have been most sympathetic to the need for independent advice to cut their grants to local advice centres. Such spending is discretionary and in times of financial cutback priority has to be given to meeting statutory obligations. Consequently the provision of advice services in general, and money advice services in particular, has been extremely patchy. In general, provision is best in the inner cities, where a range of different services exist, and worst in rural areas where consumers face a long and expensive round trip to the nearest source of help. The provision in Northern Ireland, outside Belfast, is particularly bad.

This haphazard development means that many people in debt are denied access to sources of help and advice. The case for money advice is now widely accepted, as is the recognition that needs far outstrip current provision. There is also a good deal of evidence that can be used for the strategic planning of service provision. What is lacking is the political will to do so.

One of the real strengths of the development of independent money advice services in the voluntary sector has been innovations in working methods. The time has come, however, for an evaluation of the effectiveness of different approaches so that scarce resources can be used to best effect.

Finally we return to where we started this chapter: to the stigma of debt. Six out of 10 of people with problem debts had sought no help or advice, not even from family or friends. Only a third of debtors had consulted a formal adviser, most often an independent advice agency or a bank manager. Those who *had* sought advice tended to be pleased with the help they received, especially that from advice agencies. So it seems unlikely that people do not seek advice because the services are thought to be unhelpful or incompetent. By far the most common reason, given by two-thirds of those not seeking advice, was a reluctance to discuss the problem with anyone else.

Only by establishing a better and more general understanding of the causes and nature of debt will we begin to overcome this deep-seated problem and move to a position where credit is used beneficially. We hope that our research and this book will contribute to improving that level of understanding.

References

1. A.B. Atkinson and J. Micklewright, 'Turning the screw: benefits for the unemployed 1979-88' in A. Dilnot, and I. Walker (eds), *The Economics of Social Security*, Oxford University Press, 1989

2. See for example M. White, *Against Unemployment*, Policy Studies Institute, 1991

3. R. Berthoud, *Selective Social Security*, Policy Studies Institute,1986

4. *Inquiry into British Housing: Second Report*, Joseph Rowntree Foundation, 1991

5. S. Duncan and K. Kirby, *Preventing Rent Arrears*, HMSO, 1983

6. J. Hills, R. Berthoud and P. Kemp, *The Future of Housing Allowances,* Policy Studies Institute,1989

7. Derived from 'The effects of taxes and benefits on household income 1988', *Economic Trends,* March 1991

8. *Revised Proposals for Legislation on Credit Marketing: a Consultative Document,* Department of Trade and Industry, 1991

9. E. Kempson and R. Berthoud, *Credit Records of People Living at the Same Address,* Policy Studies Institute,1991

10. *Consumer Credit Act 1974: Unjust Credit Transactions,* Office of Fair Trading, 1991.

11. R. Berthoud and T. Hinton, *Credit Unions in the United Kingdom,* Policy Studies Institute,1989

12. S. Tester, *Social Loans in the Netherlands,* Policy Studies Institute,1987

13. R. Berthoud, 'The Social Fund – is it working?' *Policy Studies* Vol 12(1) Spring 1991

14. National Consumer Council, *Credit and Debt: the Consumer Interest,* HMSO, 1990

15. *A Survey of Debt Advice Provision in the UK,* National Consumer Council, 1990

16. T. Hinton and R. Berthoud, *Money Advice Services,* Policy Studies Institute,1988

17. *'Report of the Money Advice Funding Working Party',* Finance Houses Association, 1990

Appendix 1 The survey sample

This report is based on personal interviews in 2,212 households: 1,732 households in Britain and 480 in Northern Ireland. The fieldwork was conducted in the summer and autumn of 1989 by the experienced interviewers of PAS Survey Research Ltd in Britain, and Ulster Marketing Surveys in Northern Ireland.

The sample was selected in three ways, with slight differences between Great Britain and Northern Ireland.

Great Britain

A) A national random sample of addresses from the Post Office Address File. A representative sample of 94 postal sectors was selected, with probability proportionate to number of addresses, from a complete list of all sectors in Britain. The list had been stratified by region, and (within region) by an index of urban/rural. An equal number of addresses was selected in each of the 94 sampling points. Where more than one household was living at an address, both households were included in the sample. There are 844 household interviews in this sample.

B) A second random sample of addresses in the same 94 postal sectors, selected by the same method. This time the interviewer conducted a preliminary screening, and interviewed the household only if it fell into one of the groups known to be at risk of debt: non-pensioners with children, unemployed or on low-pay. There are 602 household interviews in this sample.

C) Random samples from the arrears lists of several creditor organisations:

- a bank (including its credit card subsidiary)
- a building society
- a finance house mainly concerned with revolving credit offered by high street retailers
- a finance house mainly concerned with one-off agreements to finance car purchase and home improvements
- a utility
- seven local authority housing departments

286 Sample C debtors are included in the analysis.

Northern Ireland

A) A random sample of addresses from the Rating Register for Northern Ireland. This is directly equivalent to sample A in Great Britain, except that the selection covered the whole of Northern Ireland, without a preliminary selection of sampling points. There are 386 household interviews from this sample.

There was no sample B in Northern Ireland.

C) Random samples from the arrears lists of two creditor organisations:

- a building society;
- the Northern Ireland Housing Executive.

32 Sample C debtors are analysed in the tables.

D) A random sample of people who had been interviewed for an earlier survey, the Financial Research Survey, and who, within their income group, were heavy users of credit. 62 interviews from this sample are included in the tables.

Interviews

In all samples, the interview covered the income, spending, credit and debt of the 'householder', that is the person who owned or rented the accommodation. Where a householder was married the transactions of both husband and wife were covered. The actual interview was given by the one who was mainly responsible for dealing with money matters; as often as possible both husband and wife were interviewed together.

The survey of 'householders' does not cover those adults who live in someone else's household as 'non-householders' – adult children, other relatives, friends or boarders. In sample A, interviewers were instructed to administer a second questionnaire if they identified a non-householder over 18. 160 of these non-householder interviews were completed. They have not been included in any of the general analysis of the survey, which always refers to householders. The non-householders are, however, compared with householders of similar age and marital status in Chapters 4 and 8.

Response

If a survey of a random sample of the population is to provide reliable estimates, a high proportion of the people originally selected to take part should provide information. If not, there is a risk that those who did take part might be different in some way from those who did not.

The most important samples are A and B, because these provide the benchmark for all the analysis. The results were as follows:

		Samples A and B	
Addresses selected		4924	
minus	not traced/demolished	582	
	ineligible households (sample B)	1341	
plus	extra households	91	
	non-householders	202	
Total potential interviews		3294	100%
minus	no contact	249	8%
	refused interview	925	28%
	other non-interviews/ analysis rejects	145*	4%
Achieved interviews		1975	60%
minus	non-householders	143	
Interviews analysed		1832	

* Estimated from incomplete records

The response rate was 60 per cent of the potential number of interviews. This is less than has been obtained on other surveys, but this was an exceptionally detailed enquiry into people's financial circumstances, and it is not surprising that many were reluctant to take part. Both PAS and UMS went to considerable lengths to obtain as many interviews as possible from people who had not taken part when first approached.

Whatever the explanation, there is a risk that the results of the survey are less accurate than they would have been if a higher response had been achieved.

The effect of non-response on the accuracy of the sample cannot be measured. Checks on the results, however, provide little direct evidence that the sample is seriously biassed; the indications are that refusals to participate were just as common among middle and upper income households as among those with low incomes. Where comparison with other sources is possible the data from this survey have proven to be remarkably consistent. For example, we obtained almost the same measure of the ownership of consumer durables and the numbers of wage earners in households as the Family Expenditure Survey.

The samples (C) selected direct from the records of creditor organisations were more complex, and less successful. A selection of 1043 names and addresses yielded 326 interviews for full analysis. Factors contributing to the loss included:

- *refusals:* either in response to the letter from the creditor announcing the survey, or direct to the interviewer on the doorstep. But overt refusals seemed no more of a problem for sample C than they had been for A and B.

- *removals:* many of the debtors were no longer resident at the address provided by the creditor, and could not be contacted. Previous surveys have identified the same difficulty.
- *no contacts:* a number of other debtors were not contacted by the interviewer after several calls. These may also have moved; or they may have been reluctant to open the door.
- *inconsistency:* about one seventh of the people in this sample did not report any arrears, even though they had been identified as debtors before being selected. There are two possible reasons for this discrepancy: the creditors' records may have been inaccurate (out of date, or based on administrative arrears which their customers did not think of as debts); or some of the people we interviewed may have withheld information about their debts. Either way they have not been included in the analysis at all.

We conclude that this direct method of sampling would not have been satisfactory as the primary source of information about debts and debtors. It was samples A and B which provided the core of the sample. Analysis showed that the composition of Sample C was remarkably similar to the debtors identified within Samples A and B. The direct selection method was, therefore, a successful way of supplementing the sample, though it would have been inadequate on its own.

'Weighting'

The complex sample design was needed to ensure (on the one hand) that the survey provided a representative sample of all households in the United Kingdom and (on the other hand) that we included sufficient numbers of the types of household which were of special interest. The success of the design is indicated by the fact that the tables include a total of 1,072 'problem debts'; it is estimated that the same number of interviews with a straightforward sample of the population would have yielded only 497 'problem debts' for analysis.

It is necessary to readjust the balance of the sample in order to make it correctly representative. This process is known as 'weighting'. The non-technical reader does not need to know how this was done; it is important to know that it was done, so that the biasses built into the sample design have, as far as possible, been ironed out. Weights were calculated:

- to recombine samples A and B to form a single representative sample of British households;
- to adjust sample C to convert it from a sample of debts to a sample of debtors;
- to adjust sample C again to get the correct balance between debts to different types of creditor;

- to combine sample C (GB) with samples A and B to get the correct balance between debtors and non-debtors;
- to combine samples C and D (NI) with sample A to get the correct balance of credit use and debt;
- to restore the correct balance between households in Britain and Northern Ireland.

The principle behind the weighting is that samples A and B, which form a random sample of all households, show us how many debtors there were, and how many owed money to each type of creditor. Sample C allows us to analyse indebtedness in more detail, but does not contribute to the estimate of the incidence of debt. Similarly, Sample D allows us to analyse the patterns of credit use in Northern Ireland in more detail, but does not contribute to the estimates of the level of credit used.

The number of interviews and the weighted total are both about 2,200. Since there are about 22 million households in the United Kingdom it is convenient to think of each unit in the analysis as representing about 10,000 people. This is the basis for the 'grossed up' estimates of, for example, the total number of debts in the United Kingdom.

Appendix 2 Multivariate analysis of credit and debt

In order to contribute to our understanding of the influences on the use of credit and the extent of debt, the data were subjected to multivariate analysis, using the Limdep computer program. The analysis was undertaken by Michael Joyce, on secondment to PSI from the Economics Division of the Bank of England.[1]

Both credit and debt were analysed using a 'probit' equation, which uses characteristics of a household such as age, income, tenure and so on to find the best estimate the probability of a household using credit, or having a debt. The basis for estimation is a maximum likelihood function. The technique is a standard form of econometric analysis where the dependent variable can only take two values (eg yes or no)[2]. In the analysis of credit in Table A1, a variant called 'ordered probit' is used, which takes account of multiple credit use.

The lay reader is not expected to understand the methods underlying the analysis. But Tables A1 and A2 can be read as follows:

- For each variable mentioned in the table, the probability of using credit or having a debt is higher (+) or lower (–) for households with this characteristic than for the remainder of households. The multivariate analysis confirms that this is systematically true, after taking account of the possible influence of all the other variables.
- Where a variable has numeric values (age, income, housing costs etc), the model shows that the probability of credit or of debt consistently rises (+) or falls (–) as the value of the variable increases. Squared or logarithmic terms indicate that the relationship follows a curve rather than a straight line.
- The t-ratio indicates how confident we can be that the observed association did not arise by chance, for a sample of this size. If the t-ratio is greater than 2 (strictly, 1.96), the finding is significant at the 95% level of confidence. T-ratios between 1 and 2 have been included in the tables, but should be treated as no more than indicative.

Consumer credit

The model aims to predict the likelihood of a household using one, two or more 'active' sources of credit during the year. The clear findings from Table A1 are that:

- Use of credit was strongly associated with age. The probability of credit use increased up to the age of about 35, after which it declined slowly.

The shape of the relationship between Age and log(Age) is illustrated in Chapter 4, Chart 4.11.

- Single people, especially men, used less credit than couples.
- The number of credit sources increased with income.
- Households with savings in excess of £1,000 used relatively little credit, all other things being equal.
- Outright owner-occupiers used fewer sources than would have been expected on the basis of their age, income and so on.
- Although several of the variables in the model were significantly associated with the extent of credit use, the equation as a whole was not particularly powerful at explaining the variation between households. The 'Pseudo-R^2' of 0.15 compares unfavourably with the analysis of debt in Table A2.

Debt

The model aims to predict the probability of a household having any problem debt during the year, but takes no account of the number of debts. The clear findings from Table A2 are that:

- The probability of debt fell with age. The squared relationship means that this effect became greater and greater with advancing age.
- Families with children were more likely to have debts than those without.
- The probability of debt fell as income rose. Again, the slope of the curve was steeper at higher levels of income.
- Households with no savings were substantially more likely to report debts than those with any savings. It might be argued that savings are simply the opposite of debt, so that the model is circular. The right hand column of Table A2 recalculates the significance of each of the other variables if savings are left out altogether.
- Householders who had been in employment throughout the past three years had a relatively low probability of debt.
- Tenants, especially council tenants, had more debts than owner-occupiers. It is important to stress, though, that the 'extra' debts of council tenants consisted almost entirely of rent arrears. The probability of having non-housing debts was not significantly higher for council tenants than for other households with similar characteristics.
- Increased housing costs were associated with an additional risk of debt.
- Increased consumer credit commitments were associated with an additional risk of debt; but this effect reduced rapidly at higher levels of commitment. The main difference was between those with any commitments and those with none.

- The 'Pseudo-R^2' (0.45) shows that the model had substantially more explanatory power than the similar analysis of consumer credit had been. One way of illustrating this is to set the model to identify the 12 per cent of households with the highest probability of debt (because 12 per cent was the proportion who actually had a debt). We calculate (not shown in the table) that three-quarters of both debtors and non-debtors could be correctly classified by the equation.

Table A1 The probability of using a number of credit sources

	+/–	Coefficient	T-ratio
Demographic variables:			
* Age of householder	–	0.09	7.0
* Log(Age of householder)	+	3.10	5.5
* Single man	–	0.33	3.4
Single woman	–	0.16	1.6
Four or more children	–	0.31	1.5
Economic variables:			
* Net weekly income	+	0.02	3.3
No savings	+	0.09	1.1
* Savings £1,000 or more	–	0.43	5.4
Householder has variable earnings	+	0.10	1.2
Householder has been employed for past three years	+	0.12	1.3
Householder has had new job in past three years	+	0.16	1.7
Housing variables:			
* Outright owner	–	0.36	3.6
Private tenant	–	0.15	1.4
Total housing costs	+	$2x10^{-5}$	1.4
*** Constant**	–	7.15	4.7
Method of estimation	Ordered probit		
Log likelihood	–1538		
Pseudo R^2	0.15		
Sample size	1055		

* Significant at 95 per cent level of confidence.

Table A2 The probability of having a problem debt

	+/–	Coefficient	T-ratio	(T-ratio without savings)
Demographic variables:				
* (Age of householder)^2	–	$2x10^{-4}$	2.5	(4.2)
Single man	+	0.26	1.2	(1.2)
Single woman	+	0.24	1.2	(1.2)
* Has any children	+	0.70	3.9	(2.9)
Household newly formed in past three years	+	0.19	1.0	(1.0)
Widowed in past three years	+	0.71	1.5	(2.3)
Separated from spouse in past three years	+	0.53	1.7	(1.7)
Economic variables:				
* (Net weekly income)^2	–	$1x10^{-3}$	2.3	(3.2)
* No savings	+	0.70	4.0	na
* Householder has been employed for past three years	–	0.41	2.3	(3.3)
Householder is currently unemployed	+	0.45	1.8	(2.2)
Householder has had new job in past three years	+	0.25	1.5	(2.0)
Housing variables:				
* Council tenant	+	0.63	3.2	(4.5)
* Other tenant	+	0.52	2.3	(2.4)
* Total housing costs	+	$2x10^{-4}$	2.4	(2.6)
(Housing costs)^2	–	$1x10^{-5}$	1.5	(1.2)
Budgetary variables				
* Credit repayment commitments	+	0.04	4.3	(6.9)
* (Credit commitments)^2	–	$5x10^{-4}$	3.3	(5.1)
Weekly budgeting period	+	0.27	1.7	(2.9)
Has a current account	–	ns	ns	(2.3)
*** Constant**	–	2.53	5.6	(6.6)
Method of estimation	Probit			Probit
Log likelihood	–235			–380
Pseudo R^2	0.45			0.40
Sample size	1055			1692

* Significant at 95 per cent level of confidence.

References

1. A fuller statement of the findings is available: *Credit and Debt in the United Kingdom, working paper 6, Results from the Econometric Analysis.*

2. A standard textbook is R.S.Pindyck and D.L.Rubinfeld, *Econometric Models and Economic Forecasts*, McGraw Hill, 1981

Index

If a particular definition has been used in the writing of this report then this will be listed at the beginning of each heading before the main alphabetical sequence.